BorderGate

Tim

TO: Rathert

Best Wishes!

BorderGate

✦

The story
the government doesn't want you to read

Darlene L. Fitzgerald & Peter S. Ferrara

iUniverse, Inc.
New York Bloomington Shanghai

BorderGate
The story the government doesn't want you to read

iUniverse books may be ordered through booksellers or by contacting:

iUniverse
1663 Liberty Drive
Bloomington, IN 47403
www.iuniverse.com
1-800-Authors (1-800-288-4677)

Because of the dynamic nature of the Internet, any Web addresses or links contained in this book may have changed since publication and may no longer be valid.

ISBN: 978-0-595-38984-1 (pbk)
ISBN: 978-0-595-83425-9 (cloth)
ISBN: 978-0-595-83366-5 (ebk)

Printed in the United States of America

Contents

Introduction

This book is based on a true story. The disturbing events that you are about to read really did happen. Names of some operations, locations and government employees have been changed in order to protect agents who are still working for the Department of Homeland Security. This story culminated in a landmark case in Federal Court. The most significant and shocking testimony from that trial—"Fitzgerald—Nunn versus Department of Homeland Security"—is transcribed on line at "www.bordergate.net." America is less safe now than it was before we were attacked on September 11, 2001. "BORDERGATE" will tell you why.

"All that is essential for the triumph of evil is that good men do nothing"

—Edmund Burke

"You have not converted a man because you have silenced him"

—John Viscount Morley

"It is dangerous to be right when government is wrong"

—Voltaire

1

No Girls Allowed

"What counts is not the size of the dog in the fight, it's the size of the fight in the dog"
Dwight D. Eisenhower

If there ever was such a thing as a typical American small town, it could have been Fort Thomas, Kentucky. Lying just across the Ohio River from Cincinnati, it was like a Norman Rockwell Saturday Evening Post magazine cover: a collection of neat, single family homes on quiet, tree-lined streets with names like Oak and Elm and Maple. When our soldiers came back from World War Two, they settled in thousands of sleepy little towns just like Fort Thomas. Putting their guns and uniforms away, these men married their high school sweethearts, got whatever jobs were available, and quietly set about to raise their kids in the freedom they had fought and died to defend. They were living the post-war American dream.

Darlene Fitzgerald's father Kelsie was just such a man—a veteran of the bloody battles in the South Pacific who had fought the Imperial Japanese Army on Guadalcanal. Now all he wanted was to play baseball with his sons on a clear blue Saturday morning. Kelsie stood in the doorway of his living room with a baseball glove in one hand and tossing a ball up in the air and catching it with the other. He looked at two of his sons and his little daughter sitting on the couch watching a football game on television.

"Who wants to play some catch, guys? It's too nice a day to sit in front of the boob tube." Both sons were interested only in the sport of football, and didn't even look up at their father. It was little Darlene who jumped up excitedly.

"I'll play, Dad," she shouted. "I'll play!" Kelsie looked longingly at his sons, the disappointment plainly showing on his rugged face. Then he shrugged, turned to his daughter, and smiled sadly, glad that at least one of his kids showed some interest.

"Okay, Dar," he said softly. "Boys, would you lend your sister a glove?" Darlene's brothers mumbled something that sounded like "okay" without taking

1

their eyes off the screen. Kelsie's little girl scampered off to their room, returning in a flash with a glove that was too big for her hand and enough enthusiasm to overlook it. Father and daughter went out into the back yard and began tossing the ball back and forth. Kelsie, who had once played minor league baseball, was startled to discover that his little nine year old could throw the ball a lot faster and more accurately than most boys her age. As the days passed and summer approached, Darlene and her dad practiced more and more. He was impressed with how quickly his daughter was learning to pitch a baseball.

Kelsie would round up all the little neighborhood boys and get a game going just so he could watch his daughter pitch. One day, one of the local Little League hotshots named Brian saw Darlene pitching and couldn't resist mocking her effort. "A girl pitching baseball?" he sneered. "It'll never happen!" Just as Darlene turned in his direction and started to respond, her father beat her to the punch.

"Hey Brian," Kelsie said "I hear you're a pretty good ball player. You want to give our little team some practice lessons in how to hit?"

"Sure," Brian said with a sly smile on his face. "I'll be happy to show your rag-tag team here a little thing or two." Brian removed his glove from the end of his bat and stepped up to the plate, taking a few mighty practice swings. As he did, Darlene's father walked out to her and squatted down to speak confidentially with her.

"Do you really want to play baseball?" he asked. Darlene nodded "yes". "Then you really need to put this little turd in his place and strike him out in front of all these little boys. That's how you'll get to play in the league. If you strike him out, I'll try and get you in. You can do this. Remember what I told you: there is only one thing worse than fear and that is regret." As he spoke to his daughter, Kelsie was thinking back to his days as a "frog man" in what would later become the Navy Seals. He had joined in part because he had never liked swimming. "You can do this," he repeated, and walked back to the sidelines.

Darlene turned to face her opponent. She had never pitched against an older kid like Brian before. She glanced at her father, who quietly gave her a "thumbs up." The chant of "batter, batter, batter" rose from the kids on the field. A gathering crowd began watching the little girl on the mound. Darlene looked again at Kelsie, and he flashed the signal for a fast ball inside. She entered her windup and delivered her first pitch. Brian watched in shock as the ball whizzed by. "Steee-rike," yelled the parent umpire from behind the plate.

"Aw, that was just a lucky pitch," one of Brian's friends shouted from the sidelines.

Brian smiled in relief, stepped out of the batter's box to take a practice swing, and stepped back in determined to knock that little girl right off the pitcher's mound. Darlene reared back and threw another fast ball.

"Steee-rike two," the umpire called out. The playing field fell silent for a moment, and then Darlene's squad again began to cheer her on. Brian was visibly angry as he stepped out of the box and took a couple of really strong practice swings. When he was sure that he was ready, he stepped back up to the plate, a look of grim determination on his face. Darlene stared at him, readying herself for the next pitch.

"You can't let her strike you out, man," Brian's friend yelled from the side-lines. "She's only a girl. C'mon, Brian, blast one!" Darlene gazed at the plate, focusing on the catcher's mitt which offered her a target on the outside corner. She remembered her dad telling her that the ball will go where your eyes are look-ing. Darlene looked over to her father, who subtly gave her a signal for a change-up, where the ball comes in more slowly than the delivery would indicate. She went into a slow, direct windup. Keeping her eye on the catcher's mitt, she gave it her best shot. Brian swung with all his might and finished his swing before the ball even got to the plate.

"Steeeeriike three!" cried the umpire. "You're out!" Darlene closed her eyes and breathed a huge sigh of relief. Kelsie ran out to her and proudly lifted his lit-tle girl into the air as her teammates and the nearby crowd of onlookers cheered. Disgusted with himself, Brian turned, picked up his glove, and beat a hasty retreat.

A few weeks later, Kelsie took his daughter by the hand one morning and said softly: "Let's go get a haircut." Darlene's hair was very long and she was both con-fused and curious as to why her dad wanted her to get it cut. In the past, her mom had always done this sort of thing. Darlene sensed that her dad was whis-pering this to her because he didn't want her mother to hear. She quietly went with him, and didn't quiz him until after they were in the car and well on their way.

"Dad, why are you taking me to get my hair cut?"

Kelsie never took his eyes off the road. "Tomorrow is our first baseball game and this league doesn't officially allow girls to play. There's no specific written rule forbidding girls from playing, but none have ever tried before you. I thought we could hedge our bets a little by not bringing too much attention too fast to your long hair." Kelsie flashed a nervous smile at his little girl, hoping she would understand and go along with the program. Darlene squinted her eyes as if giving the matter serious contemplation. She pulled down the passenger seat visor, and looked into the little vanity mirror on the inside. After gazing at her hair for a few moments, Darlene flipped the visor back up.

"You know, Dad, I've been tired of this old long hair for months. It's too hard to brush and keep clean anyway. But mom's going to have a conniptions fit when she finds out." With that she shot him a confident smile.

Kelsie patted her head. "Don't worry, Dar. We'll jump off that bridge when we get to it. Anyway, by then the deed will be done, and it'll be too late. Just let me handle mom."

"You're a brave man, Papa," Darlene said, too young to know how brave her dad really was. Later that evening, Darlene was lying on the hallway floor just outside her parents' bedroom, eavesdropping on them under the crack of the door as she had done many times before.

"Kelsie, are you crazy?" her mom asked in an angry tone. "She's just a little girl! She's got no business playing baseball with a bunch of boys! It's bad enough that she's got four older brothers and is the only girl in a whole neighborhood of little boys. Now you're encouraging her to be even more of a tomboy than she already is."

"Now momma," Kelsie soothed, "it's just a game. If she's good enough she should be allowed to play. Shoot, Joy, she's gonna be one of the best pitchers in the league, and more importantly, she loves to play."

"You cut her hair just like a little boy's," Darlene's mother Joy complained. "We'll be the laughing stock of the whole town if you let her play like that tomorrow!"

"Oh so that's it," Kelsie replied. "This is more about your status in this town than it is about making that little kid happy."

"No, that's not what I'm saying. She's going to go out there and get laughed at. How's that going to make her happy?"

"They'll stop laughing right after she shuts down that first batter."

"I hope you're right, for her sake!"

Darlene crept back to her room and went to bed. The next day brought the first official game of the season, and the league's opening day ceremony for all the teams. The baseball park was packed with proud parents watching as each team made the traditional run around the bases. This went off without a hitch, as no one noticed that one of the players was a girl. Little Darlene looked just like all the others as they trotted around the diamond. But all of that was about to change.

At game time, Kelsie and his team went into the dugout with all their equipment. He held his breath after sending his team out onto the playing field, but again no one noticed that Darlene was among them. The first batter stepped up to the plate. Darlene glanced over at her dad as he gave her the sign for the first pitch. Her teammates started up the regular chatter of "No batter, no batter" as Darlene struck him out in three pitches.

The other team's coach—Ward Douglas—began to look closely at this pitcher who had just struck out his leadoff hitter one-two-three. Then Darlene did the same thing to his number two hitter, firing a fast ball right by him when the count had reached one ball and two strikes. Douglas sauntered over to the on-deck area and was giving his third batter some pointers when he heard one of Darlene's teammates yell: "Go get him, Dar!"

"What did he say?" Douglas asked his on-deck hitter.

"What did who say," his player replied.

"Did that kid call their pitcher Dar?"

"Yeah Coach. She's a girl. Didn't you know?"

Coach Douglas immediately stood up and called: "Time out, ump." He motioned for the umpire to join him on the sideline for a conference. After a few moments of heavy discussion and Coach Douglas pointing a finger at the girl on the pitcher's mound, Kelsie walked over to join them. Darlene stared expectantly as her father adamantly defended her playing.

The umpire abruptly ordered both coaches back to their dugouts and shouted: "Play ball!"

After Darlene struck out Douglas' third batter, the coach angrily refused to let his team take the field. "No girls allowed," he said in a loud, angry voice. The umpire approached him and told him to get his team out onto the field and continue the game. Coach Douglas refused. The umpire was losing his patience.

"Either get your team onto the field or you will forfeit the game," he warned. "C'mon, Ward, you know there's nothing specific about girls playing or not. My hands are tied."

"Bulls—t!" the Coach fired back. "This is bulls—t and you know it! This is Little League Baseball—boy's baseball! You got any idea of the precedent you're setting here, ump?"

The umpire reacted with some anger. "You know, Ward, if that little girl had pitched a lousy inning and hadn't struck out your leadoff hitters, we wouldn't be having this conversation. You know it and I know it, so either take the field or lose the game by default." After a beat, the ump repeated: "What's it gonna be, Coach?" Coach Douglas stormed back to his team's dugout and angrily began stuffing their equipment into their equipment bag. The boys on his team began to whine and complain to him that they wanted to play.

He yelled at them: "I said to pack up your stuff!" Darlene watched sadly as the other team did what their coach told them. The umpire called the game, giving Kelsie's team—and its female pitcher—their first win of the season. The other players on her team began to cheer, but Darlene felt bad as she slowly walked off the field.

Kelsie tried to comfort his little girl. "Don't worry about it, Dar. They'll just have to get used to it."

"But dad, I don't want to win like that. I want to play, not have the other team just quit," she said as she looked up into the stands and saw her mother shaking her head with an "I told you so" expression on her face. When Darlene saw this, she lowered her head and felt bad all over. Kelsie shot his wife an angry glance, and raised Darlene's chin up so she looked right into his face.

"If you want to play, Dar, then you'll play. I promise you—you'll play! Just don't quit and don't ever let anybody tell you that you can't do something just because you're a girl! Nothing ever got done by quitting. Just don't quit no matter what happens and you'll get to play!"

Back home later that day, Darlene's mother took her aside. "I don't want you to get the wrong idea," she began gently. "I'm just trying to keep you from getting hurt."

"But I want to play, mom," Darlene said softly. "I know I can do it."

Joy Meadows thought for a moment. She got a faraway look in her eyes. Then she looked at her daughter with a wistful expression. "Can I tell you a story?" she asked.

"Sure, mom."

"A few years before you were born, I had a very good job. It was during World War Two. The one your daddy went overseas to fight."

"Against the Japanese, right?"

"Yes, that's it. Well, while the men were off fighting that war, a lot of us women who stayed in this country took the jobs the men left when they became soldiers. I had the job of supervising some other workers in a factory. I was pretty good at it, too."

"I bet you were, mommy."

"Well, when the war was over and the men came back, they took that job away from me and gave it to a man."

"Even though you could do the job?"

"Yes. And it bothered me for a while to take a different job. It hurt my feelings a lot. It taught me that sometimes a girl can get hurt when she competes against the boys. That's why I didn't want you to play ball, you know, against the boys. You might get hurt."

"I understand, mom. But I know I can do this."

Joy looked closely at her daughter. "Okay, Darlene. But if you do get hurt—"

"I won't, mommy. I promise." Joy could see Darlene had made up her mind. "Well, you're certainly your father's daughter." With that, she gave her little girl a hug and watched her as she went out of the room. "And mine, too," Joy said softly to herself.

Kelsie met Darlene in the hallway. "Did your mother tell you to quit?" he asked.

"No," Darlene replied. "She said to be careful and she gave me a hug."

Kelsie was relieved. "Ah, well—good. Always listen to you mother. But remember what I told you—"

Darlene finished his sentence: "Don't quit!"

"That's my girl," Kelsie said as he laughed and headed off toward the kitchen. It was a day Darlene has never forgotten, a day that changed her life forever.

2

The Jinx

"I've written 17 novels, and I've found out that fiction can't keep up with real life."
John Grisham

Seventeen years later, on a crisp December evening in the Arizona desert, a human head—detached from its body—flew through the cool, dry air. Its eyes were wide open even as its brain was dying. Was it still capable of thinking as it landed in the soft sand, rolled a couple of feet, and came to rest by an aloe plant? When did it stop hearing the rumble of the column of tanks that shut down their motors just twenty feet away? As the life force quickly drained away, did the open eyes see anything at all as the eerie darkness of a moonless night became the permanent darkness of death? Had there been a scream?

A few miles away, near one of the least-publicized installations of the United States Army, a telephone rang by the bedside of a young Army Lieutenant in the Military Police. Darlene Fitzgerald fumbled for the phone, looking at the small clock by her bed. It was ten after one in the morning. Still only half-awake, she spoke unsteadily. "Hello? Yes—yes—holy cow! I'm on my way!" She leapt out of bed and quickly put on her uniform, overcoat, and gloves. Darlene ran to her car. She jabbed several times with the key, opened the door, jumped inside and took off without waiting for the engine to warm up. Gravel shot out from behind her tires as she sped off down the road.

Before long, Lieutenant Fitzgerald approached a range of terrain used for tank maneuvers. Driving toward several flashing lights, she could see a cluster of "M.P."-marked vehicles arranged so that their headlights shone on two Army tanks. Other tanks were scattered about as she made her way through the bizarre scene. A small group of men came walking towards her. Besides some Military Police, there was an Army Criminal Investigator from the CID named Jack Roland. Roland was the only one there not in uniform. Darlene could see her breath as she asked: "Okay, boys, what have we got here?"

Jack Roland came up close. He was twenty-four years old, handsome and muscular, and had a big grin on his face. He was chewing a huge wad of bubble gum and blew a large bubble, which he quickly deflated before Darlene could pop it.

"Dar, you're not gonna believe this one," he said amiably. "It's the jinx, I tell you. It's the jinx." Roland popped another bubble.

"Roland, will you stop with that jinx crap already, and quit smacking that damn gum!"

"Hey, it was you that guilted me into stopping smoking. So it's either the smoking or the damn gum," he replied.

"All right, all right, what's the scoop here?"

"What we got is a bunch of deuce (police slang for intoxicated) reservists from the 3333 Armored Cavalry Unit out of Phoenix running tank maneuvers in the black (without headlights)." He continued to fill in some details as the group made its way over to the two tanks illuminated by the M.P. vehicle headlights. "As best as I can tell, they were running single file doing about forty miles an hour when the lead tank here must have seen a deer or something and threw on his brakes. The tank following behind couldn't stop in time and rear-ended the lead tank. Well, you see the tank turret and how the barrel of the second tank is right in line with the manhole of the driver of the lead tank?"

Darlene immediately grasped what had happened. "You've got to be freaking' kidding me!"

"No ma'am, it took his head clean off. Want to have a look-see on top?" Roland and Darlene climbed up on top of the lead tank and she shone her flashlight down into the manhole. She saw the headless, lifeless body of the driver inside. There wasn't as much blood as she had expected, although it's hard to see blood in a dark area. It looks like black oil and is hard to make out.

"Where's the head?" she asked. Roland pointed with his light toward a spot about twenty feet away, where another of the M.P. sedans was shining its headlights. There on the ground was a round, oddly-shaped object covered in dirt. The two investigators sat down on top of the tank and pondered how to write this up on a report. Roland spoke.

"Well, the tank Company Commander, a Major Price, is as plastered as his troops. They are all pretty much in shock from the accident, so we've just got the basics I told you."

They were quiet as they looked around the accident scene and over at the lifeless head in the sand. Then Darlene broke the silence and took charge

"Take everybody from the tank unit over to the M.P. station and make sure you rights waiver every one of these rat bastards in writing. Then I want every swinging' one of them to be field sobriety tested and run on the Intoxilyzer (a breath analyzer which measures the blood alcohol level of drunk driving suspects). Start with their idiot Company Commander. Also have three M.P.'s cordon off and tape this entire crime scene, and guard it for tonight. We'll have to complete this investigation at first light. I want our TAI's (Traffic Accident Investigators) out here at dawn along with O'Leary from D.P.S. (Arizona Department of Public Safety). We're going to write this up initially as a vehicular manslaughter charging the driver of the second tank. Then charge the Company Commander with Contributory Vehicular Criminal Negligence, Conduct Unbecoming, and anything else you can think of to stack onto that moron." Roland nodded in agreement and the pair climbed down off the tank.

"Are you gonna take care of the notifications or should I?" he asked.

"You notify the next of kin and I'll tip the J.A.G. (Judge Advocate General) and everyone else."

"Oh man," Roland whined. "Why do I always have to get the next of kin?" Darlene turned to him and stuck out her hand to play the guessing game "Rock, Scissors and Paper." "Hey Dar, you know I never win at this." At the count of three, Roland stuck out his hand making the sign of "paper" as Darlene displayed "scissors." "Dammit," Roland muttered as he blew and popped another bubble, "dammit to hell!"

"Sorry, sucker," Darlene taunted as she turned and walked to her car. She drove back to her apartment to catch a few hours of sleep. Then at dawn, she again headed out from the sleepy little town of Sierra Vista, Arizona . Nestled against the snow-capped Huachuca Mountains in the southeastern corner of the state between Tucson to the northwest and Nogales to the south on the Mexican border, Fort Huachuca is one of the best-kept retirement secrets in the Army. For many a senior officer, it's the last stop in a successful career, finishing their service in an old west resort-like setting worthy of a painting by Frederick Remington. The Coronado National Forest stretched to the north and the Sonoran Desert flowed from the Mexican border to the south. Remote, historic, and beautiful it was. But that wasn't all.

Fort Huachuca has a few secrets of its own. Besides being a kind of military Club Fed out in the desert, it is also the home of the United States Army Military Intelligence School. The fort is popularly known as Spook Central, and has a mysterious reputation for hiding lots of clandestine operations, secret units, and specialized training. The sun was just peeking over the horizon as Darlene pulled into the M.P. main gate. The guard on duty saluted her as she yawned back at him and returned his salute. She rolled down her window and the guard gave her a "high five."

"Hey, Ma'am, was is los (German for "What's up?")?" he asked.

"Wer weiss (German for "Who knows?")," she replied.

"That's not what I hear, Ma'am. I hear you got hit with that jinx again last night."

Darlene laughed and added: "Am ende seiner Kunste sein ("I'm at my wits end")."

"Das ist pech ("That's bad luck")," the guard said with a wry laugh, pointing an accusing finger at her.

"You guys watch too much television," Darlene said as she drove past him onto the Post. She walked into a historic frontier building whose floorboards creaked as she went down a long corridor and up to the M.P. desk, where the troops on duty joked with her about the jinx as they handed over the daily blotter. "Are they here yet?" she asked.

"Yes Ma'am," a soldier replied, "including that new Marine Colonel." The M.P. blotter is a report completed every morning listing the prior day's events and crimes. Darlene was reading it as Rosa, her secretary, rushed out of her office clutching a sheet of paper.

"You really need to read this before you go into your meeting, Ma'am" Rosa said. "I didn't want you to be blindsided by it." Darlene read the memo. It had been written by a man she hated, Army Captain Francis Ward Nedaheiger, and part of it was designed to humiliate her by volunteering her services to the visiting Colonel's mission. This was something you never did without first discussing it with the person whose name you're putting forward. It was typical. Disliked by everyone around, Captain Nedaheiger was known as "Knee High" as much for his outsized ego as well as his short stature. Francis—a name he hated to be called, preferring "Frank"—was the kind of weasel even other weasels don't like. Whether it was insecurity brought on by being small or just a plain old mean streak, Nedaheiger had even once made his own father, a career Army man of lesser military rank, salute him in front of his entire command. Darlene suspected Frank of having some kind of Napoleon complex since he always insisted on being in charge and pulling rank.

Darlene and Captain Nedaheiger had gotten off on the wrong foot at a dance at the O'Club (Officers Club) when they first arrived at Fort Huachuca. Known as the "Hail and Farewell" formal dinner, it was a monthly event to welcome new officers and bid goodbye to those leaving the Post. At the dance, Nedaheiger's advances toward Darlene were rebuffed and from then on he exhibited a grudge against her. It didn't take much to get Nedaheiger on your case, anyway.

The meeting was led by Lieutenant Colonel Rockwell, the Provost Marshall (Chief of Police) of Fort Huachuca. He was a greying 56 year old former infantry commander whose secondary M.O.S. (job description) was in the Military Police. In order to qualify for "full bird" (after the insignia for higher rank) Colonel status, Rockwell had to serve at least one tour of duty in the Military Police. He didn't know much about law enforcement, and was grateful that those who did, like Lieutenant Fitzgerald, had gone to great lengths to help him out and make him look good in that capacity. He treated Darlene almost like a daughter and she in turn really liked the man.

Colonel Rockwell introduced the group to Marine Colonel Kenny Green, a tall, tough 40 year old veteran whose previous assignment had been with the NSA (National Security Agency) as a Counter Terrorism Task Force Officer. Colonel Green had come to Fort Huachuca to organize a Counter Terrorism Task Force which would affect all the Army posts along America's southwest border. From the first moment he saw her, there was a special chemistry between him and Darlene. Nearing the end of the meeting, Green summed things up and made a pitch: "I propose we call this Task Force Thunder, since "Huachuca" is the Apache word for thunder, and to ask if any of you would volunteer to come aboard as we get this thing off the ground."

"I've read all the relevant materials with respect to your assignment," Darlene responded. "I'd be honored to be assigned to your task force, sir." Nedaheiger rolled his eyes condescendingly, although he was somewhat baffled by Darlene's coolness knowing she must have read his memo. This served Darlene's plan to keep the little twit off balance.

"I can't let you have our girl full time, Colonel Green," Colonel Rockwell said, "but I will approve delegating some of her duties to other personnel so she can work with you. Speaking of work," he continued, turning toward Darlene, "what's going on with the headless tank man?"

"Sir," Darlene replied, "we've submitted charges for indictments to J.A.G. In fact, Agent Roland and I have to be there in about thirty minutes for Article 32 (court martial proceedings under the Uniform Code of Military Justice) hearings on these guys."

Roland slid copies of the rights waivers across the table to the Colonel. "Well, what did these fine soldiers have to say for themselves after they sobered up?" Rockwell asked.

"As soon as they sobered up, sir," Roland said, "they immediately lawyered up as well. The tank driver at first refused the Intoxilyzer test, so we took him to the hospital and drew blood. He was shocked that we could do this under military law, but then clammed up on advice of counsel."

As everyone stood up at the meeting's end and began leaving, Darlene was joined by her secretary Rosa and they began chatting. Nedaheiger threw Darlene a dirty look and approached Colonel Green. "Sir, I have some ideas that I'd like to share with you regarding how to justify the manpower you'll need for this task force."

Green immediately sized up Knee High as trouble and brushed him off. "Oh, that's fine, Captain. Just give my secretary a call and we'll set something up."

Colonel Rockwell stepped in to help. "Colonel Green, weren't we going to grab a couple of tennis rackets?"

"Sure," Green replied. "I hear the O'Club has some really nice courts. We shouldn't have a problem getting one at this time of day." Nedaheiger did a slow burn as both his plan to humiliate Darlene and to ingratiate himself with Colonel Green had failed.

He was further upset to watch Colonel Green ask Darlene: "Hey LT (Army slang for lieutenant), I hear you swing a pretty mean racket. You want to join us?" Darlene and Colonel Green exchanged smiles.

"Sure Sir," she replied, "that is—if I can get out of these Article 32 hearings on time."

"Great, LT, and maybe you can fill me in on this jinx business I keep hearing about."

Colonel Rockwell began to laugh. "Well, it's simple, really. This post is haunted and the ghosts have latched onto Darlene and Roland. It seems they've managed to piss off these ghosts so that every time they pull duty agent and officer together, some extreme sort of crime, rape, robbery, murder, or suicide befalls their shift. No kidding, it's like clockwork: Fitzgerald and Roland pull duty and all hell breaks loose." Everyone laughed except Knee High, whose anger level at being left out was rapidly rising.

"Fairy tales. Just fairy tales and coincidence," Darlene said, on her way to the J.A.G.

A half hour later, she and Roland made their presentation to the judge. The tank driver and Company Commander were indicted on all charges and released on half a million dollars bail. Darlene glanced at the two indicted soldiers and whispered to Roland: "Career over."

"Not just career over, but life over," Roland responded.

Darlene shot Roland a hard glance. "It pays to be sober, Roland!"

"Don't even compare me to them, Dar. Don't even!" he replied angrily.

Two days later, Roland, Detective Logan O'Leary of the Arizona Department of Public Safety (DPS) and Darlene reported to Greeley Hall for their first official Operation Thunder Task Force meeting. O'Leary, as everyone called him, was a handsome guy in his mid-forties who'd been with the DPS police force for twenty years. As they entered the Pentagon-like building which also housed several Army intelligence units, they passed through ever-tightening rings of security where you needed special clearances and I.D. badges to go on. If Fort Huachuca was Spook Central then this was its heart. The trio went down long sterile corridors with brightly polished marble floors. Darlene's spit-shined pump heels clanked noisily on the floor, and she embarrassedly began to walk like an Indian—toe to heel. As she tiptoed, she suddenly glanced up and saw the face of Colonel Green laughing at her as he looked out into the hallway. Darlene knew he was laughing at her and immediately piped up. "I guess you need to have your ass handed to you again on the tennis court, Sir."

"Hey, I was just wondering what was making all that racket out in the hall. I should have known it was you," he laughed.

Colonel Green motioned for the group to come into the conference room adjacent to his office. Other members of the task force were already assembled. "Here come the jinxes," somebody said as Roland and Darlene entered. The jinx story had traveled throughout the camp. Captain Nedaheiger was one of the last to arrive. Then Colonel Green began the meeting.

"All right everyone, let's get started. Evelyn (his secretary), can you take the minutes for us?" He introduced everyone in the room, then laid out some ground rules. "All future discussions whether written or spoken will be considered classified as Top Secret communications and will be handled as such. All communications both verbal and written will be on the record unless specified otherwise by notifying Evelyn that something is off record." As he made each point, Green looked carefully around the room to make sure everybody understood and agreed. "Additionally, for the purpose of ease of communications, this task force will dispense with the formal rank references and speak on a first name basis. We'll be spending a lot of time together and I think this will add to the comfort level of free-flowing ideas. Is everyone okay with this?" It was okay with everyone—except Nedaheiger.

"Well Sir," Knee High began, "don't you feel it necessary to maintain a chain of command so that lesser-ranking personnel won't be confused?" Nedaheiger shot a pointed glance at Darlene.

Colonel Green's expression said "You've got to be kidding me," but his words were: "Frank, no I don't. We're all adults here. I think we can handle it.." Everyone stared at Nedaheiger with disapproval on their faces. Some even snickered at his pettiness. Knee High was about to experience yet another Maalox moment as Colonel Green continued.

"Now to get us started, I've asked Darlene to give us a briefing on some very interesting research she's completed on a local self-proclaimed terrorist organization. Darlene?"

Lieutenant Fitzgerald moved to the head of the table and stepped in front of a large projection screen as Captain Nedaheiger shifted uncomfortably in his chair, wondering what a 1st Lieutenant was doing giving a briefing and not a more senior officer, such as himself for example. His face darkened as Darlene continued, clicking a remote projector switch to advance slides which supported what she was saying.

"Good morning everyone. My information today is regarding an organization entitled Posse Comitatus. The origins of this name stem from a Latin based legal term for a law that was enacted some years ago entitled the Posse Comitatus Act, 18 U.S.C. (United States Code) 1385. This is a Reconstruction Era criminal law proscribing use of military to "execute the laws" except where expressly authorized by Constitution or Congress. Limits on the use of military for civilian law enforcement emphasize supportive and technical assistance (e.g. use of facilities, vessels, aircraft, intelligence, tech aid, surveillance, etc.) while generally prohibiting direct participation of DOD (Department of Defense) personnel in law enforcement activities (e.g., search, seizure, and arrest). This law establishes a clear line for the military to engage in certain law enforcement investigative or disciplinary acts against civilians without a clear military connection. This task force, for example, can conduct investigations and take certain limited actions for two reasons. Number one, we are targeting only terrorist organizations, which are exempt from this law because of their clear threat to national security. Additionally, we've taken extreme measures to grant security clearances to our local detective from the Arizona DPS (Department of Public Safety). This gives us multi-jurisdictional powers that also extend well past Posse Comitatus."

"This organization—Posse Comitatus—has thus far to our knowledge not engaged in any terrorist acts. They have, however, engaged in illegal acts. These acts are of great concern to us by their very nature. These acts consist of committing burglaries of homes and businesses for the specific purpose of stockpiling weapons and ammunition. The head of this organization is a former Army NCO (Non Commissioned Officer) named Wayne Gilbert. Gilbert is a 52 year old white male, six feet one inch, 170 pounds. He was a former Army Ranger who served in a Special Forces Unit for two tours of Vietnam. It seems that Gilbert had some type of beef with the government stemming from his less than honorable discharge following his second tour in Nam. Our records reflect that Gilbert was originally brought up on charges for aggravated assault on a senior officer. This all-around nice guy had a "hook" (Army slang for someone high in rank who uses their position to help out someone of lesser rank) who helped him reduce his charges to a mere dishonorable discharge. Gilbert served no time for his offense, yet still had the nerve to be angry with the Army. Our intelligence indicates that Gilbert now resides in Tucson, Arizona, and makes his living as a demolition expert for construction companies. This puts him in clear, legal contact with very powerful explosive materials, which is of great concern. Additionally, Gilbert is known to try and recruit other individuals who have just been kicked out of the armed forces into his organization. He's been quite successful at this and his organization may have hundreds of members." Darlene continued her presentation for forty-five minutes, then asked for questions. Nedaheiger's hand shot up. "Yes, Francis?"

Nedaheiger bristled at his own name, sighed angrily, and responded. "That's Frank, Lieutenant, Frank," he said, emphasizing the word "lieutenant" to try and put Darlene in her place. "And what exactly were all your sources for this information?"

"Well, Frank," Darlene replied, "I had access to the files of State and local law enforcement as well as the FBI."

"So what did you do," Knee High sneered, "just pick up the phone and someone from all these agencies just handed over all this information to you, a mere M.P. lieutenant?"

Before she could reply Colonel Green spoke. "Frank, Darlene met personally with these law enforcement agencies, as well as having full access to our NSA (National Security Agency) files."

"And just how did she get access to NSA files?" Frank snapped.

"I cleared her," Colonel Green replied icily, clearly angry with Nedaheiger's unprofessional behavior at the meeting. "I made sure she had all the information she needed." He looked squarely at Frank and added: "I can assure you that this information is as accurate as it gets. If you wish to question this further, please feel free to schedule an appointment with Evelyn to discuss it with me in private. Okay, Frank?" Captain Nedaheiger sat back in his chair embarrassed as he noticed the expressions of contempt glaring at him from around the room. It had not been a good day for Knee High.

3

Ghosts

"Life is but a walking shadow"
William Shakespeare

After the meeting, Colonel Green approached Darlene as she was talking with Roland and O'Leary. "We need to chat about something," he said.

"Well," Darlene replied, "Roland and O'Leary have offered to buy me lunch—"

"Hey wait a minute," O'Leary said, "we thought you were buying us lunch."

"I can settle this," Green said with a smile. "Let me join you and I'll pick up the tab."

"Aha," Roland laughed, "whoever said there's no such thing as a free lunch?"

Shortly afterward, the four sat down together at a steak house in Sierra Vista, the little town just outside Fort Huachuca. "So how long have you all known each other?" Green began.

Darlene took a sip of ice water. "I've known O'Leary for nearly two years, and Roland a lot longer." She took another sip while watching with concern as Roland gulped down his scotch on the rocks. He motioned to the waitress for another drink.

Green continued: "And how long have you known Captain Nedaheiger?"

"Too long!" Detective O'Leary grimaced as he replied.

"So what's his story?" Green asked. Darlene abruptly excused herself to go to the salad bar as O'Leary continued with the Colonel.

"Captain Nedaheiger," O'Leary said, "or Knee High as we call him, is a walking Napoleon Complex. He's a wannabe cop who couldn't get into the M.P.'s for some reason. He has a real attitude toward anybody of lower rank. I'm sure it just killed him when you had Darlene give that briefing on the Posse Comitatus and not him."

"Darlene showed initiative by going out and getting this information on her own and putting together a good briefing on short notice. Had Frank shown the same initiative I'd have given him the same opportunity, something I'll be telling him personally tomorrow."

"Why—are you seeing him tomorrow?"

"Yes. Evidently he took me up on my offer and immediately made an appointment with my secretary for 0800 sharp. Man, there's always one in every group."

Darlene returned to the table with her salad. "One what?"

"One troublemaker," Colonel Green replied. "I have a PHD in psychology and I can tell you the Captain has some real problems." He turned to face Darlene directly. "You're one of them. He's got the hots for you and it's really bugging him."

Darlene was startled by this news. "No freaking' way! The guy hates me and the feeling is mutual. He's always trying to put me down and embarrass me in front of everyone."

Colonel Green continued calmly. "Just listen to me. I know how things appear to you but believe me—I'm right about this. I've seen it before. He's got the hots for you real bad and resents the fact he can't have you." Darlene looked around the table with an astonished expression.

"The Colonel's right about this, Darlene," O'Leary said. "Knee High thinks by putting you down he's leveling the playing field, so to speak. They really should conduct some kind of psychological screening for these M.I. (Military Intelligence) Officers and weed out guys like Francis. He's the type you read about in the newspaper after a bunch of bodies get discovered buried in some lunatic's backyard and the neighbors all say what a nice, quiet, inconspicuous guy the axe murderer was."

"I've been watching him too, Dar," Roland added. "From day one he's made it a point to be at every meeting on post you attend, whether they have anything to do with him or not. To me it's pretty obvious he wants you."

Darlene fidgeted nervously in her chair, then stood up. "Sorry guys, but I've got to cut this short. I have to be back on the headless tank man investigation this afternoon and—"

"Oh come on," Roland interrupted. "Sit down and finish your lunch. We're just trying to give you a heads up about Knee High, that's all. We don't want you to get blindsided by anything the little moron might do." Darlene reluctantly sat down and quickly ate her salad.

"That reminds me," Colonel Green said, changing the subject, "you guys are supposed to fill me in on this jinx business I keep hearing about."

"I can tell you all about it, Kenny," O'Leary said.

"Don't listen to this ghost story bull, Colonel," Darlene said as she finished her salad. "This is the 80's, O'Leary. Don't exaggerate." She got up and motioned to Roland to get going with her as she headed out of the restaurant.

Roland responded by downing another scotch, grabbing his stuff, and getting up. "Damn girl," he muttered good-naturedly. "I never get to eat, sleep, or rest around her. I better go after her. Thanks for lunch, Colonel."

Roland hurried off as Green watched him with a concerned expression. Then he turned to O'Leary. "Does he always drink like that?"

"He's got it under control, Kenny. He's a good agent. Now about that jinx," he continued, trying to get Green's mind off Roland's drinking, "the first thing you need to know is that Fort Huachuca has a lot of history behind it. In 1886, General Nelson Miles used it as his advance base and supply post for the pursuit and capture of the Apache Chief Geronimo. After they captured Geronimo in the early 1900's, the fort became the headquarters for the 10th Cavalry. That was the first black cavalry mounted unit. They called them the "Buffalo Soldiers," and they rode into Mexico on an expedition with General John J. Pershing going after Pancho Villa."

"Is that why they called him Black Jack," Green asked.

"That's it," O'Leary continued. "Pershing eventually became Army Chief of Staff in the 1920's and even won a Pulitzer prize for his memoirs."

"What's all that got to do with this jinx stuff?"

"I was just getting to that. It seems that way back then a couple of Buffalo Soldiers had what some say was consensual sex with a white general's daughter, and when her daddy found out about it she cried rape. These two soldiers were convicted—unfairly many said at the time—but back in those days black life was considered pretty cheap. They built a special building over by the graveyard just to hang the poor bastards. I'll show it to you on our way back to the post. Now to make a long story short, right after Darlene and Roland arrived here, some NCO (Non Commissioned Officer) played a practical joke on them. Darlene wanted to get him back only better. She found out the guy was real superstitious and believed the post was haunted."

"Do a lot of people think so?"

"You'd be surprised how many do. Anyway, one night when she and Roland were on duty together, they got that NCO to ride in an MP sedan with them at midnight and drove on their rounds over to the graveyard. See, these two dead Buffalo Soldiers weren't even allowed to be buried in the main cemetery. Instead, they lie in a couple of unmarked graves about fifty feet away from it. Roland faked engine trouble and they all got out to look under the hood. Darlene and

Roland had bribed a couple of soldiers to lie on the hanged men's nearby graves under dark poncho liners, and when they suddenly rose up this NCO just about had a heart attack. He went screaming all the way back to the M.P. station. Of course, Darlene and Roland bust a gut laughing and no, I'm not done yet."

"Jesus," Green said, "some prank!"

"Shortly after that, whenever Dar and Roland work together—which is always because nobody else will work with them—we have some huge trouble like murder, aggravated assault, robbery—"

"Or decapitation by tank turret?"

"That's it, Kenny. Rumor is that Darlene and Roland disturbed the graves of those hanged soldiers, and now they're jinxed." O'Leary went back to eating his lunch.

Colonel Green thought about this story for a minute. "You don't really believe in this jinx crap, do you?"

O'Leary put his fork down. "Well, sir, I got to tell you. I've been a cop working with the MP's on post for about eleven years now and I've never seen anything like it. Serious crimes have increased dramatically since the jinx and it's always when Darlene and Roland are working."

"Have you ever witnessed anything strange on post yourself?"

"Funny you should ask, Kenny. One night I was in the C.I.D. building working with Roland and Darlene on an accident report. It was hot and about 0200 hours and we had the windows open hoping a breeze would cool things off. Those buildings are so old they've been declared historic sites, you know. So we're typing away and then we hear the sound of boots coming up the wooden stairs outside, and walking over to the screen porch door and we hear it open. We all heard it open because it's rusty and makes a real racket. We figured it was an MP from downstairs bringing us a report. But when we opened the inner door to let the guy in there was nobody out there. We looked all over the place, but there was no sound of anybody running away—nothing. It was the damnedest thing I've ever seen or heard, and I've seen some strange stuff."

Green stared at O'Leary with a dumbfounded expression. "Detective, you don't strike me as a particularly crazy fellow. Are you telling me that you actually believe in this jinx and ghost stuff?"

"Sir," O'Leary said soberly, "I can only relate the facts to you. That's what an investigator does. But I'll tell you this much: I don't believe in mere coincidence anymore. And as much as Darlene and Roland try to distance themselves from this, it just seems to follow them around. Maybe it's the dismal past they share together."

"What dismal past are you talking about?" Green asked.

"I don't know, sir, I mean, I think I may have said too much already. They are both very good friends of mine as well as colleagues. This is pretty personal. Maybe they should be the ones to tell you."

Colonel Green sat back in his chair in disappointment. "They're in love with each other, aren't they? It makes sense. That's why I can't even step up to bat with her. She's in love with him."

O'Leary laughed and shook his head. "No, no it isn't like that. You've got the wrong idea. I mean, they do care about each other a lot but, uh, that is—" O'Leary stopped talking.

Colonel Green broke the silence. "I can clearly see that you're protective of Darlene. Look, I'm not trying to rush into anything. I just want to get to know her. I promise I'm not out to hurt her or anything—I respect her way too much for that."

"Well, you're right that Roland and I are protective of her. She's one of the first MP Officers us locals have been able to work well with. She's a really good kid, and she's been through a lot for somebody so young."

Anxious for answers, Colonel Green asked: "Been through what? Did somebody die or something?" O'Leary quickly looked away. Green added: "That's it, isn't it?"

O'Leary looked back at the Colonel. "I shouldn't be telling you this, but you'll find out anyway. Better you get it from me than some screwed up version from somebody else. Darlene was engaged to a guy who was also Roland's best friend from back when they were kids. The three of them were inseparable. Well, the fact is that Darlene's soul mate and Roland's best buddy was killed by a drunk driver in a motorcycle crash just over a year ago. And neither one of them has been the same ever since." Colonel Green stared blankly down at his plate, lost in thought. Then O'Leary added: "It's hard to compete with a ghost, isn't it?"

After an awkward pause, Colonel Green looked back up at O'Leary. "You're right. I can't compete with that, and I don't intend to. I'll just back off, and if the time is ever right maybe I'll try again someday." The two men sat quietly for a spell, and Green signaled to the waitress for the check. They got up, grabbed their coats, and headed for the door. "Does this ghost have a name?" Green wondered.

"His name was Nathaniel Westfield." This remark stopped Green dead in his tracks.

"Any relation to General Westfield?"

"His only son."

"Wow!" Green said quietly. "A general's kid. What was he like?"

"He was a good kid. A real professional officer. Never rode his daddy's coat tails or anything like that. A real class act."

"I bet he was even good looking, too, huh?"

"'Fraid so, Colonel. Blond hair, blue eyes. He could have been a model for one of those magazines. Funny thing is, though, the kid didn't have an arrogant bone in his body. He was soft spoken, even kind of shy. Everyone liked him and I can see why Darlene fell for him." As they made their way out to the car, O'Leary tried to brighten the Colonel's dark mood. "Kenny, it's been over a year now. Maybe you shouldn't just give up so easily. Hell, it might even be good for her to become interested in somebody else. She's too young to be living like a nun."

"And you're sure that she and Roland are just friends?"

"Sir, I know Roland. He's a standup guy and would never dishonor his best friend like that. But to get to her you're going to have to go through him and that won't be easy, my friend." The two men got into Green's car and drove away, lost in thought.

At five o'clock the next morning, Darlene and Roland met for a jog up into Black Tail Canyon, one of the most beautiful spots on the post.

"Do you still dream about him?" Roland asked.

"All the time. I still miss him," Darlene answered. They slowed down to a walk and Roland put his arm around Darlene. He spoke softly. "There's something I've been meaning to tell you about the tank accident investigation."

"What is it, Roland?"

"When we interviewed the drivers of the tanks, I asked them if they could see what it was the driver of the headless guy's tank threw on his brakes for." Roland stopped, put his hands on his hips, gazed up at the sky, and took a couple of deep breaths. "They said they saw a dark man on a horse."

"How's that?" Darlene asked.

"The drivers of the tanks said a dark man in some kind of uniform and riding a horse suddenly darted out from nowhere and ran right in front of them."

Darlene gave a nervous laugh. "And what did this moron whose turret took the guy's head off blow on the Breathalyzer?"

"Yeah, that's what I thought too. But he only blew a point zero seven. So I mean, yeah, that's impaired but he wasn't stinking drunk like the rest of them. And get this, the headless victim's tank driver BAC (blood alcohol level) came back at point zero eight—and that's not stinking drunk either."

Darlene pondered this bizarre information. "What about vision? Did any of them have glasses or contacts they forgot to wear?"

"No. They all had no mention of impaired vision on their records."

"So what are you telling me, Roland?"

Roland placed his hands on his hips, looked up and down the canyon as if searching for an answer, bit his bottom lip and said: "I don't know what I'm saying, Dar. I just know that they saw something and it wasn't a deer. I looked all over the accident scene for tracks and there weren't any. It had rained the night before and the ground was soft. If it had been an animal there would have been tracks. But there was nothing. I photographed the whole area."

Darlene looked Roland straight in the face. "Then it's a lie. They had to invent some kind of alibi to cover their own stupidity, so that's where this stuff about a dark horseman came from."

Roland began walking slowly back down the canyon road as he answered in a dubious tone of voice. "Yeah, that's probably it. You're probably right."

Darlene watched him pull ahead of her, and she was frightened for him. Roland had been fighting an alcohol addiction for quite a while and she feared this could push him over the edge. She hurried up to his side, and as they both began jogging more briskly down the road she asked: "How'd you write it up?"

"I just took down their statements verbatim and drew no conclusions on what they said. Only I left out the part about me not finding any tracks." They continued in silence for a while. Then Darlene tapped Roland's shoulder.

"This is what we do, Roland. We process death. We don't pass judgment on it. We just process it."

Roland's face showed grief and frustration brought on by months of personal anguish as they continued down the canyon. Silently they disappeared into the darkness.

4

Madness

"Who knows what evil lurks in the hearts of men? The Shadow Knows."
From the radio drama "The Shadow."

At 0700 hours that same morning, Colonel Green walked into the reception area of his office. His secretary Evelyn hadn't arrived yet, but sitting on a couch was Captain Nedaheiger. Green looked at his watch and gave Nedaheiger a puzzled look. "I thought our meeting wasn't until 0800, Frank. Did I miss something?"

Nedaheiger snapped to attention. "No sir. I'm just early."

"Relax, Frank. It's okay. I'd offer you some coffee but Evelyn's not in yet. Come on into my office." They entered Green's office and the Colonel motioned for Frank to sit in the chair in front of his desk. Kenny couldn't help but notice how small Frank looked in the large chair, and had to suppress a smile. "So what's got you up so early?"

"Well sir, I have some questions about Task Force Thunder and the direction that it's taking. I'm concerned about such a junior ranking officer having so much more responsibility. I think it would be better suited for a more senior ranking officer, sir."

Colonel Green sat back in his chair, took a deep breath, and put his feet up on his desk as he contemplated how to respond. Finally he said: "Frank, how long have you been a captain?"

"Six months, sir."

"First Lieutenant Fitzgerald will be promoted to captain in just a few days, Frank. That means you outrank her by a mere six months. I consider that kind of comparison as splitting hairs. Don't you?" At a loss as to how to respond, Nedaheiger just shrugged his shoulders. Colonel Green sat up and took his feet off the desk. "May we speak frankly, Frank—no pun intended?" Frank stared at Green, leery of what was coming next. "Look Frank, your jumping to conclusions about how I'm running this task force causes me great concern. I mean, what makes you think I'm giving Fitzgerald any special authority?"

Nedaheiger shifted nervously. "Well, you let her control the very first meeting."

"Ah, I see. So you think that if someone gives an information briefing at a meeting that they are in control?" Without waiting for an answer Green continued. "This is exactly what I'm talking about, Frank—your misperception and jumping to wrong conclusions. Just because Darlene showed some initiative and put that briefing together—on her own, I might add—doesn't mean that I've endowed her with any more responsibility than anyone else. That having been said, I've got to tell you I was impressed with her ability to get this intelligence so quickly and put together such an informative briefing. I see that as initiative and taking advantage of an opportunity—an opportunity you have the same shot at."

Colonel Green picked up a memo off his desk and handed it to Frank. "Isn't this your memo in which you put Darlene's name on the list of people recommended for this task force?"

Frank glanced at the memo he had hoped would embarrass Darlene. "Yes sir."

"Well then Frank, answer me this: why would you recommend someone and then question their abilities?" Captain Nedaheiger twisted nervously in his chair. "It's a rhetorical question, Frank. You don't have to answer. Let me tell you what I see. I see a guy with some deep-seeded insecurity and self-esteem issues. It makes you uncomfortable when you can't use your rank as some kind of security blanket, if you will. Additionally, I think you feel threatened by Fitzgerald's success—and I don't just mean in her briefing. I mean in the Army as a whole. You're projecting, and in a big way, that you're jealous of her."

That got Nedaheiger out of his chair. Trying to control his anger, he spat out: "Sir, with all due respect, I didn't come here to be psychoanalyzed by the National Security Agency. I hardly think you're qualified, sir—with all due respect."

"Well Frank," Green said calmly as he stood up behind his desk, "that's where you're wrong. Actually I'm very qualified. I have a PhD in psychology and practiced counseling in the Marines for several years before being recruited to the NSA. So Frank, I do know what I'm talking about. I've seen this type of thing many times before." A long awkward pause followed. Then Nedaheiger turned and briskly walked out of Green's office. The next day there was a memo written by and requesting that Captain Frank Nedaheiger be removed from Task Force Thunder. Colonel Green sighed, shook his head, and signed the memo.

The following morning, SP4 (Specialist 4th Class) John Lucas Washington stood at attention in front of his company commander—Captain Frank Nedaheiger. SP4 Washington was dressed in his class A uniform, an Army business professional suit. With him was his JAG (Judge Advocate General) attorney. Nedaheiger read Washington his Article 32 hearing rights waiver, which is similar to the Miranda Rights advisory used in civilian law enforcement. Then Knee High, in a very authoritarian tone of voice, asked: "Soldier, do you understand each of these rights as I have read them to you?"

"Yes sir," Washington replied.

"It is my understanding that you, on the advice of your counsel, have elected to accept the plea bargain of a dishonorable discharge out of the service in lieu of a Court Martial. Is that correct?"

Washington's eyes filled with anger and hatred even as they welled up with tears. He gave his JAG lawyer a pitiful look, like a little boy being taunted by a big bully. The JAG officer merely nodded at him to continue, as if to say that this was his only recourse to get out of the trouble he was in. Washington looked down at the floor like a broken man. He managed to choke out the words: "Yes sir."

Nedaheiger had a smirk on his face. He was enjoying this. "Okay Mister Washington," he said, emphasizing the word "mister" in its civilian context, "then you need to sign right here." He passed Washington a document which the former SP4 sadly signed. Then Nedaheiger slid the paper across his desk to the JAG officer to witness with his signature. The lawyer signed the paper and slid it back to Captain Nedaheiger. Frank placed the paper in a manilla folder, which he vertically tapped loudly on the desk as if to signify the finality of the situation. The JAG officer stared at Nedaheiger and shook his head sadly, scarcely believing how much this little piss ant of a captain was getting off on humiliating this soldier. But Nedaheiger wasn't finished. He stood up and walked around to the front of his desk, where he stood facing the disgraced Washington, who in turn snapped to attention. The JAG officer knew what was coming next. Nedaheiger's de-ranking ceremonies were legendary on the post. He was the only officer anybody knew of who performed this degrading ritual.

"Captain," the lawyer asked, "is this really necessary?" Nedaheiger gave him a stern look as he began ripping the rank and insignia off of Washington's uniform. Washington stood firm and stuck out his jaw as he tried to face this situation with some remaining shred of dignity. A single tear streamed down the side of his face.

That afternoon, Washington was escorted off the installation. The man looked like a zombie as he walked slowly up the road, carrying his duffel bag. He checked in at a cheap motel on Fry Boulevard, unpacked his few belongings, and stared blankly for over an hour out the window of his drab room. Then he noticed paper and a pen on a small wooden desk nearby. He went over and sat on the battered folding chair at the desk and began to write. His face was a mask of both intense rage and bewilderment. Something inside the man had died. Something else had been created. He kept writing.

Two weeks later in the post duplex housing, SP4 Linda Francis of the Army Intelligence unit was arguing with her boyfriend, SFC (Sergeant First Class) Raymond Thomas of the Army Engineer Company. Raymond was speaking to Linda in a voice of controlled anger. "You've got to report this to Knee High," he told her. "I really think this guy Washington could be dangerous." Linda began to cry softly. Sergeant Francis put his arms around her and tried to comfort her. "Look, you've got to quit blaming yourself for what happened to Washington. The guy had some serious mental problems before you ever entered the picture. If it hadn't been you he decked that NCO over it would have been someone else. You're probably not even the first woman he's obsessed over. It's not your fault. Look at me," he said softly, lifting her chin up so that their eyes met. "If I decked the dates of every woman who ever dumped me I'd be in Leavenworth for the rest of my life."

Linda smiled weakly, then buried her face in his chest. "You're right," she said. "I need to tell someone about these bizarre, scary letters. I just wish it wasn't Knee High—I mean Captain Nedaheiger. See, you've even got me saying Knee High. I'm gonna slip up one day and call him that to his face. It's just that Nedaheiger is such an asshole and a woman hater. He's the last guy I want to tell my troubles to."

"I know," Raymond replied, "but this is the Army, and like it or not he's your chain of command."

The next day, Raymond and Linda entered Nedaheiger's office for a preset appointment.. Already present in the office was the Company First Sergeant Alvin Phalen, known as "Top." Linda and Raymond went in with their hats held under the right arm of their neatly pressed uniforms Class A uniforms. They snapped to attention in front of Nedaheiger's desk. Frank looked up from his chair. "At ease soldiers, at ease," he said. "Now what can we help you with?"

Top, Raymond and Linda also sat down in a formal manner. Linda looked at Raymond with a puzzled expression, but he gave her a reassuring look as he began to speak. "Sir, for the last two weeks Specialist Francis here has been receiving these bizarre letters from her ex-boyfriend John Washington." He handed Frank a pile of hand written letters. "These letters are causing us great concern, sir. They are threatening in nature and get more and more bizarre as time goes on." As Sergeant Thomas continued, Nedaheiger glanced over the letters in a flippant, disinterested manner, then handed each page over to 1st Sgt. Phalen. Phalen looked at each frantically scribbled letter with growing concern. Sergeant Raymond couldn't help but notice the manner in which Nedaheiger seemed to be glossing over the letters' content.

"Well, sir," Raymond continued, "we were wondering if we should take these letters to the MP's." Sergeant Phalen glanced up from what he was reading, looked at Nedaheiger, and his expression darkened in anticipation of what he thought Nedaheiger's reaction would be.

Nedaheiger casually looked over the last page he was holding, passed it to Phalen, and a sinister smile crept across his face. "Well Sergeant Thomas and Specialist Francis," he said in a soft, controlled tone of voice, "I'm sure that won't be necessary." As he continued speaking, he got up from behind his desk, came around to the front, and slowly began escorting the couple towards the door. "I can assure you that in all probability this is no real danger at all. Washington is simply trying to reconcile a broken heart and a bruised ego by expressing himself in writing. Now all of us have experienced a broken heart at some time or another, and we all eventually get over it. I'm sure that Mr. Washington will get tired of writing and simply move on. Until then, we'll keep on top of this matter, and I assure you that everything will be fine. If you have any more problems, just call on old Top here, and we'll see what we can do. You did the right thing by using your chain of command and coming to us first." Nedaheiger shook their hands and whisked them out the door. The he turned and looked at Phalen, who was staring at him with an expression of disbelief and extreme concern on his face. "What do you think, Top?" Nedaheiger asked.

"Sir," Phalen replied, "did you really look at some of these letters? I mean really read them?"

"I saw enough, Sergeant. This guy Washington's just full of hot air and sour grapes. Not to mention he's also a big coward. He doesn't have the balls to follow through with all that stuff. He's just a loser shooting his mouth off."

"Sir, I'm not so sure. Those letters read like a real psycho wrote them. I think this guy Washington may have snapped or something." Captain Nedaheiger looked at Top and simply shook his head indicating both "no" and a smirk that belittled the Sergeant's fear.

Later that day, SP4 Linda Francis and SFC Raymond Thomas were wandering through a local swap meet in Sierra Vista. As they browsed among the hodge-podge of stuff for sale, it was obvious they only had eyes for each other. What they did not see was the shadowy figure of former SP4 John Washington as he followed them at a discreet distance. Washington watched the couple as they walked, held hands, and sampled foods at some vendors' booths. With every smile the two lovers made, with every little kiss they exchanged, Washington's face grew angrier and more sinister. Washington had dark circles around his sunken eyes. He hadn't slept in days. He clutched a worn photograph of Linda in one hand. When he couldn't stand to watch the couple anymore, he stepped behind a wall and slowly began tearing the picture into little pieces. "You bitch," he said softly to himself. His eyes welled up with tears. "You little whore!" That night, John Washington again sat behind the little desk in his dingy motel room and wrote frantically, his rage growing with every word.

5

The Promotion

"A woman is like a tea bag—you never know how strong she is until she gets in hot water."
Eleanor Roosevelt

Two days later, the members of Task Force Thunder were having another meeting. Again the subject was the terrorist group called Posse Comitatus. Colonel Green held a memo in his hand. "Well," he told his assembled team, "based upon Darlene's conclusions about our bunker security, this problem needs to become one of our first priorities, along with the inspection of the reserve depots on this list. I mean, the lack of security at these depots is scary. I'm surprised they haven't been hit already." He looked pointedly at Darlene.

"I'll get with JAG and see what their regulations say," Darlene said. "And also with Johnny over at the Engineers. I'm sure they'll both have plenty of input on this."

"Okay," Colonel Green said, "and thanks everybody for your good work. We're getting a handle on this and not a moment too soon." Green glanced at his watch. "I think that's enough for today. But remember that time isn't on our side. Let's plan on having this information by our next meeting. Now, if you're hungry, you'll notice that there's chow on the table in the conference room. I'm not sure exactly what delicacies are in store for us, but the line forms on the right."

The group rose and, while chatting among themselves, made their way over to the buffet. Darlene found herself between O'Leary and Roland, who were leaning in close to her in an attempt to resume a private conversation they had been having before the meeting began. They spoke in low tones, but privacy is rather scarce in a room full of investigators.

"Darlene," O'Leary said, "I think you should go with him. He seems like a really nice guy. You know you like him. What are you waiting for?"

In a whisper Darlene said: "Do we have to discuss this here? Can't this wait a few minutes? Okay with you, Roland?"

"I don't know, Dar," Roland said. "Maybe O'Leary's right. Maybe it really is time. I mean, you've got to get back in the saddle sometime."

Darlene was incredulous. "Back in the saddle? What is that? You've been watching too many westerns. Besides, I really don't think this is the place—"

"Look," Roland continued, "I can't believe that Nathan would want you to be lonely forever."

"Who says I'm lonely," Darlene replied. "I have you guys, don't I?" She mockingly batted her eyes, first at one man, then at the other. Then in a serious tone she added: "But really, I'm too busy to have a relationship now. No kidding. So gimme a break!"

"One date does not a relationship make," Roland replied. "Nobody's suggesting you run out and marry the guy. It's just a date."

As the lunch line came to a temporary halt, Darlene faced Roland. "Oh really, Roland? Then why haven't you been going out on dates, hmmmm? Anyway, you don't have to look out for me forever. I can take care of myself. But I'll make a deal with you. You show up at this stupid thing with a date and I'll go with the Colonel."

Now it was Roland's turn to squirm. He looked at his two friends and then shrugged his shoulders. "Okay, okay. It's a deal. You go with the Colonel and I'll find somebody, too." He stood there trying to convince himself that this was all a good idea.

Colonel Green joined them on line. "So who's going with who where and when?"

There was a brief but pregnant pause.

"Who's on first and what's on second?" O'Leary said, breaking the tension. They all laughed.

"We're talking about Darlene's promotion party, sir—" Roland said.

"That's Kenny," the Colonel interrupted.

"Well, yes sir, uh Kenny," Roland stammered. "See, I'm bringing a date and you're bringing Darlene."

Darlene was clearly embarrassed. "Gosh, Roland," she said, gently shoving an elbow into him, "he may not want to take me—and I can find my own damn date! Geeesh!"

"I'm sure you can," Colonel Green said with a smile, "but I would love to take you if you're willing." O'Leary looked at Darlene and his expression told her to go for it.

"All right, all right, I'll go," she said in a submissive but cheerful tone of voice. Colonel Green took hold of her empty plate and along with his laid them on a table.

"Can I talk to you for a moment, Darlene—outside?" he asked. They stepped into the hallway. The Colonel took a deep breath. "Look, don't let anyone pressure you into anything. I really do want to go out with you. I mean it's probably no secret. A blind man could tell I have a pretty enormous crush on you. But I also know what you've been through. And I know that you might not be ready yet, and I understand that." Darlene stared at the floor, tracing the swirling lines of the marble with her foot as she listened. "Consider it an open invitation," he continued, "or that I'm merely your taxi service for your party. No strings attached. No pressure."

"Well," Darlene said, looking up at him with a smile, "as long as I don't have to tip you at the end of the evening. I'll be happy to go with you, no strings attached." She put her hand out and they shook hands on the deal and returned to the conference room and had lunch.

That night at about midnight, Roland's phone rang, startling him awake. It was Darlene calling, and she was upset and wanted him to come over to her apartment. Since they lived in the same building complex, it was only a matter of minutes before they were curled up on her couch in front of the fireplace. He guessed what was troubling her.

"You had another dream about Nathan?"

"More like a nightmare," she said.

"Come on, tell me about it."

"I'll tell you after you answer a question for me."

"Shoot."

"Why haven't you been dating? Is it because of me? Because you think you have to take care of me?"

Roland thought for a moment, and tucked Darlene's head under his chin protectively, closed his eyes and gave her a hug. "If I wanted to be dating someone, I would," he said.

"Nice dodge. You still didn't answer my question. Because I don't want you to feel that you have to take care of me. I'm fine, Roland. Really."

"I know that," he said. "I'm fully aware of the fact that you don't need anyone. I'm not here because I believe you can't make it without me. I know you could. I'm here because I want to be, not because I feel I have to be. Do you understand that?"

Darlene thought for a moment. "Roland, what do you think happens to us when we die?"

Roland was thrown a little by her question. "What do you mean? I don't know what you're asking me."

"I mean, do you believe in God and in heaven and hell and all that stuff, or what?"

"This has to do with your nightmare about Nathan, doesn't it? What did you dream about?"

"You're answering a question with a question," Darlene said. "Okay. It was bizarre. It was the most bizarre nightmare I ever had. I was in a room—a bedroom, I think. There was blood everywhere. There was a body lying on the floor face down. I sensed that there was something definitely sinister about this body, like it was evil or something. I went to roll the body over and Nathan grabbed my arm and yelled No! No! Then I woke up. I know it must sound stupid as I'm telling it to you now, but as I was dreaming it, it was really scary. But the weird thing is—as scary as it was I didn't want to wake up and leave Nathan. Even in my nightmares I don't want to leave him. All I want to do anymore is sleep, and try to find him in my dreams. But just when I find him, I wake up. It's so frustrating." Roland looked on with concern, and kissed Darlene on top of her head.

"I want you to go on this date with the Colonel," Roland said. "This isn't good—what you're doing to yourself—and Nathan would be furious that I'm not helping matters."

Darlene gave Roland a serious look. "Roland, Nathan wouldn't want you wasting your life taking care of me, either," she said.

"I don't consider this wasting my life," he replied. "You have to know how I feel about this—about you. I feel trapped. I can't fall in love with my best friend's girl. I just won't. But I can't help how I feel about you, either, and I can't stop wanting to take care of you. I think I need to take care of you more than you need taking care of. Does any of this make sense to you."

"I understand more than you think," Darlene said as she buried her head in his chest. There was a long pause. Then Darlene continued. "You still didn't answer my question. What do you believe happens after we die?"

Roland stared blankly into the fire, lost in thought. "I used to have some idea," he said at last, "but I don't anymore. I mean, I think there's something else, something afterwards, but we're not supposed to find out about it until after we die. Coming to this place in the desert and seeing the things we've seen, and then Nathan's death, they've all changed what I used to believe in. I think there's something else that happens to us—but I'm not sure what." Roland shook his head, dissatisfied with his own answer.

"Do you think we're really jinxed because of that stupid joke we played? Do you think we're really haunted or that Nathan's trying to contact us?"

"If you had asked me that six months ago, I would've said you're crazy," Roland said softly. "Now I'm not so sure. If it's true that we are jinxed or haunted or some damn thing, then at least I'm not alone, huh?" He looked at Darlene and smiled.

She smiled back. "Yeah, misery loves company, right?" They snuggled close together on the couch for a while in silence, then Darlene said: "Roland, are we going to be okay?" He squeezed her affectionately.

"Don't worry. I won't let anything happen to us. I'm not going through that again. I couldn't handle losing somebody like that—like you—again." There was another long pause. "What are you thinking about now, Dar?"

"All right," she replied, "I'm going to lay something on you that's kind of out there. Roland, you were a science major. So think like a science guy and don't make fun of me for what I'm going to say, okay?"

"I promise."

"Okay, here goes. You know how everything in our universe is set up with its opposite? Like there's never an in without an out. There's never an up without a down. There's never happy without sad. There's never a forward without a back." Darlene gazed up at Roland to see how he was processing this line of thinking. He struggled not to laugh.

"Go on," he said. "I'm listening."

"Then how is it that we can only go forward in time? I mean, it just doesn't make sense. Everything else in our universe has its opposite. So then why can't we move backward in time?"

Roland saw that Darlene had placed a lot of thought and importance in all of this, and thought carefully before he answered. "You're right. It doesn't make any sense. Scientifically speaking—and not scientifically speaking. You got a point. It really defies logic. We should be able to move forward and backward in time." They looked at each other for a moment, not knowing what to say. "You've obviously put a lot of thought into this. Why?"

"I don't know," Darlene said. "I just thought—I just thought we should be able to move backward in time. I wish I could go back."

Roland laid down on the couch, gently pulling Darlene on top of him. It wasn't a sexual move, just comforting. "This is really all just about Nathan, isn't it? Don't you think that every day of my freaking' life I wish I could go back in time and do things differently?"

"Exactly," Darlene said. "Scientifically speaking, it should be possible."

Roland sat back up on the couch, gently sliding Darlene off of him. He rubbed his face in obvious distress. "So what do you want me to do, Dar? Figure how to go back in time so I can undo the most incredible screw-up of a lifetime?"

"I'm sorry," she said, angry with herself for torturing him this way. "I don't mean to say this to hurt you or anything. I was just thinking about it, that's all. And I just wanted to see what you thought about it." Roland got up and walked to the kitchen, where he saw a bottle of scotch on the table. He picked it up and began looking for a glass. "Please don't, Roland! I didn't mean to upset you. I just needed to talk about it after my nightmare. I'm sorry. I'll never bring it up again."

Roland held the bottle in his hands in anguish. "Why do you keep this here, Darlene?" he said angrily. "I mean you know I'm struggling with this stuff. Why the hell is this here?"

Darlene followed him into the kitchen and gently took the bottle out of his hand.

"I don't keep this here, Roland. The last time you got plastered you left it here." She walked over to the sink and began pouring out the liquor. "You were so smashed you don't even remember leaving it here." She finished pouring it down the sink and when it was gone just stood there, almost frozen. Roland's face blushed red with embarrassment.

He turned and walked back into the living room, grabbed his coat, and began fumbling through his pockets for his keys. Darlene snapped out of her brief trance, put the bottle down and followed him. "Don't do this, Roland."

He spun around in anger. "Jack!" he shouted. "God dammit, my name is Jack! You never call me by my first name, Darlene. Why is that?"

"I'm sorry," she said softly. "No one calls you Jack. Everyone calls you by your last name. It's just one of those cop things. Like everyone calls O'Leary O'Leary. I never thought about it. I'm sorry. I'll call you Jack if you want me to."

Roland put his hands on his hips and made an effort to control his frustration, took a deep breath, and looked up at the ceiling. "You don't remember," he said in a somber tone, shaking his head sadly. "You used to call me Jack before Nathan died. You called me Jack. Then it became Roland after Nathan was killed."

Darlene gave him a puzzled look, trying to remember how it had been. "I'm sorry, Ro—" She caught herself. "Jack. I didn't even realize I did that." She walked over and stroked his arm gently. "Honest, I didn't know I did that. I'm sorry. But what's your point, Jack?"

"My point is that I think you did that subconsciously to create some sort of wall between us. Like you were setting some new ground rules or something. How the hell am I supposed to know why you did that? I'm no mind reader." He continued fumbling through his pockets for his keys as Darlene walked over and sat back down on the couch, staring straight ahead in a daze. Roland found his keys and then looked at her sitting there so quietly. He walked to the door and turned to her. "Look, we'll talk about this tomorrow. I just can't deal with it right now." He waited for her to say something, but she just stared ahead silently. She wasn't angry—just stunned. "Okay, Darlene?" he said in a slightly louder tone. "Tomorrow. We'll talk about this tomorrow, okay?"

"No," Darlene replied softly. "No we won't. We'll never be able to have a real conversation about how we feel about this." Her eyes filled with tears and she looked down at her feet, hoping he wouldn't notice that she was crying. "Every time I try to talk to you, this is how you react. You're my best friend, and if I can't talk to you about this—then there's no one."

Roland squeezed his eyes shut and pressed his head against the door. Taking a deep breath, he spoke softly to her. "Maybe that's the problem."

"What do you mean," Darlene said, looking up at him.

Roland straightened up and said in a calm voice: "Nothing. I didn't mean anything. I'm sorry. I know I'm an asshole for not being able to deal with this with you. Look, I gotta go. I just gotta get out of here before I say or do something I know I'm gonna regret later on. I'm great at that you know—regret, I mean. I've fined tuned it into an art form. Hell, I'm even better at it than I am at drinking." He looked at her to see if his little joke made her smile. It didn't. Instead, Darlene got up from the couch and walked over to him and unzipped his jacket.

"You're not going anywhere like this," she said. Roland grabbed both her arms as a swell of emotion overcame him. He gripped her arms tightly and looked up at the ceiling as if waiting for some sign from above. Then he looked into her eyes and saw fear there. Roland immediately released her, letting out a small, strange scream of frustration. Then he turned abruptly and quickly let himself out of her apartment without looking back. It was as if he knew that if he turned back around and went back to her something bad might happen.

He hurried quickly through the cold darkness back to his apartment, slamming the door behind him after he had gone inside. Then, without taking his jacket off, he began pacing back and forth. He walked over to his telephone and quickly dialed.

"O'Leary," he said hoarsely into the phone, "it's me. I need a party, man, come and get me. Yeah, ten minutes is great. I'll meet you out front." Roland hung up the phone and stared at it with some misgivings. Suddenly, the phone rang, startling him. But he just stared at the phone and waited for his machine to answer. It was Darlene calling.

"Pick it up, Jack," she said in a tinny voice through his small speaker. "It's me. I'm worried. C'mon, Jack, I know you're listening. Pick it up." Roland leaned over the phone and squeezed his eyes shut. Then he placed his head against the wall as he listened to Darlene plead with him to answer. He rubbed his forehead in torment, and then turned and walked quickly out his door.

6

Killing Time

"The mass of men lead lives of quiet desperation."
Henry David Thoreau

At two o'clock the following Saturday afternoon, John Lucas Washington clandestinely entered Fort Huachuca. It wasn't a difficult thing to do. He simply crawled through a hole in the fence around the fort. He was wearing camouflaged fatigues and was armed with a .357 caliber revolver, which he had tucked into his waist underneath his shirt. Nobody noticed him as he sauntered over to the duplex of SP4 Linda Francis. He hid in a line of trees at the back of the duplex, carefully looking around to see if anybody had spotted him. A short time passed. When he was sure he hadn't been observed, he walked quietly up to the back door. Washington removed a key from his pocket, unlocked the door, and let himself in. Seconds later there was a muffled scream. Then there was only silence.

Five hours later, Darlene Fitzgerald was sitting in her apartment trying to put a flower pin in her hair. She stared at herself in her make-up mirror. Every time she placed the pin in her hair she stared at her reflection, frowned slightly, and tried putting the pin in another spot. Instead of her uniform, she was wearing a green velvet dress. Tonight there was going to be a promotion party for her, celebrating her having risen to the rank of Captain. The party was being held at the O'Club, as they called the Officers Club on the base. At last she found a spot where she thought the pin looked just right. Or did it? She wasn't sure.

Her concentration was broken by the sound of a knock on her door. She glanced at the clock on her dresser. "He's early," she said out loud to herself, and got up to answer the knock. Opening the front door, she was surprised not to be looking at her escort for the evening—Colonel Green. Instead, she saw that it was Roland, looking like a schoolboy on prom night holding a small white box. He smiled at her.

"Avon calling," he said, bowing slightly as he offered the white box. Then, noticing how nervous she appeared, he added: "Well, aren't you going to invite

38

me in?" Darlene grabbed him by the arm and jerked him inside. "Hey, are you all right?"

"Do I look all right?" she answered. "I'm a mess. This is going to be a nightmare!" She looked at Roland in his dress blue formal attire Army uniform. "But damn Jack, you look dashing." He grabbed her and pulled her close to him, staring deeply into her eyes.

"And you look beautiful," he said in a low, sexy tone. "This Colonel doesn't know how lucky he is, the rat bastard. Here, I got you something." He gave her the little white box, smiling as she opened it. Inside was a beautiful wrist corsage. He took it out and placed it on her wrist. Then, still smiling, he added: "You know we're duty again at midnight tonight, don't you?"

Darlene frowned. "Boy, you sure know how to kill a moment. Don't remind me, please." Roland moved closer to her. It was painfully obvious he wanted to kiss her on the lips, but instead he just gave her a peck on the forehead. Darlene's body felt hot all over as she struggled with the disappointment of his control. Roland forced himself back from her arms, trying to collect himself. He looked away in embarrassment.

"Look," he said. "this Colonel—he seems to be a pretty nice guy. You're going to have a great time."

"Thanks Roland—Jack. You're too good to me," Darlene said as she lowered her head and played nervously with the corsage.

"Congratulations on the promotion, babe," he said as he opened the door and started to leave. He stopped and stared at the open door as if he wanted to tell her something else, but instead went out and started down the apartment complex stairs.

As he was walking down the steps, he met Colonel Green, who was walking up. Green stopped and looked at Roland in surprise. Roland stopped, stepped back, and lowered his head. "Evening, Sir," Roland said in a sheepish tone. Green gave him a strange look.

"What's going on, Roland?" he asked.

"Just making sure she's okay, Sir."

"Roland, call me Ken. Are you sure everything's all right?"

"Sure, Sir, sure it is." Roland began to pass by Green when the Colonel reached out and stopped him.

"Roland, I thought I had a green light here. Am I making a mistake?"

"No Sir. No mistake. She's waiting for you." Roland couldn't hide the anguish on his face as he forced a fake smile. He started to walk on, then stopped and said without looking up: "Take care of her."

"I will, Roland, I will," Green said softly, then turned and finished climbing the stairs as Roland went down and walked quickly away. Green looked over the railing as Roland walked away. Then he turned around and knocked on Darlene's door.

Later that night at the O'Club, Roland was by himself at the bar, drinking heavily. He would take a swallow and then look mournfully across the room to the dance floor as Darlene and Colonel Green spun happily around to the music, stopping here and there as she was congratulated by the others at the festive affair. As the night wore on, however, Darlene couldn't help but notice that Roland was getting plastered. When she saw him heading for the bathroom, she excused herself from the Colonel and intercepted Roland away from the others and out in the hallway. When she grabbed him by the arm and spun him around, he fell clumsily against the wall.

"You lied to me," she said accusingly. "You don't have a date, do you?"

"Hey how, is my favorite Captain," he said with slurred speech. He reached for her to give her a hug, but she crossed her arms across her chest and refused to be hugged. "Uh oh, she's mad" he said, weaving back and forth unsteadily, attempting to straighten up.

"That's right," Darlene said sternly, "and you're drunk again. Let's not forget that we're duty again tonight, Roland."

"So it's Roland, is it, mon Capitan? No more Jacques, eh? C'est la guerre!" With that, Roland leaned back heavily into the wall. Darlene turned angrily and stormed away.

Roland's expression changed as he watched her go. Then he turned and went into the men's room. He leaned over a sink and held on with both hands for much-needed support. Then he splashed some water on his face. When he gazed up into the mirror and saw what he looked like, he drew back a fist and punch at his reflection, breaking the mirror. "Uh oh," he said. "More bad luck." His words echoed off the tiled walls. Then he wheeled around, straightened up, and headed back to the bar.

Sitting with Darlene and a couple of other officers at a small table by the dance floor, Colonel Green looked at Darlene's troubled expression, then glanced over at the bar at Roland, who continued drinking even as blood ran down from the cuts on his knuckles.

"Did he drive here by himself?" Green asked. Darlene nodded yes. "Okay Darlene, you stay here. It's your party, You can't leave. I'll take him home and come back for you."

They stood up and Darlene gave the Colonel a big hug. "Thanks, Kenny," she said. "You're a real class act."

"Yeah, yeah," he said, forcing a smile, "just remember you owe me big time." He gave her a wink and a genuine smile as he motioned to O'Leary, who had been watching, to give him a hand. The two men met as they walked over to Roland at the bar.

"Hey buddy," O'Leary said to Roland when they got to him, "it's time to take you home."

Roland gazed at them with glassy eyes. "Hey, it's my besht buddy Detective O'Leary," he slurred. Roland attempted to hug O'Leary but lost his balance. O'Leary and Green caught him before he could fall, however, and the two gently guided him out of the party. They poured Roland into the back of O'Leary's car. Roland was singing "The Caissons Keep Rolling Along" as they drove him home. Once inside Roland's place, Colonel Green found some hydrogen peroxide and, after rinsing off Roland's bleeding knuckles, poured some of it on them. He then found a bandage and neatly bound up Roland's hand. They had no sooner tucked him in bed than Roland simply passed out.

As they drove back to the base, Green opened up to O'Leary. "I'm wasting my time here, Detective. That kid's in love with Darlene and it's tearing him up to see me with her. Not to mention that she has feelings for him as well. I don't get it, O'Leary. Why is she with me tonight and not with him? C'mon, pal, do me a favor and fill me in. What gives?"

O'Leary let out a long breath, and rubbed his eyes as he stared at the road ahead. "Roland had his chance," he said. "But it's like I said—he won't be any more than friends with her, whether she wants to or not. I just don't think he'll cross that line no matter how badly he wants to."

"So you're agreeing with me that he does want to?"

"Kenny, Roland's been in love with Darlene since he met her. But she's Nathan's girl. He won't cross that line."

"I don't get it. Why not? The kid's been dead for over a year now. What else is going on here that I don't know about?"

"Look. they're just two screwed up kids who haven't been able to reconcile this situation that they're in. Colonel, you and I have a few years on them and a world full of wisdom they don't have. Roland's a great guy, but he's never going to be able to handle a relationship with his dead best friend's girl. He knows that, and he wants Darlene to move on, painful as that may be for him. Roland won't get in your way."

"I'd say he already has, O'Leary. I've been in his shoes. He's hurting real bad. Darlene sees this and she wants to help him. Look at what happened here tonight. Case in point." They sat quietly together as they made their way back to the base.

O'Leary broke the silence. "Just give it some time, Ken. Roland's a big boy and he'll get over this. It's just that right now, if you're going to have a relationship with Darlene you're going to have to deal with Roland. You're a psychologist. Can't you help the boy somehow? Help him get over Nathan's death as well as Darlene? If you can. the two of them will be better off for it, for sure. Just be the good guy that you are and you'll surely win Darlene over."

Green thought for a moment. "You're forgetting one thing: technically, they both work for me now. That puts a monkey wrench into the whole thing. I can't have one of my key investigators getting plastered every time he sees me with another of my key investigators. Damn, what am I doing here? I ought to have my head examined."

"Physician, heal thyself," O'Leary said, breaking the tension. They laughed as they pulled back onto the base.

At just before midnight that night, Colonel Green walked Darlene up the stairs to her front door. Gently, he kissed his newest Captain good night, then turned and went back down the stairs. Darlene entered her apartment, went into her bedroom and sat down on the end of her bed. She glanced over at her dresser and saw an old picture of Roland, Nathan and her that had been taken in better days. She lay back quietly and began to cry.

At about two that morning, her phone rang. At the same time, her pager went off. Darlene switched on the light by her bed and picked up the phone. "Ma'am," a nervous voice told her, "you need to get in here." It was the MP desk sergeant at the base.

"What have we got?" she asked.

"I'm not sure exactly, but it doesn't sound good. The parents of one of our female Intel (intelligence) soldiers have called here several times. They're worried that they can't get a hold of her, and that earlier today the girl's ex-boyfriend had answered the phone. According to the parents, the ex had been threatening and stalking her. Right after the last disturbing call from the mom we got a call from one of the girl's neighbors. They said they thought they heard a gun shot."

"Okay," Darlene replied. "Have an MP drive over there and park about a block away from where this girl lives. Have him stay on the radio and watch the house until I get there. I'll get Roland, and we'll be right over. I have my radio and I will be monitoring."

"Yes, Ma'am," the sergeant said. Darlene hung up the phone and a few minutes later was banging on Roland's door. When he failed to answer, she let herself in with a key. She ran into his bed room and began shaking him awake.

"C'mon, Roland, wake up! We got a duty call!" Roland was still intoxicated from the party, and very sleepy. He grabbed Darlene and pulled her on top of him, and began kissing her passionately. She began kissing him back, and then abruptly stopped herself and remembered why she was there. "Snap out of it, Roland!"

He woke up. "I knew it was just a dream," he said as he raised up and shook himself awake. "I knew you'd never kiss me like that." Darlene surprised herself with the strength she had in pulling him out of bed and pushing him into his shower. She snapped on the cold faucet and Roland screamed as the water soaked him. "Why are you doing this to me, woman?"

"Roland, you've got ten seconds to sober up and get a move on! We got a duty call and it sounds pretty grim! We got a girl missing, a stalker, and shots fired so get your ass in gear, soldier!"

In a matter of minutes, Darlene and Roland were driving onto the post, listening to Darlene's MP police radio. She turned out her lights as they pulled up along side of the parked MP unit near SP4 Francis' house, and they rolled down their car windows. MP Charles Scott rolled his window down so they could talk.

"Evening Ma'am. Evening Roland," Scott said. "It's all quiet. Haven't heard a thing and I haven't seen a thing. There seems to be a living room light on—tv, maybe."

"All right, Scott," Darlene said. "Roland and I will quietly approach the front of the duplex and you go around the back. We'll reckon the situation and then knock at the front door." MP Scott nodded yes and got out of his car. Darlene parked in front of his vehicle and she and Roland got out . As the three made their way toward the house, she noticed that Roland now appeared quite sober. Darlene couldn't help wondering as they walked if it was the cold shower, the cold mountain air, or the astonishment of their kiss that had jolted him sober.

When they were near the house, MP Scott whispered: "The duplex adjoining our target is empty." Darlene and Roland nodded at the soldier, who began making his way around to the rear of the building. Roland and Darlene crept up to the large front window of the target house, one on each side, and carefully peeked in through the lace drapes. They saw a small male child, approximately five years old, sitting directly in front of a television. He seemed to be frozen in place, just staring at the tv. Behind the child was a couch, where they could see two legs dangling casually over the arm rest. Underneath the couch, there appeared to be a puddle of something dark. Darlene and Roland looked at each other apprehensively.

A voice came softly over the radio. "I'm in position in the rear," Scott whispered.

"Roger that," Darlene replied quietly. "We have one small child in the living room and one possible adult lying on the couch behind him. We are making entry now." She and Roland made their way to the front door, pulled out their weapons, and knocked.

"Military Police," Roland yelled as he looked through the small vertical window in the door. "Open the door." He could see what appeared to be a female lying on the couch, motionless. As he knocked again, and louder, and began to yell a second time, a definite gunshot rang out. He and Darlene dove off the porch and took cover behind a vehicle parked in the driveway.

Darlene snapped on the radio. "Scott, are you all right?"

"Yeah," Scott answered. "Did you guys hear that?"

"Yeah," she replied. "Get out of there, Scott. Come around front and take cover!"

Darlene continued. "MP Desk to 03, MP Desk to 03, shots fired. Need backup immediately!" Darlene then handed her radio to Roland. "I got to get that kid out of there."

"Not without me, you're not," Roland replied. Just then, MP Scott dove behind the vehicle and joined them. Darlene turned to the MP.

"Scott, hang tight. We got to get that kid out of there." She and Roland traded looks that combined apprehension with determination.

"Okay, on three," Roland said. He counted three and the two of them ran to the door. He turned the knob and it was unlocked. The pair rushed into the living room, grabbed the child, and ran back outside and behind the vehicle. Gasping for breath, they handed the child over to Scott. The child was quiet and in shock. As they caught their breath, three MP units arrived with lights on and sirens blaring.

"What about the person on the couch?" Scott asked.

"We saw one female, face down on the couch and in a pool of blood," Darlene said.

"I think she's dead."

"Damn, I hate working with you," Scott said, looking through them with a blank stare.

"Take this kid to the hospital now!" Darlene said to one of the arriving MP's. The other MP's crouched down with them behind the vehicle in the driveway.

Darlene turned to them. "Use your vehicles to block off both ends of the street, get the rest of the CID office out here, and turn off those damn sirens!" As another MP vehicle pulled up, Darlene ran over to it and crouched behind the door on the passenger side. "Does this vehicle have a P.A. system?"

"Yes Ma'am," the MP inside answered.

Darlene motion to Roland to join her, and he ran over and crouched down beside her. "Here's what we're going to do," she said. "That female might just still be alive in there. We have to get her out and get her to a hospital now." She pointed at the driver of the MP car. "You start talking to the shooter on this P.A. Tell him he's surrounded and he must come out now. Use this P.A. as a diversion while Roland, Scott and I go back inside and get this woman." She and Roland ducked and made their way back to where Scott was waiting by the vehicle in the driveway. "Dude, we're going back in," she told Scott. "I'll go in low and cover from the hallway wall. The shot came from the northwest side of the house, and I should be able to cover you guys from that wall. You two get that girl and get out. I'll hold that position until you do, and don't wait all damn day to do it, got it?" The two men nodded yes in response.

Darlene motioned to the MP in the vehicle to start the diversion with the P.A. As soon as he began doing this, the trio ran back into the house. Darlene took up her position by the wall leading to the back bedrooms as Roland and Scott snatched the female off the couch and carried her out of the house. In what seemed like hours but was in fact only seconds, they returned to where Darlene had positioned herself in the living room hallway. They all were pumped full of adrenaline and were gasping for breath.

"The girl's alive," Roland said. "Just barely, but alive."

"Good," Darlene replied between gulps of breath. "Now let's clear this house."

The three of them moved slowly and tactically through the building. The kitchen was first. They saw a charred pan burning on the stove. MP Scott turned off the burner under the pan, grabbed a dish towel, and moved the pan to a different burner. They then went tactically down the hallway, using only hand and arm signals and body language to communicate. They entered the first bedroom. It was obviously the child's room. There was a trail of blood from the end of the hall to this bedroom, then leading back into the living room. They could see blood dripping from the side of the child's bed.

Their fears grew as they made their way down the hall to the second bedroom's closed door, where they took up positions on either side. Roland tried to force the door open, but something was blocking it. He managed to get it open about two inches. Darlene got down on the floor and looked through the crack. She could see what appeared in the darkened interior to be a body dressed in military camouflaged fatigues. She raised one finger at Roland and Scott, then pointed at the floor signifying one body down. Then Darlene and Roland slowly, carefully pushed open the door until there was an opening wide enough for them to go through. They could see inside where blood was smeared on the hardwood floor where the body had been dragged by the door. Roland used his fingers to count one-two-three and on three they entered the room tactically and with force. Once inside, they immediately saw another male sitting on a bed. This male was slumped over against the wall beside the bed. He had at least one shot to the head and appeared dead. They continued to clear the room, moving slowly and carefully until it was obvious that there wasn't anybody else there.

Roland bent down and checked the pulse on the body lying face down on the floor. This body also had what appeared to be an exit wound to the left temple of the head. Brain matter was smeared with blood along the left side of the dead man's face. Roland got some on his glove, and grimaced as he wiped it on the dead man's back. Lying on the floor next to the right hand of the body was a .357 caliber revolver. Roland glanced up at the others and shook his head no, indicating that there was no pulse.

MP Scott moved slowly to the body on the bed. As he felt for a pulse, Scott began staring into the dead man's open eyes. Scott froze in what was a kind of trance. When Roland noticed this, he snapped his fingers loudly, jarring Scott back into the task at hand. Scott then shook his head no, indicating no pulse. The three investigators moved back out into the hallway and down to a closet and yet another bedroom, both of which were clear.

Once the duplex had been cleared, the trio holstered their weapons with considerable relief. Darlene got on her radio and signaled those outside that all was clear in the building. "Code 4," she said, still out of breath from the tension of this grisly task. "We got two more bodies. Somebody get the coroner." Then they went back to the bedroom where the two bodies were. There they were joined by the MP's and a CID agent.

"Wow," Roland said, "this is some crime scene now." He turned to the MP's and CID agent and backed them back out into the hall. "I can't have everyone traipsing in here." Pointing at the two MP's, he continued: "You and you guard the front and back doors. No one else gets in here, you hear? No one!" To the CID agent he said: "Get some help and have them tape off this entire duplex and the yard surrounding it. I don't want anybody going through the yard, either. Then get me two boxes ASAP." These are metal boxes containing equipment used by crime scene investigators." The agent nodded yes and took off in a hurry. Roland walked back to the bedroom where Scott and Darlene were still standing.

As he entered, Darlene said: "Damn, there's blood everywhere. It's going to be a long night." The three of them stared at the blood which appeared to be smeared everywhere. Then the CID agent returned with the CSI boxes.

"Let's photograph everything first, before anything gets moved," Roland instructed. "In fact, let's get video on everything inside the duplex and outside before we have a bunch of folks running through it all and before anything gets touched."

"Yes Sir," the CID man responded. "I've got the video cam inside my trunk. I'll be right back." The investigators on scene proceeded with their various tasks. When everything had been carefully videotaped and photographed, Roland and Darlene went back into the bedroom where the two male bodies were. A voice crackled on Darlene's radio.

"The girl is still alive," it said. "She's been flown to Tucson Medical Trauma Center."

Roland crouched over the body of the man lying face down behind the bedroom door. He was studying the body carefully. As he did, the scene reminded Darlene of the nightmare she recently had: blood everywhere and a dead body lying face down on the floor, just like this one. As Roland reached over and was about to roll the body over, it was not Nathan but Darlene who yelled.

"No! No! Don't touch him, Roland!" She ran over and grabbed her partner's arm. "Look," she continued, "his arm is tucked under his body. He's got something clutched in his hand!"

Roland froze, then glanced up at her. "So what do we do now?" He and Darlene scooted back on their butts away from the body. They stared at the corpse and then at each other, trying to figure out what to do next.

Darlene got an idea. "Let's get the kid's small mattress from the other room and put on Kevlar vests. We'll crouch behind the mattress and Kevlar and get a broom handle or something and roll this guy over."

"Okay, Dar. I guess it wouldn't hurt to dot our i's on this one." He and Darlene went to the front of the house, where the other CID agent and MP Scott were working. "Look, guys," he continued, "we may not have a Code 4 (All Secure) situation. The body behind the door has something tucked under him, possibly in his hand. I want everyone to clear out as Lieutenant—I mean Captain Fitzgerald and I clear the situation. Scott, you hustle out to the cars and bring us back three Kevlar vests. Then get E.O.D. (Explosive Ordinance Disposal) on the phone and tell them we might have a job for them. Tell them to get a can (a metal cannister designed to place explosives inside) over here." That was all Scott and the CID agent had to hear. They hightailed it out of the house.

Darlene and Roland went to the child's room and got his mattress. As they entered the hall with it, they were joined by Scott, who had brought the Kevlar vests. Scott laid the vests down on the floor.

"Thanks, Scott," Roland said. "Now get the hell out of here. You too, Darlene. I can handle this myself."

"Roland, don't make me pull rank on you," Darlene said. "You need help. There's no way you can hold the mattress, three vests, and roll over the body all at the same time. I'm staying and that's an order!"

Roland shot her a pained look. "There's no way I can stop you from doing this, is there?" Without answering, Darlene grabbed one end of the mattress and one Kevlar vest. Roland grabbed the other end and the remaining vests and they carefully carried them into the bedroom with the suspicious body. Roland put his load down and tipped over a small desk so that its top was parallel to the body in question. The he leaned the mattress against the front of the desk.

"Wise move, Weedhopper," Darlene said. Roland couldn't help but smile and shake his head slowly. Darlene hung the three Kevlar vests over the mattress and then went to the hallway closet. She found a sponge mop, and went back into the bedroom and handed it to Roland.

He took the mop and, staring at the body, said: "You know, if there's nothing under this guy we're gonna look like a couple of paranoid idiots."

Darlene answered: "Better two paranoid idiots than two stupid dead cops."

"Can't argue with that," Roland said. Then he took the sponge mop and from behind the Kevlar'ed mattress carefully maneuvered the sponge mop portion into the armpit of the body. It was not something they had practiced, and it took some doing, but he finally had hooked the sponge mop into position where he could roll over the body with it. "If this doesn't work, I mean if there's something there and we don't make it—"

Darlene place her gloved fingers over his mouth. "I know, Jack, I know." They received a transmission over the radio.

"Ma'am, E.O.D. has the can in place in the back yard, just beyond the porch."

Roland looked at Darlene with an expression of dread, turned slowly to the body, took a deep breath, and rolled the body over with the mop. As the corpse slowly rolled over, they could see that a grenade was clutched in its left hand. The pin had been pulled, but the hand was still clutched tightly around the spoon of the grenade, incapacitating it. When they saw the grenade, Roland and Darlene dropped the mop and crouched behind the mattress, breathing heavily.

"Congratulations," Darlene said, "we're not idiots. But we got to get that pin back into that grenade or we're both toast." Roland extended his arm and gave Darlene a strange look. She understood the gesture. "You want to play rock, scissors, and paper?"

"Don't worry," Roland replied. "You always win at this. Winner goes for the grenade. What do you say?" They played and for the first time, Roland won by pulling scissors to Darlene's paper. "I beat you," he said almost gleefully. "Wow. I really beat you."

"How about two out of three?" Darlene asked.

"No way, Jose. You're not cheating me out of this victory." Roland rushed over to the grenade and held the man's hand in his own, also wrapping it around the grenade.

"I got it! I got it!" he shouted. "I got the spoon!"

"You may end up a lucky stiff, Jack," Darlene said. "Let me see if I can find the pin for you." Darlene looked near the dead man's body and through his pockets. Finding nothing, she went to the other corpse. There, about a foot from that body, she found the pin. She crawled over to Roland holding the pin carefully. They were both breathing heavily. Darlene's hands were shaking as she attempted to delicately maneuver the pin back into its hole and prevent the grenade from exploding. Failing to do this, she sat back for a moment, still breathing heavily.

"You can do this, Darlene," Roland said. "Dammit, you can do this!" Darlene crawled back to Roland and, steadying herself, managed to get the pin back into the grenade. "You got it, Dar! Now get back behind the mattress in case the pin doesn't hold." Darlene paused, but before she could argue he yelled at her. "Do it!" Darlene crept back behind the barricade and peeked over the top. Roland slowly removed the grenade from the dead man's grip. Then he got to his feet and walked carefully out of the room, out the door of the duplex, and carried the grenade over toward the cannister by the porch. Two E.O.D. specialists were crouching behind a large black metal shield as they watched Roland moving slowly to the can.

"Okay Sir," one of the E.O.D. men said, "take it slow and easy. When you get to the can, just gingerly drop it in and then grab some dirt." His voice was steady and calm and it helped Roland relax as he approached the can. Roland nodded and moved closer and closer to the can, staring at the explosive device he held in his hand. He could hear his heart beating out of his chest. Despite the cold, sweat beaded down his face. He got to the can, dropped the grenade, dove for the ground and covered his head.

After a few seconds of dead silence, an E.O.D. specialist moved to the can, sealed it, and announced over the radio: "All clear, all clear." Roland continued to lie on the ground in relief and exhaustion from his ordeal.

"Thanks, Nathan," Roland said out loud. "Thanks, buddy." Then he jumped to his feet and ran over to the E.O.D. men shouting "Yeah! Yeah!" at the top of his lungs. They were all "high-five-ing" each other in joy. Darlene and the others bolted out of the back door and ran over to Roland. Darlene jumped into his arms. He spun her around, all the time yelling "Who's the man? Who's the man?"

As the excitement of the moment melted, an E.O.D. specialist carried the can with the grenade away. Roland, Darlene, and the others slowly came back down to earth as they remember that they still had a very difficult crime scene to process. They worked until the next morning. As Roland was carrying yet another bag of evidence out a co-worker came up to him.

"Colonel Rockwell wants to see you and the Captain ASAP for a briefing," the man said. "He said he was getting pressure from the post commander wanting to know what's going on."

"Okay," Roland replied, "I'll give him a call." He motioned to Darlene to join him, and together they walked back into the house. "The old man wants a briefing," Roland explained. "He's getting heat from upstairs for the scoop." They went inside and called in to Colonel Rockwell, who told them to be in his office in two hours ready to fill him in on the details. After hanging up, Roland told Darlene: "Look, we're pretty much done here. We can let Scott and Jarvis finish up while we take showers and grab some coffee."

"Okay, but before we go I want you to see something." She led him back to the bedroom with the two bodies. Crouching over Washington's body, she pointed over to the hole in the wall nearby. "Roland, look at that entry hole of the round in the wall. Now you see how his knees are in relation to that hole. This guy was leaning forward in a kneeling position when he shot himself." Darlene demonstrated what she meant. "The trajectory of that slug came from less than three feet off the ground."

Roland whistled softly. "Man, that took some kind of guts for this bastard to think through something like that—to pull the pin and then grasp a grenade in one hand while you lean forward and blow your brains out with the other. The guy was leaning forward so he'd land on the grenade and cover it with his body."

"That's not guts. That's pure evil, to booby trap yourself like that. The S.O.B. wanted to make sure he didn't have far to fall so whoever found him would get blown up when he rolled the body over. Pure freaking' evil is what it was."

Two hours later, Darlene and Roland, cleaned up and wired on coffee, were sitting at a large conference table in Colonel Rockwell's office. As Rockwell's secretary took down every word, Darlene and Roland filled in Rockwell and the Post Commander, full bird Colonel Mitchell.

"The Reader's Digest version of what we have," Roland explained, "is that the BCD'd (bad conduct discharged) Washington sneaked back onto the base through a hole in the south mountain fence on the Mexican border. He had made a copy of a key to SP4 Francis' place which he secretly kept after they broke up, so when he gave her the original back he kept the duplicate. She didn't think to change the locks. Washington held the couple at gunpoint for at least twelve hours. He tortured them. The sicko must have made Sergeant Thomas watch while he sexually assaulted Francis, then he shot her in the mouth. It's a miracle she survived after he shot her again in the stomach. That's when she crawled out of the bedroom, into the hall, through the child's room and into the living room where she bled all over the couch. While this was going on, Washington did God knows what to Thomas as he held him at bay with his .357 revolver. We have front sight marks from the gun inside Thomas' mouth and Thomas' blood on the barrel of the gun. Thomas' front teeth were knock out from having the gun barrel jammed into his mouth." Rockwell and Mitchell winced as they heard these gruesome details.

Darlene took it from there. "We also have bruises matching the barrel and gunsight of Washington's weapon on both temples of Thomas's head. Both Thomas and Francis also have blunt force trauma injuries to various parts of their bodies, as well as cigarette burns. Now all of this took place while the minor child was in shock, frozen in the living room in front of the tv. The third shot heard by the neighbors was the one called in about 0130, and we believe that was the fatal shot to the head of Sergeant Thomas. It was shortly thereafter we made entry to the house when the fourth shot occurred, a self-inflicted wound to the head of Washington. He had grasped a grenade tightly into his chest, pulled the pin, knelt down on both knees, and leaned forward when he shot himself in the head using his other hand."

"How do you know he was on his knees?" Colonel Mitchell asked.

"The exit wound from Washington's head and the trajectory of the round into the adjacent wall would suggest he was in fact kneeling sir," Darlene answered. "Probably to insure that he would land on top of the grenade with the spoon intact so that when we arrived and turned his body over: boom!"

Mitchell shook his head in disbelief. "Damn! What a sick, evil bastard!" Roland gave Darlene a nod to continue.

"Since the perpetrator had been BCD'd and was now a civilian, we've already contacted Detective O'Leary of DPS, and he's out at the crime scene now giving us a hand. O'Leary has secured Washington's off-base motel room in anticipation of a search warrant. We've been up all night and both scenes are secured. So Roland, MP Scott and I are going to grab a couple of hours of sleep and then we'll get back at it. Additionally, Roland and I will attend Washington's autopsy tomorrow morning." When she had finished, Darlene leaned over and asked the Colonel's secretary: "Can I have a copy of that transcript? I can use it in my report and save myself some writing." The secretary smiled and nodded yes.

"What are you going to do with the grenade, Captain?" Colonel Mitchell asked.

"Sir, we're having the serial number traced to see if it was stolen from any of our depots. We're concerned that a civilian had possession of such ordnance, which is another reason for searching Washington's room."

Mitchell stood up. "Great work, soldiers! Now get some shuteye. You guys look terrible. Oh by the way, I heard about the jinx. Maybe we shouldn't let you two work together so we can have a little peace and quiet around here." He smiled sadly and shook his head. "Drive on, troops, and keep us informed."

"We'll give you another briefing on their progress after Washington's autopsy tomorrow," Colonel Rockwell added. The meeting broke up quickly.

Roland and Darlene drove out to the crime scene for a last look before getting some sleep. As they pulled into the driveway, O'Leary walked over and leaned on their vehicle by the driver's side window. "It's the two hexed cops," he said. Then he made a cross with his fingers and added: "Back, back you cursed heathens!"

Darlene and Roland were not amused. "Ha-ha. Yuck it up, asshole," Darlene said.

"Oh come on, soldiers, You know I love you guys."

"Yeah, right. How's it going?" Roland asked.

"Man, this is some pretty gruesome stuff you guys got here. This Washington was a real sicko. Anyhow, based on what we got so far it'll be no problem getting a warrant. I'm headed back to the office to start writing. By the way, you guys look terrible. Get a couple hours of sleep and then I'll call you." O'Leary and Roland high-fived each other. O'Leary held on to Roland's hand and gave him a serious look. "Roland, I'm glad things turned out okay with the grenade and all. I know that must have been pretty intense, man."

"It was out of hand, man, totally out of hand," Roland said.

O'Leary stepped back and gave them a casual salute as they backed the car out of the driveway. He watched as their car rolled up the street, rounded the corner, and disappeared from view. Turning slowly around, he gazed at the quiet little residence which had witnessed such horror. "Geez," he said aloud to no one. "Geez." He walked back into the house.

7

The Connection

"Security is mostly a superstition. It does not exist in nature......
Life is either a daring adventure or nothing."
Helen Keller

O'Leary waited four hours before calling Roland on the phone. "Good morning Sleeping Beauty, this is your fairy godfather bringing you good tidings of great joy."

Roland sat up in bed and rubbed his eyes. "Man, quit mixing up your fairy tales. What time is it, anyway?"

"Thirteen hundred hours (1 pm). Get your lazy ass down to my office for a search warrant briefing."

"1300?" Roland yelled. "Why'd you let me sleep so long?"

"Because you're ugly," O'Leary laughed, "and sad and tired."

Roland hung up the phone and called Darlene. Half an hour later, they were in O'Leary's office along with a couple of investigators from the Department of Public Safety. After a short briefing, O'Leary told them: "Let's saddle up, folks." They all proceeded to the motel where Washington had been living. Darlene and Roland gave a copy of the search warrant to the motel manager who obediently opened the killer's room up for them. O'Leary noticed Washington's journal lying on the desk, began reading it, and then spoke to the others in a serious tone of voice. "You guys better come over here and check this out."

Roland and Darlene looked over O'Leary's shoulder and read the crazed ranting Washington had written down. It contained detailed descriptions of how and where he had stalked SP4 Francis and Sergeant Thomas, along with some of the things he was going to do to them before he killed them. Washington also noted that he had called Specialist Francis and she had warned him that she would be meeting with Captain Nedaheiger to complain about being threatened and harassed.

Darlene rubbed her forehead in disgust. "That f_ _ _ ing Knee High! She went to him for help and he did nothing!"

O'Leary was incredulous. "So you guys never got a call from him or anything?"

Darlene and Roland shook their heads. Roland spoke: "What a piece of crap that Nedaheiger is!"

"Yeah," Darlene agreed, "and there's a word for this. It's called contributory negligence resulting in a homicide. The little bastard's gonna pay for this!"

"Well sports fans," Roland said after a moment of stunned silence, "what now?"

"We go after the little prick," Darlene said, "that's what we do."

Roland smiled in agreement. "And the fun just never stops." One of the DPS officers walked over and handed O'Leary a document. O'Leary looked at it and handed it to Roland, who glanced at it and handed it to Darlene. "Like I said," Roland continued, "the fun just never stops."

Darlene took the paper and quickly read it. "You've got to be f_ _ _ ing kidding me," she said. The paper was a storage locker receipt from nearby Bisbee, Arizona, stapled to a credit card receipt. The name on the credit card was Wayne Gilbert, the same name as the leader of the terrorist organization Posse Comitatus. "I'll call Colonel Green," Darlene said. "He's not going to believe this!"

At 0800 the next morning, Darlene, Roland and O'Leary were at the Coroner's Office observing the autopsies of Washington and Thomas. In the dull, monotonous voice of a man who has seen death in all its bizarre forms, the coroner was speaking into a hand-held recorder as he listed the injuries to Thomas' body inflicted by Washington. There were sixteen cigarette burns and numerous bruises to the head and genitals caused by the barrel of a gun. In addition, most of Thomas' teeth had been broken out by the front sight on the gun's barrel being rammed repeatedly into his mouth by Washington. The bullet wound to Thomas' head was from a shot fired at point blank range and the entry was surrounded by powder burns. This entry wound corresponded exactly to the exit wound at the back of the dead Sergeant's head. The coroner would pause occasionally in his investigation to take a healthy bite from a bacon, lettuce, and tomato sandwich, which he would wash down with a sip from a can of Mountain Dew. He glanced over at Darlene and Roland, who were looking at him with some astonishment. "Damn good sandwich," he told them, and belched softly. "Washington's chemical tests all came back negative, indicating he had no intoxicants or drugs in his body for at least forty-eight hours prior to committing these offenses." He belched again and patted his stomach. "I'd say that Washington was stone cold sober when he had his little party on this poor guy. Took his time, too, I'd say." His work completed, the coroner clicked off his recorder and went back to his lunch.

A couple of hours later, Darlene and Roland were giving another briefing in Colonel Rockwell's office. Also present were Task Force Thunder Commander Kenny Green, Post Commander Colonel Mitchell, the JAG Commander Colonel Rosenberg, and local DPS Post Commander Major Forrest. The men listened to the briefing in disgust and were particularly upset to hear of Captain Nedaheiger's apparent failure to contact the MP's or CID when he learned about the stalking and threats against SP4 Francis and Sgt. Thomas.

"So you want to go after Nedaheiger?" JAG Commander Rosenberg asked.

"Absolutely," Darlene replied. "We think it's about contributory negligence resulting in a homicide, conduct unbecoming, and anything else we can nail on that little weasel."

Rosenberg nodded in agreement. "If Nedaheiger knew this was going on and failed to act, he should be made an example of. We don't need that kind of thing in the Army if chain of command is to have any meaning."

"What about the storage locker in Bisbee?" Colonel Rockwell asked.

Colonel Green answered. "Since Wayne Gilbert's name is on the receipt, Darlene, Roland, O'Leary and I are of the consensus that this inquiry should continue as a Task Force Thunder investigation given the involvement of Posse Comitatus. To my knowledge, it will be the first U.S. terrorist murder investigation conducted by a counter terrorism task force."

"We're already on board in the task force anyway," Roland added. "This thing looks like it's gonna go well past a murder-suicide."

"It's a good place to start spending some of the funding we've got," Colonel Green added, "and I agree that we're only at the beginning of a much bigger story than one homicidal maniac and a couple of innocent victims."

"We're on our way over to the storage locker in Bisbee," Darlene told Colonel Green as they were leaving Rockwell's office. "And then—"

"And then what?"

"And then I get to go ten rounds with Knee High in an interrogation room."

Colonel Green took Darlene's arm and fixed her with a steady gaze. "I can tell you're really looking forward to that, my little friend."

"What goes around comes around, Colonel," she replied.

Bisbee, Arizona, is a small, historical copper mining town overlooking the Mexico-U.S. border about forty minutes southeast of Fort Huachuca. The copper had been exhausted long ago, and now the town lived off the occasional tourists who wandered through on their way elsewhere. It had also once been a haven of the Charles Manson gang, and a few members could still be seen wandering around with X marks branded on their foreheads. Local gift shops sold t-shirts with "Bisbee: Rubble Without A Cause" emblazoned on them. Others in the tiny population included retired couples, aging hippies, starving artists, and assorted tramps and losers who couldn't or didn't want to get out.

Darlene, O'Leary, Roland and Green stood in the manager's office of the storage locker facility. The manager fit into the 60's hippie throwback category.

"What's happenin', dudes?" he said pleasantly.

O'Leary showed him the search warrant. "We want to look into this locker."

"Okay by me, detective dude." He led them to the locker in question and unlocked it. "Whaddya lookin' for, if I may ask?"

"Just playing a hunch, son," Colonel Green replied. "Now maybe you want to step back while we open it."

"No prob, Colonel dude."

O'Leary opened the door and he and Roland stepped inside, where Roland threw on the light switch. Everybody's jaw dropped as they looked upon a mountain of weapons and munitions, including grenades, grenade launchers, mortars, explosives, and a huge cache of rifles, machine guns, and ammunition.

"Hello," Colonel Green said. "Welcome to my world."

Roland walked over to a little cluster of gas masks and lifted one up to his face. "Trick or treat?" With that, the investigators gave each other hi-five's.

"Folks," Colonel Green said, "we got some phone calls to make. Dar, you get hold of E.O.D. O'Leary and Roland, you get us some uniforms to load this stuff up and escort it back onto the base. I'll secure a location to store it while we track down all the serial numbers and see where it came from."

O'Leary turned to the facility manager. "Son, have you seen this man before?" He showed him a photograph of Wayne Gilbert.

"That's him, dude, that's the cat who rented the place. Yeah, it was him and another guy wearing an army uniform."

"Bingo," O'Leary smiled. "People, we have ignition!"

Darlene raised her hand, put a finger to her to her lips, and squinted her eyes, deep in thought. Colonel Green also motioned for silence.

"Wait everybody," he said with a smile, "the hamster in her head is running in the wheel a mile a minute."

"What if—" Darlene wondered as she drew the three investigators aside in a huddle, "what if we leave everything where it is and set up video surveillance to see who comes for it." She pointed outside at the video cameras on the rooftops of some of the storage lockers. "We could arrange to beef up the cameras, maybe even hide one in here, then see who adds or subtracts from this pile of goodies. It might be surprising to see who shows up."

"Me likee!" O'Leary added, then turned to the facility manager. "You'll help your Uncle Sam catch some bad guys, won't you Woodstock?"

"Damn straight! This is cool!"

Colonel Green became serious. "Look, son," he told the manager. "The people who put this stuff here are extremely dangerous. You haven't seen anything and you don't know anything, right?"

"Right on, major dude."

"He's not kidding," Roland added. "These folks won't hesitate to kill you if they think you can mess them up."

"I haven't seen anything and I don't know nothin', okay? Like, I don't even see you now!" the manager replied.

"Okay," Colonel Green said. The manager beat a hasty retreat as Green continued.

"We better work fast. It'd be just our luck if somebody sees what we're up to and let's the cat out of the bag."

"O'Leary," Darlene said, "go with the manager and make sure he's air tight. Roland and I will take some Polaroids of this stuff and get some serial numbers so we can start tracing it. Then we'll get the hell out of here. We better leave somebody here watching this stuff or it'll walk off camera or not."

As O'Leary turned to follow the manager, he said: "I'll get some plain clothes guys down here ASAP. I'll call from the manager's office. Then our agencies will have to take turns providing the manpower U.C. (undercover operatives) to surveil this."

"I'll see to it," Colonel Green replied. Darlene and Roland quickly took some pictures and jotted down those serial numbers which hadn't been scraped off. Then they checked the facility's video cameras to make sure they worked properly. Everybody took off as soon as O'Leary's plain clothes men arrived and took up their positions out of sight.

The following day, Darlene, Roland, Green, and two burly MP's walked into Captain Nedaheiger's office. Darlene smiled pleasantly at the man she loathed. "Captain, you need to come with us." First Sergeant Phalen walked into the office.

"What's all this about?" Phalen asked.

"Top," Roland replied, "you'll need to follow us, too." Top shot Nedaheiger a look that unmistakably said they were in deep trouble. Then the entourage went outside, where several MP-marked patrol cars were waiting, engines running. Nedaheiger was placed in one unit, Sergeant Phalen in the other. Darlene broke away from Green and Roland and went back to Phalen's car.

"I'll ride with Top," she told them. "Meet you at the station." She smiled at the men and Roland nodded at her, knowing what she was up to.

"Yeah," he said. "We'll see you there."

During the brief car trip, Darlene sat in the back seat with Sergeant "Top" Phalen. "I guess you know what this is all about," she told him calmly. Top squirmed in his seat as Darlene continued. "Top, listen very closely to what I have to say, and then think on it for a while before you answer. I have enough on Nedaheiger to bury him in Leavenworth 'til hell freezes over. There's contributory negligent homicide, conduct unbecoming, failure to follow lawful written orders, conspiracy and a partridge in a pear tree. Unfortunately, there's also enough to bury you right along with him." As she spoke, Darlene could see by Phalen's expression that his spirits were sinking lower with each charge. "But I've done some homework on you, Top, and you're not Nedaheiger. In fact, you're a damn good leader. It's really sad that your first big mistake may also be your last. Now get this: I don't want to put the screws to you if I don't have to, so do yourself a big fat favor. If you'll corroborate our story on Knee High, I think we can come to a mutual agreement that'll benefit everybody except the little twerp. It's not like you're protecting Alvin York or Audie Murphy here. Think about it." Darlene sat back and she and Phalen finished the trip in silence.

Their car arrived just as Captain Nedaheiger was being led up the steps into the Criminal Investigations Department office. After a few moments, Darlene gave the car's driver a nod and he got out and opened the door for them. She walked the forlorn Phalen up the creaky stairs as he hung his head in despair. She led him to an interview room which contained a small wooden table, two deliberately uncomfortable wood chairs, and a large mirror on the wall.

"Sit in that chair, Sergeant," she said, indicating the chair which also faced the mirror, and then left the room. Darlene walked down the hall to where Roland, O'Leary and Colonel Green were standing. Roland led them into a conference room where they could speak privately. A CID secretary brought them some coffee.

"So what did he say," Roland asked about Sergeant Phalen. "Is he going to play ball?" Darlene relished the moment, slowly emptying numerous packets of sugar and quite a lot of cream into her cup.

"Damn, Darlene," O'Leary jeered, "have a little coffee with your cream and sugar!"

"Don't worry," she answered calmly. "He'll cooperate. I want to let him and Knee High sit in their interview rooms for a while. Let'em both think that the other one is being interviewed first. They'll be dying to know what the other one is saying. Give'em a little time for the panic to settle in."

Colonel Green took a sip of coffee and smiled. "Darlene, I admire your keen understanding of the workings of the human mind."

"What you're really saying is you admire what a bitch she is," Roland corrected.

Darlene looked down at the paperwork she was holding and rubbed her forehead conspicuously with her middle finger so that Roland could clearly see it.

Colonel Green laughed. "So we sit here, drink coffee, eat muffins, cap on each other and shoot the breeze while Nedaheiger and Phalen imagine the worst." Darlene looked up and smiled.

"Damn girl," Roland said. "I hope I never really piss you off." As they continued to chat and relax, Nedaheiger and Top sat in their little rooms facing mirrors they were each convinced concealed the prying eyes of their captors when in fact nobody was behind them. About twenty minutes went by.

Darlene glanced at her watch. "I guess our little pots have had long enough to come to a boil," she said with a wicked smile on her face. "I want to talk to Phalen first, while Knee High stews just a bit more." The group got up and sauntered down the hall, pausing to step behind the mirror looking into Captain Nedaheiger's room. They could see him squirming in his chair and looking around nervously. Then they continued down to look through the mirror at Sergeant Phalen. He, too, looked like he was a kid who had been caught with his hand in the cookie jar and had been told by his mother to "wait until your father gets home!" As they observed him, the group was joined by a CID secretary who handed Roland some paperwork and then departed.

"Here you go," Roland said, handing the papers to Darlene. "It's the printout of the UCMJ (Uniform Code of Military Justice) charges and the proffer (legal agreement commonly used for cooperating subjects) you asked JAG to write."

As Darlene checked the papers, Colonel Green spoke about her to the others. "She has a certain dark side to her, doesn't she?"

"That's what I like best about her, Sir," Roland replied. Darlene left the group to walk around to the entrance to Phalen's conference room. She carried a cup of coffee and a bagel for the Sergeant, along with the documents she had just read over. She gave Top the food and asked him: "Can I get you anything else before we get started?"

"Not unless you can get me out of here right now," he replied.

"Well, Top, that's just what I'd like to do. But first we have to attend to a couple of things. I have to read you the charges that are being alleged against you under the UCMJ, then I have to read you your Article 32 rights and this waiver. After that, the rest is up to you." Slowly and deliberately, Darlene read the list of charges being brought against Sergeant Phalen. With each charge, Phalen could see his career going right down the drain.

When she had finished, Darlene asked: "Now you do understand each and every charge that I have read here today, don't you Sergeant Phalen?"

"I understand," Phalen reluctantly replied.

Darlene turned the charge sheet around, slid it across the table to him, and pointed at the line on the bottom. "I need you to sign there," she said, passing him a pen. "It states you have read and understand the charges." With his hand visibly shaking, Top signed the paper. Darlene quickly snatched the paper from him and began reading him another. "Sergeant Phalen, under the Uniform Code of Military Justice you have the right to remain silent. Anything you say may be used against you." Darlene continued to read him his rights as he stared blankly at the table.

Roland, O'Leary and Green watched this happen hidden behind the mirror. "Jesus," O'Leary said softly, "he's already been reduced to a shell of a man. Look at him. He'll sign anything now."

"Yeah," Roland agreed. "A little fear goes a long, long way."

Darlene finished reading Top his rights. "If you wish to waive each of these rights I've read to you, and you wish to cooperate fully with our investigation, I need you to sign right here." She passed Phalen another sheet and he signed it. The Sergeant then buried his head in his arms on the table. Darlene felt sorry for him. "Top, you're doing the right thing. The worst is just about over now. If I were in your shoes, I'd do this."

Phalen looked up at her. "Then why do I feel like such a weasel?"

"The only weasel in this whole thing is that rat bastard Nedaheiger, for putting you into this situation. No self-respecting soldier would have done this to you. He's the one who has to answer for this. You know it and I know it."

"I know you're right, Captain," Phalen said. "Let's cut to the chase and get this over with. What's next?"

Darlene sat back in her chair and turned on a tape recorder which was lying on the table. "I have to record this interview. Regulations. Now just tell me in your own words what happened." With that, Phalen recounted the whole story of how Specialist Francis and Sergeant Thomas had come to Captain Nedaheiger with their complaint looking for help only to have their concerns fall on deaf ears.

Phalen also said for the record that he had told Nedaheiger that he should go to the MP's and had been rebuffed. The whole ordeal took Sergeant Phalen about half an hour to lay out, after which Darlene left with the recorder and signed documents. She joined the group still huddled behind the observation mirror.

"Okay boys," she said cheerfully. "Knee High next."

After complimenting her on the interview, Colonel Green asked: "Darlene, given you relationship with Nedaheiger do you think you should be the one interviewing him?"

"My relationship with him is exactly why I should do it," she said. "Here's my plan: I'm not really going to interview him. That's what he expects. He would perceive an interview as us not having a real good case against him. He'll think we need him to cop to something. That isn't so. He can be charged right now. Remember, he's a legend in his own mind and he's pretty sure he can outsmart a mere girl, so I'm not going to play his game. I'm just going to check mate him and take the wind out of his sails right away."

The men listened to this with increasing interest.

"This I got to see," Roland said.

"Watch and learn, boys. Watch and learn," Darlene added with an impish grin.

"Like I said before," Green said, "you do have a dark side."

Darlene went into the conference room where Nedaheiger sat nervously, as again the others watched from behind a mirror. She sat down opposite him with a confident expression. "Good morning, Captain. Sorry to have kept you waiting but I had other business to attend to first."

"What's this all about, Fitzgerald?"

"Well, I'm going to read to you a list of charges under UCMJ, and then I'm going to read you your Article 32 Rights Waiver Warnings. Then I am going to officially relieve you of your command and place you under post house arrest, pending final investigation."

As she proceeded calmly along on her duties, Darlene hid her pleasure at the deep shade of red that was washing over Nedaheiger's enraged face.

"You can't do that," he exploded. "You have no authority to do that!"

"The post commander has already signed the order," Darlene replied, leaning a little closer to him. "An Article 32 hearing of indictment is being held tomorrow morning at 1000 hours at my request, Captain."

Watching Nedaheiger's darkening expression, Roland told the others behind the mirror: "I better get in there. Knee High looks like a caged rat." He walked into the interrogation room and positioned himself between Darlene and Nedaheiger.

Darlene continued calmly. "Here is a list of charges against you. I suggest you read along with me." When she had finished reading them, she added: "You have a right to an attorney and Captain, I suggest that you exercise that right immediately." With that, Darlene neated the folder she held by tapping it edgewise on the table in the same arrogant manner Knee High had at his meeting with Washington's victims. She looked at him with an expression of utter contempt. Nedaheiger just lost it.

"I knew it would be a disaster when they let women in the military," he sputtered.

Darlene smiled and she gathered the papers together with her coffee cup and leaned across the table, baiting him.

"Why Francis," she said acidly, "I should think that you of all people should be grateful they let women into the Army. That's when they reduced the height standards, which is the only reason you're sitting here right now, Knee High."

Nedaheiger exploded out of his chair and lunged across the table at Darlene. Roland quickly jumped between them, pushing Knee High back toward his chair.

"Go ahead, moron, hit me," Darlene pleaded. "I'll put you in Leavenworth for an extra decade or so." Nedaheiger suddenly realized what she was doing and sat back down, still seething.

Roland told her: "Will you please get out of here and let me handle this?"

"No problem, Roland," Darlene replied, dangling the incriminating charges in front of her. "I have everything I need right here." She walked to the door, but could not resist turning around and adding: "Oh and Francis, remember that one of the orders clearly states that you are not to discuss this case with anyone, and I do mean anyone, other than your attorney." As she left the room, she was met by Colonel Green and O'Leary in the hall. They were smiling and shaking their heads.

Seconds later, Roland exited the interview room, walked up to the group and gave Darlene a disapproving look. "You do that again and I'll kill you myself," he said. They all went into another conference room. "Okay," Roland continued. "You've scared the crap out of him. Before I left him, I slid the phone over to him and told the little rat he better call an attorney. So what does he do? He refuses and tells me he wants to talk to Darlene again. You were right, Dar. He thinks that by beating you in a battle of wits he can get himself out of this mess."

"It's called empowerment," Green said. "Darlene placed herself in a position of power over Nedaheiger and didn't give him a chance to take any of that power away. I have to admit it was a nice piece of work."

"Oh do stop," Darlene said with mock humility. "You're making me blush." She fanned herself frantically and broke the tension as they all had a good laugh. Darlene was surprised at how much of a rush she felt after humiliating Knee High the way she did. But all of that passed quickly as they turned again to the task at hand.

"Now, Professor, what's your next move?" the Colonel asked Darlene.

"We'll have Knee High escorted back to his house in a marked unit and take Top back to his barracks in an unmarked unit for a little additional psychological warfare. Let Top take over the unit for a while and make sure that information leaks back to Nedaheiger. In the mean time, we have to brief Colonel Rockwell, the Post Commander, DPS and JAG tomorrow morning at 0700 before we indict Knee High at 1000 hours. By then, maybe we'll also get lucky and get a break on our surveillance of that storage locker in Bisbee."

"About that," O'Leary added, "I sent an unmarked unit by Wayne Gilbert's house and business in Tucson this morning. I told them to cop some plates and not take a burn (cop slang for being discovered by crooks while on surveillance)."

"Great work, everyone," Colonel Green said. Then looking at Darlene and Roland, he added: "Maybe the jinx is finally starting to wear off of you two. We'll reconvene at 0700 tomorrow."

8

A Fine Mess

"Lord, what fools these mortals be!"
William Shakespeare

At 0630 the next morning, Darlene was already at her desk having some coffee when O'Leary knocked at her door.

"Come in, come in," she said. "Man, you're early. Tell me some good news."

O'Leary smiled and threw some documents on her desk. "Read'em and weep." Darlene looked at the papers as O'Leary continued. "My guys up in Tucson got some plates yesterday. Seems that Mr. Wayne Gilbert of the Posse Comitatus has several vehicles, all of which have been driven down into Mexico on a regular basis. Additionally, my guys observed a Consolidated Freight tractor-trailer making a delivery at Gilbert's business. I took the liberty of contacting a friendly source at Consolidated and he ran the manifest for me. Gilbert's delivery was picked up from a U.S. Customs in-bond warehouse in Douglas, Arizona. It had been delivered there by rail."

Darlene looked up from what she had been reading. "What do you mean 'by rail'?"

"You know—choo-choo: rail," O'Leary replied in a condescending tone of voice. "The shipment originated from Agua Prieta via rail, crossed in Douglas, and landed in-bond there. Consolidated picked it up and delivered it to Tucson."

"Well how in the hell is he getting this stuff past Customs?"

"Good question. In fact, the million dollar question is how have all his shipments made it past Customs without ever being checked?" O'Leary pointed at one of the documents and continued. "Look here. Consolidated keeps a record of all secondary shipments. Secondary is a Customs terms for shipments that have been opened and searched. As indicated by the zeroes you see prominently placed here, none of Mr. Gilbert's many imports has ever been secondaried by Customs."

"So what are you telling me, O'Leary? Are you saying U.S. Customs has been bought off?"

"I'm not sure. But I am damn sure we need to find out."

Just then Roland poked his head into Darlene's office. "What's going on, guys?"

O'Leary and Darlene got up and, gathering the documents, headed for the door.

"Like you always say, Roland, the fun just never stops," Darlene said.

Roland spoke as the trio walked down the hall together. "Well, folks, there's more. We've run about half of the few serial numbers we got off the munitions in the Bisbee locker and have confirmed that most of it was stolen from our reserve Army depots."

Darlene paused in the hallway. "Then let me get this straight. This stuff is stolen and then smuggled south of the border?"

"Probably to let it cool off," O'Leary said.

Darlene thought for a moment. "Then Gilbert goes to Mexico, meets with his fence, buys this stuff, and then smuggles it back across the border into the U.S.?" she asked.

"All under the blinded eye of U.S. Customs," O'Leary replied.

"No f_ _ _ ing wonder we have such a huge drug problem in this country," Darlene said as they resumed walking towards their meeting. "You can get anything you want into the U.S.!"

Minutes later, the primary members of Task Force Thunder were in Colonel Rockwell's conference room updating Colonel Green, Post Commander Mitchell, JAG Colonel Rosenberg, DPS Commander Forrest, and Colonel Rockwell. When they had been briefed, Colonel Mitchell asked: "What do you intend to do about the possible Customs problem, Colonel Green?"

"I intend to contact Customs Office of Internal Affairs and ascertain if there is any suspicion of or ongoing investigation into this in-bond warehouse," Green replied. "Then I want Darlene and Roland to develop contacts among our local railroad managers, and get briefed on how these railroad shipments are supposed to work. O'Leary has a good contact at Consolidated who'll give us a heads up on Gilbert's next shipment."

JAG Commander Rosenberg made some notes and looked up at the group.

"It appears as though you guys started out with a jealous boyfriend and ended up with Pandora's box. I'm not so sure that I'm looking forward to opening that box and seeing what's inside."

"I agree," Major Forrest of the DPS added. "It does seem like the more you dig the more you find. I mean that in a good way, though. You're doing a great job. But this thing just keeps growing."

"Yes," Rosenberg added, "I echo that sentiment also. I'm just a little shocked by what a spider's web this is turning into. Still, the good news is that you'll have no problem indicting Nedaheiger this morning. Am I assuming that you want him to cooperate, too?"

"Well, Sir," Darlene answered, "I'd just as soon jam it to him. I can't see where he'll have any more beneficial information than what we already got from Top. I think we ought to make an example of him for not reporting what those two good soldiers told him. If he'd done his job, Sergeant Thomas might still be alive today and SP4 Francis wouldn't be in the hospital fighting for her life."

"I agree," Colonel Green said. "I don't think we need to be in the business of plea-bargaining these kinds of offenses away on an officer. Nedaheiger needs to answer fully for what he has done."

"Very well, then," Rosenberg concurred. "We'll proceed as planned."

Later that morning at 1000 hours, Green, O'Leary, and Darlene sat in a courtroom. Agent Jack Roland was at a desk with the JAG Prosecutor, Major James Sanders. At the table adjacent to them sat Captain Nedaheiger, along with his JAG attorney Major Christine Kirkland. As the Judge entered the courtroom the bailiff announced: "All rise for the honorable Judge, Colonel Robert Barnes." Everyone snapped to attention.

"At ease, people," Judge Barnes said as he took the bench. Prosecutor Sanders then commenced reading the charges against Captain Nedaheiger. The Judge asked Nedaheiger if he understood the charges against him.

"Yes Sir." Then Major Sanders asked Roland to take the stand, where he swore him in. Roland laid out the facts of the case against Captain Nedaheiger. In the indictment phase of an Article 32 hearing, the rules of procedure are similar to those in a civilian court.

One police officer or detective can relate all the relevant evidence. In this context, "hearsay" is admissible as evidence. During this process, Nedaheiger's defense counsel made several objections, all of which were noted by the Judge.

There followed a fifteen minute recess. Then the Judge returned the indictment against Captain Nedaheiger. "Captain Nedaheiger, I'm compelled to forward this case to a jury of your peers in a Court Martial, based upon the evidence presented. You have ninety days to prepare your defense, after which I'll hear further motions from both sides. Hearing date for all motions, motions for summary judgment, and final disclosure are scheduled for March 17th. Until such time,

Captain Nedaheiger, you will be relieved of all your military duties and security clearances pending the outcome of this Court Martial."

Then Judge Barnes tapped his gavel and with that Nedaheiger was indicted.

Darlene made a fist and subtly punched the chair in front of her. "Yeah," she whispered. "What goes around comes around, you little rat bastard!"

"I couldn't agree with you more on that one," Roland whispered to her.

Out in the hallway, Colonel Green told his Task Force members: "Folks, I think we could use a break. I've squared it with all your commanders for you to go home, take the day off and rest. Tonight I'm buying you all dinner at the Thunder Mountain Inn." The Inn was the best and most expensive restaurant in town, and this news was happily received by the group.

As they were walking out of the building, Roland approached Darlene and motioned her away from the others. "I'm not tired," he said. "But I am a little nervous after being grilled on the stand. You want to run?"

"Yeah, I got some nervous energy I need to work off." The two met up a few minutes later at Black Tail Canyon. They jogged in silence up the trail, marveling as always at the stark beauty of the place. Finally, Darlene broke the silence. "God this place is incredible. I can see why so many officers come here to retire."

"You know what they say—best kept secret in the Army." They continued to run, and Darlene began to sense that something was troubling Roland. She slowed to a walk. Roland at first didn't notice she had fallen behind. Then, when he did, he turned and jogged back to her. "What's wrong?" he asked. "Are you okay?"

"I don't know. You tell me, Roland. What's wrong?"

Roland stopped jogging in place. He put his hands on his hips, took a deep breath, and looked to the beautiful mountains for just the right words to say. Darlene saw him struggling to speak, and added: "C'mon, Roland, you're scaring me. What is it?"

"I got orders yesterday."

"Orders? What kind of orders?"

"A few weeks ago, I put in for a tour in Germany. I mean, what's the point of being fluent in the language if you never use it?" He tried to break the tension by forcing a little laugh, which only emphasized the awkwardness of the moment.

Darlene looked at the ground in stunned silence. Then she began to walk down the path and the walk soon became a fast jog. Roland watched her for a moment, and then ran to catch up with her. They ran together for a couple of minutes, then Darlene stopped and turned to him. "Why did you do that? Why didn't you tell me before you did something stupid like that?" She turned and began running down the hill. Roland followed. When he had caught up to her, he began trying to explain but Darlene held up a hand in a gesture of "I don't want to hear it" and kept going. "Just leave me alone," she told him.

When they reached the bottom, where their cars were parked, Darlene made straight for hers and quickly unlocked it. Roland got to her after she had started her car. "You need to walk and cool down or you're going to get leg cramps," he said. She ignored him and quickly sped away as he leaned over and placed his hands on his knees, catching his breath. When she got home, Darlene dashed into her apartment, slammed the door, threw off her clothes, and jumped into a hot shower. She was crying and her deep sobs almost took her breath away. Soon she could hear Roland knocking at her front door and yelling her name, but she ignored him.

Roland used his key to let himself in. He heard the shower and walked to her bedroom, where he sat in a chair near the bathroom door and searched for something to say. "I'm sorry," he yelled over the rushing water. "It seemed like the right thing to do. I wanted you to have a clean slate with Colonel Green. He's a good catch. He's better for you than I am. We have too much history between us and I didn't think we could get past it." He waited for a moment to see if Darlene would respond. When she didn't, he tried the bathroom door. It was locked. "You can't stay in there all day. You'll turn into a prune!"

The bathroom door opened and Darlene came out in a bath robe with a towel wrapped around her head. She passed Roland without looking at him and went into a walk-in closet. Roland tried to follow, but she shut the door in his face. He backed up slowly, and sat on the bed shaking his head sadly. Darlene began dressing inside the closet.

"C'mon, Dar," Roland said, still trying to defuse the situation with humor. "It's time for you to come out of the closet, anyway."

Darlene finished dressing, took a deep breath, dried her eyes, and came out.

She sat on the bed next to him. After another awkward pause, she turned to him and began to speak at the same moment he began to speak to her. They stopped.

"Go ahead," Roland said softly.

"No, no, you go ahead," Darlene said.

"Okay. First, I'm sorry. I would never hurt you. I thought I was doing the right thing for you. He's everything I'm not. We both know you'll be better off with Kenny than with me."

"And where is my opinion in all this? You didn't bother to ask me what I think or want. What other decisions have you made for me? Why don't you just plan out the rest of my life for me?"

"I'm sorry," Roland replied. "What can I say? But I don't know what else I can do. It tears me up watching you with him and knowing I can't have you."

Darlene softened, seeing his anguish. "Look, I want you to answer something for me. Forget about our past and forget about Colonel Green. If there was no Colonel and if Nathan had never existed, what would you wish for right now?"

"Well, I mean—" Roland stammered.

"C'mon, just tell me what you really want. And I don't want to hear what you think is best for me. Be straight with me. What do you really want?"

"I think you know the answer to that question, Darlene."

"No I don't. I want to hear it. I want you to say it just once, Roland. I need to hear you say it."

Roland stood up and walked over to the window, staring off into space. "I'm in love with you. I've been in love with you since the day I met you. You fell in love with my best friend and I had to let you go then, just like I have to let you go now. I can't keep living like this. We both know what really happened that night. I caused Nathan's death. I should never have tossed him the keys to my motorcycle. I knew he was drunk. I never should have let him walk out of there, and I have to live with that. I will always feel like I stole you away from my best friend. I'll always wonder what was going through my mind when I tossed him my keys." Roland sat back down on the bed and continued looking out the window. His eyes welled up with tears. "Don't you get it? I'll never feel right about having you. It will never be right. Never. Nathan will always be between us."

Darlene sat down next to Roland on the bed, and they both looked out the window. It began to snow. She spoke gently. "How do we know it'll never be right if we don't try? Can you really go off to Europe and wonder what we might have had together? Which do you think is worse: us trying to be together or wondering what would have happened?"

Roland smiled weakly. "I should have had the guts to have this conversation before I put in for Germany. Now it's too late. I leave in sixty days. It was thirty, but I got it bumped to sixty in order to finish this investigation."

"This is a fine mess you've gotten us into, Jack Roland. What in the hell do we do now?"

"I've told you how I feel," Roland said after a pause. "Now it's your turn. What about you? I'm a big boy. You can give it to me straight. Do you want to try this or not?"

Darlene looked intensely at Roland. "Well, we have sixty days, right? I think we should make these sixty days count. I don't want to spend the rest of my life not knowing. I think I'm in love with you, Roland. I wasn't at first. Not when I met you. But after Nathan died, well, somewhere along the way it just happened. I don't even think I realized it until you told me about Germany. I don't want to lose you—not without at least trying."

Roland looked at her with a surprised expression, then smiled. "Okay, so that's it, then. We both agree. For the next sixty days, we're gonna give this a try, right?" They sat together quietly, digesting everything that had just been said. Then Roland's face took on a dark look. "What if this does work out? What if we find out that we really are made for each other. Then I go to Germany. What then?"

"Don't borrow trouble, Roland. We'll jump off that bridge when we get to it."

"Cross," Roland replied with a smile. "We'll cross that bridge when we get to it."

Darlene's stomach burned, and she felt like an elephant was sitting on her chest.

"There's just one more thing, Roland."

"What's that?"

"No more booze. I mean it."

Roland thought for a minute, knowing how hard that would be. He nodded his head yes even as he struggled with the thought. Then Darlene's pager went off. Seconds later, Roland's did as well. "I forgot," he said. "We're duty again tonight. Damn! This no drinking stuff—when exactly does it start?"

"Now, Roland. It starts right now." Darlene picked up her telephone and called the MP Station on post. She asked the Desk Sergeant: "What's going on?"

"Hello Captain. We got a wreck out towards the west gate. It looks bad. We need you guys to come on in. We've paged Roland and he hasn't called in yet."

Crossing her fingers, Darlene lied: "He's waiting for me out front. We'll be right there." Hanging up, she told Roland: "It's some sort of bad wreck out by the west gate. They want us both to get in there."

"Look, I'm dressed," Roland replied. "I'll go ahead and give you some time to finish dressing." With that, he drew Darlene into his arms and gave her a long, passionate kiss.

"I'll see you out there," he said on his way out. His kiss left Darlene breathless and a little disoriented. She quickly gathered her thoughts.

About twenty minutes later, Roland pulled up to the scene of the accident. The MP's had the road blocked off, waiting for the investigators to come. The paramedics were treating a man who was sitting on the back of an ambulance. O'Leary saw Roland and walked over to him.

"And we all thought we had the day off," O'Leary said, referring to the time off Colonel Green had told them to take. O'Leary put his hand against Roland's chest to keep him from the accident. "This is a bad one, Roland. Maybe you should get someone else out here."

Roland gave him an odd look. "What's going on?"

"It's a motorcycle accident. Two kids on a bike dashed out of a side road in front of that guy's truck," O'Leary said, pointing towards the man getting medical attention. "Both kids on the bike are dead." Roland stopped and simply glared at the road as O'Leary continued. "Hey buddy, are you gonna be all right with this?"

"I'm cool. I can handle this."

As they walked closer to the accident scene, Roland listened as O'Leary spoke into a small tape recorder he kept for report purposes. "We have a dead female, approximately eighteen years of age. She was the motorcycle's passenger, and is lying on her back in the road about twenty feet from the suspected impact location. Upon my arrival, the motorcycle was lying about ten feet southwest of the female's body and at the base of a telephone pole. The initial vehicle impact of the collision appears to have knocked the helmet off of the female's head and sent her soaring through the air a distance of about twenty feet. The subsequent impact of her head against the pavement cracked open her skull, spilling brain matter onto the road and killing her instantly. The male driver of the motorcycle had been thrown about twenty feet into the telephone pole, killing him instantly. MP's responded to the accident and immediately called medical personnel to the scene, who in turn have summoned the coroner. Upon discovering that the driver of the truck was a civilian, the MP's notified the Department of Public Safety, and I responded."

Roland stood transfixed, staring at the mangled body of the boy at the base of the telephone pole. It was a traumatic scene, and Roland was struck by how unreal everything appeared. He couldn't keep an image of Nathan's mangled body lying in a ditch from occupying his mind. "They don't look real, do they, O'Leary?"

O'Leary patted his friend on the back and looked closely into his face. They both heard the sound of another vehicle pulling up, and turned to look.

"Oh Lord," Roland said. "It's Darlene. She doesn't need to see this, not so soon after Nathan." Darlene got out of her car.

"Damn! Too late now," O'Leary said.

Roland rushed up to Darlene and, putting his hands on her shoulders, spun her around away from the scene. "Darlene," he said softly, "you don't want to go over there. It's bad."

Darlene could see the concern on his face, but felt he shouldn't be shielding her this way in front of the troops. "Roland, I'm a professional. I've seen this kind of thing before and I can handle it."

"No, not like this. It's a motorcycle wreck, Darlene. A real bad one. Please let me handle this one by myself."

"I can handle it, Roland. I have to. Everyone's watching me and I have to." She broke free of his hold and walked over to where O'Leary was trying to take some measurements with his tape measure. Roland watched her with concern, but she didn't let any emotion show. O'Leary filled her in on the accident details. She pointed at the man getting medical attention. "Has anybody interviewed him yet?"

"Only briefly," O'Leary replied. "He said the motorcycle just came out of nowhere and he just couldn't stop. That matches up with the crime scene indicators so far."

"Roland," Darlene said pointing at the driver, "make sure that the hospital gets blood from him for BAC (blood alcohol content) levels, and they should admit him at least overnight for treatment of shock." Roland shook his head yes as he watched her walk over to both bodies and visually examine each one. He and O'Leary were surprised that Darlene could handle this situation without any display of emotion, as she appeared utterly calm.

Darlene took the tape measure from O'Leary and the three of them began measuring the length of the skid marks and documenting them. Roland took the end of the measure and he and Darlene plotted the length of one of the shorter marks. Roland stared at her with sad eyes.

"You doing okay, Darlene?"

"Roland, we both know that neither of us is all right with this, but we've got to keep it together for now. We can fall to pieces later. Dude, this is what we do. We process death."

"You're right," Roland said in a monotone. "We'll have nightmares later." When they had finished, they joined O'Leary, who was beside his vehicle pulling off the coveralls commonly worn by accident investigators over their clothes.

"You guys going to be okay?" O'Leary asked.

"Man, I could sure use a drink right now," Roland replied. "And I'm getting tired of this f_ _ _ ing jinx!"

"Yeah," O'Leary said. "You guys just can't seem to catch a break, can you?"

Darlene turned and began walking to her car, trying to control her anger over Roland's remark about needing a drink. She spoke over her shoulder. "Hey, I'll see you guys tonight. Remember, Green's buying dinner. I'm kinda tired. Think I'll go home and take a nap."

Roland turned to O'Leary as Darlene drove away. "Yeah, like she's really going to be able to sleep after all this." He leaned against O'Leary's car. "Man, why do we do this? What's wrong with us that we made the decision to do this kind of demented work? You know what Darlene just said? She said we process death."

O'Leary finished writing on his clipboard and tossed it into his car through the open driver's side window. He leaned back against his car next to Roland and folded his arms.

He spoke as they both stared at the beautiful Huachuca Mountains. "You know, if you believe all the psycho-babble the shrinks have written about cops, it's because we have a `crisis personality.' We've had some kind of trauma in our lives that makes us seek this work. See, we're comfortable doing this because we grew up with this trauma we had, or some kind of bull." Roland giggled as O'Leary continued. "Hey, there must be something to this. Look at us. I know it whenever I hang out with you and Darlene and see how screwed up you are. Kind of makes me feel normal."

"Comparison therapy," Roland offered. "We should charge you money to be with us, O'Leary. But don't you think you're as screwed up as I am?"

"Who me? Come on. Man, you know I love you like a brother, but you are the most intensely messed-up cop I ever met."

"I am?"

"Damn straight. There's something severely wrong with a guy who's so deeply in love with a girl he pushes her into the arms of another man. I love you, man, but I sure as hell don't get it." O'Leary put his arm around Roland and hugged him.

Roland smiled. "Well, then you're seriously not going to believe this one, either." He paused, searching for the right words. "Remember a few weeks ago when Darlene had her first real date with the Colonel?" O'Leary nodded yes. "Well, in response to my obvious inability to handle this situation, I put in for a transfer to Germany the very next day. I leave in sixty days.

O'Leary was shocked. "You did what? Does Darlene know?"

"I was telling her this morning when we got paged in for this and yeah, she's not taking it very well. Especially since I told her I was in love with her about two seconds after I told her I was leaving." O'Leary stood up and turned to face

Roland. Before he could speak, however, Roland continued. "Man, don't say it. I know I f_ _ _ ed up big time. Believe me, I know."

"Roland, like I said, I love you, man. But take it from someone a little bit older and wiser than you. I've been watching this game of cat and mouse between you guys for over a year now. What you're doing to that girl is wrong. You're mind-f_ _ _ing her because you can't handle your own guilt and pain, and it's wrong, Roland. It's just plain wrong!"

Roland looked up at his friend with tears in his eyes. "I know. I've made a real mess of things and now I don't know what the hell to do." He sighed sadly.

"C'mon, boy, and let daddy show you some mercy and I'll buy us both a drink. We make most shrinks right about cops having a drinking problem, too." The ambulance took the survivor away from the accident scene with its lights flashing and its siren wailing. "You hear that, Roland?" O'Leary continued as they walked. "It's the music of our life."

9

Changes

"You should have seen the one that got away."
Dorothy Parker

That evening, Darlene and Roland entered the Thunder Mountain Inn and saw that Colonel Green and O'Leary were already there. As they took off their coats and sat down at the table Green had reserved, the Colonel leaned forward and spoke anxiously.

"I'm glad you guys are here. I just got a page from our folks who are watching the storage locker and guess who showed up?"

"Wayne Gilbert," Darlene answered.

"The one and only," Green replied.

"Don't worry," O'Leary said. "With your guys and my guys on them we got a good team on their tail."

Green's expression remained serious. "I told them to stay on them when they leave the locker and see where they take this stuff. They'll update us as they go, and as of five minutes ago they were all still at the storage locker."

"Well, should we even order food?" Darlene wondered. "We don't want to get paged out of here right after the waiters bring dinner."

"It's okay," Green said. "I've told the cops on the scene to just take photo's and document where things go. We should have time to eat before anything happens."

With that, everyone breathed a collective sigh of relief and picked up their menus. Green continued speaking, his face hidden behind his menu. "I hear you guys didn't get much rest today."

"Yeah," O'Leary said, "it looks like the jinx got'em again today, sir." Roland and Darlene exchanged embarrassed looks. O'Leary watched them, smiled, and continued. "Colonel, it looks like you're going to have to find a replacement for our dear friend Roland, here."

"What?" The Colonel responded. "You're leaving us, Roland?"

"Yes Sir," Roland answered. "It appears that I'm going to Germany in sixty days."

He glanced sheepishly at Darlene as he squirmed uncomfortably. She did not look up, instead focusing on her menu. A waitress took their orders.

An eerie quiet hung over the group as they ate their meals. Between waiting for their pagers to go off and end the meal and contemplating Roland's departure and its effect on things, it didn't seem like there was much to say. By the time they were finishing eating almost an hour later, the tension was so thick you couldn't cut it with a serrated hunting knife. The Colonel saw Darlene yawn.

"You guys must be exhausted," he said with a compassionate voice. "You've been going strong for days now on very little rest. Look, we've got good people on this surveillance and I'm sure nothing will be happening tonight. Now I can't order O'Leary to rest, but I can order you two and that's what I'm doing. I want you to go home and get a good night's sleep so that you'll be ready when something does happen."

"Sir, you don't have to tell me twice," Roland said.

"Yes, thank you Sir," Darlene added.

"Darlene, you barely ate," the Colonel replied. "I'm serious about this rest. You don't look well. If you guys don't get some serious rest you're going to get sick. I can't have that now. I need you too much."

As they all rose, Green signaled to O'Leary to remain. When Darlene and Roland had left, the Colonel ordered another drink for O'Leary and himself. O'Leary was uneasy.

"Ken, I can tell you have something on your mind and I think I know what it is. Look, I want to apologize for giving you the advice to pursue a relationship with Darlene. I thought it was the right thing to do. I thought it would be the best thing for everyone. I really did."

"And what do you think now?" Colonel Green inquired.

"Sir, you and I both know that those two kids are severely screwed up. Look, I never told you the complete story about that kid Nathan." Green sat up in his chair and paid close attention as O'Leary continued. "The night Nathan died, there was a fight. Roland and Nathan were at a party and they were both drunk. Darlene got mad at them and stormed out, leaving Nathan without wheels. Roland and Nathan had an argument about Darlene. Roland tossed the keys to his motorcycle to a very drunk Nathan and told him to go after Darlene. Well, you know what happened."

"Yes, but I thought you had said that Nathan was struck by a drunk driver."

"Yes, the driver who struck Nathan was drunk, but so was Nathan. The other driver crossed left of the center line and hit Nathan head on. Had Nathan not been plastered, maybe he could have made some evasive move or something. I guess we'll never know. But now you understand the extreme guilt both Roland and Darlene feel. They've never really dealt with it. They're also convinced that their actions with Nathan have brought this jinx on them they can't seem to shake. And there's more."

Colonel Green took a long drink from his glass. "Go on."

"This morning at the accident, Roland admitted for the first time that he's in love with her. I really don't think he realized just how much until he got his orders for the transfer to Germany. He put in for that transfer the day after your date with Darlene."

"Oh great!" the Colonel groaned. "It was obvious tonight that Darlene isn't handling any of this very well."

"Yeah, Roland told Darlene about the transfer this morning. He did this in the same breath as he was confessing to her that he loved her. This was right before they had to respond to the accident, which by the way involved a motorcycle and two dead kids. I guess the best way to put it is that Darlene and Roland are, well—"

"Shell-shocked," the Colonel offered.

"That's it, Kenny. Between the motorcycle accident this morning and thinking they're being punished for what happened to Nathan, they're a mess."

"Did they tell you that?"

"Not in so many words. But I know that's exactly what they feel."

"Well," the Colonel said after a pause, "what do I do now?"

"Sir, I don't know what to tell you. I just know that I'm sorry I gave you such bad advice in the first place. I like Darlene, and Roland is like a little brother to me. I thought they'd be better off going their separate ways, romantically speaking. There's just too much haunting them. I thought I was doing the right thing, and now everything is a mess."

"Poor Darlene," the Colonel said. "What's she going to do now?"

"Like we said, the two of them are just shell-shocked." O'Leary and Green sat quietly, sipping their drinks, lost in thought.

Roland was pulling into Darlene's parking area to let her off. Ever the gentleman, he walked her to her door. As she opened the door to her apartment, Roland stood outside. You could see his breath in the cold air. "Are you all right, Roland?" Darlene asked.

"No. No I'm not all right. I don't want to lose you," he said sadly. Darlene looked at him freezing in the doorway and took his hand to pull him inside.

He resisted, saying: "Are you sure this is what you want?" She pulled him inside, closed the door, wrapped her arms around him, and they began kissing passionately.

At 0800 the next morning, both Roland and Darlene's pagers went off. They looked up from under the covers of her bed. "Uh-oh," Darlene said groggily as she looked at her pager. "It's Colonel Green." She called his number on her phone. "Good morning, Sir. What's up?"

"They just placed Wayne Gilbert and another guy under arrest in Tucson," Green replied. "We've got to get up there right away."

"I'll page Roland and O'Leary right away," Darlene said. "We'll all meet you at the front gate." She hung up the phone as Roland gave her a disapproving look.

"I noticed you didn't just hand me the phone," he said. "Now what? I got to call him back, too?" He slid across the bed and reluctantly began dialing. When Colonel Green answered, Roland acted as if he hadn't been with Darlene and agreed to meet at the gate.

After he hung up, he turned to Darlene. "Who's going to break this to the Colonel—about us, I mean?"

"You know it has to be me," Darlene replied. "But not like this. You know it would have been wrong for me to simply hand you the phone. I'll tell him today." They got out of bed and began dressing.

"What are you going to tell him," Roland asked.

"I'll simply tell him the truth, that you and I have cared about each other for a long time, and have decided to try a relationship that is more than just being friends."

Roland took Darlene in his arms and gave her a gentle kiss. "You think he'll understand? I mean, technically we're both working for him."

"He's a good person. He'll understand."

O'Leary drove Darlene and Roland to the DPS Command Post in Tucson where Wayne Gilbert was being held. Colonel Green met them there. As they entered the office, CID Agent Glover and DPS Detective Encarta greeted them at the door.

Encarta began briefing them as they walked to a small conference room and sat down. "Gilbert and this other guy Stockman, also ex-military, delivered two U.S. Army issue .45 caliber semi-automatic pistols with the serial numbers scraped off to the storage locker in Bisbee," he said. "This was of course right after they breezed across the border in Douglas with the two firearms in tow."

"I can't believe this," Darlene said. "Talk about a waste of the taxpayer's money! What are these border Feds doing all day—sleeping?"

"You know what, Darlene," O'Leary said with a laugh, "I think you should become a Customs Agent and go down there and fix this! That's what I think!"

Darlene fixed him with a steely gaze. "Well just maybe I will, O'Leary, just maybe I will."

"You know it's not a real border or anything," O'Leary added. "It's just an imaginary border. There's no fence or anything. Just open spaces for miles, most of which are not patrolled by either Border Patrol or Customs.

"I get that," Darlene responded patiently, "but these guys are driving right through what's supposed to be a check point, and they're just waving them through. Damn! I just don't get this!"

"Well, Ma'am," Encarta said, "now you know what our agency has been dealing with for years here in Arizona. O'Leary's right. It's just an imaginary border until the politicians wake up and decide otherwise."

Darlene angrily shot back: "Just wait until one of these crazy, inbred, home-grown terrorists stick a ton of TNT up their elected assess or blow up the White House or something. Then the morons will wake up. I mean, just look at the arsenal this little group of half-witted bandits has collected," she said, referring to the Posse Comitatus.

Colonel Green tried to calm things down. "Darlene, some of our government officials have seen this threat, which is how I came to be here in the first place. That's why the NSA (National Security Agency) is funding this task force. We need cases just like this one to bring attention to this problem." The group paused in reflection. Then Encarta continued.

"Okay, well so far they (Wayne Gilbert and his companion Stockman) have both lawyered up. We've secured their businesses, homes, vehicles, etc., for search warrants. We're going to need more bodies. We have at least four locations to search today."

"Yeah," Darlene agreed, "and probably more depending on what we find at these locations."

"Well, we should be able to write piggy back warrants for any additional locations stemming out of those," Roland said. "We just have to be careful not to poison the tree (legal term from "fruits of the poisonous tree", meaning the improper seizure of evidence) or they'll all get tossed. Yeah, that can be a real problem with piggy backs. The good thing is that this all started on post with the murders where I don't need a warrant. From there we got paper on everything thus far, and we've not had to interview any suspects yet. So in a legal sense, if we watch our p's and q's and don't go beyond the scope of the warrants, we should be fine."

"Lets make sure that before we hit these places we've thoroughly briefed the troops doing the searches," Colonel Green added.

"Good idea," O'Leary chimed in, "and I also told our paper writer to make the warrants as broad as possible."

"How broad?" Darlene asked.

"Anywhere where anyone could possibly hide a grenade pin we can search," O'Leary replied. "In other words, we can toss the places." At this everybody smiled at what seemed to be good progress in the investigation.

Several hours later, Task Force Thunder served search warrants at four different locations. These search warrants yielded two more piggy back warrants on two additional residences. One additional suspect was taken into custody and charged with the illegal possession of firearms. At each location illegal firearms, munitions, ammunition, cash, and documentary evidence were seized. All the suspects in the case had made numerous border crossings in their vehicles. By the end of this long day, a very tired group of cops gathered at a little pub in Tucson to catch a bite to eat and to gather their thoughts.

"O'Leary," Colonel Green said, "we need to talk to your Customs contact alone and in person tomorrow. I don't want him to bring anyone else with him. Darlene's right. This border stuff is out of control.."

"My contact is with Customs IA (Internal Affairs)," O'Leary replied. "Just wait until you hear the horror stories this guy has about that agency. He's kind of young, but he's a real good guy. I think we can trust him."

"Great," Green said. "See if you can get hold of him and set up a meeting for tomorrow morning. Darlene and Roland, make sure this evidence gets bagged and processed properly. With the kind of homes and rides (vehicles) these guys have, they are heavily funded and will be able to hire some big guns for attorneys."

"Yeah, that's true," Darlene said, "until I trace their bank accounts, seize all their assets, and take all their money away." She smiled deviously and wringed her hands in mock glee.

"At this point, with what we've found, the burden of proof will be on them with respect to how they acquired these assets legally. I'm going to begin a net worth probe on them first thing tomorrow. Too bad the rats lawyered up so fast. I'd have a field day interviewing them."

Colonel Green looked at Darlene's sinister expression, smiled, and shook his head.

"Like I said, you got kind of a dark side to you, don't you." Everyone laughed. They finished their late supper, made final plans, and began to depart.

"Sir," Darlene asked Green, "would you mind if I caught a ride back with you?"

"Be my guest," he replied, looking her deeply in the eyes.

As they drove back from Tucson, Green spoke quietly to Darlene. "You look real tired. I know you've been burning the candle at both ends with this task force investigation along with all the other stuff you guys have caught lately."

"Yeah, I am really tired. For the last six months or so, Roland and I haven't been able to catch a break. Every time we have duty, somebody dies." Darlene became quiet and stared out the window, lost in thought, for several minutes.

"I get the feeling you have something you want to tell me," Colonel Green said at last. "Something that I'm not going to want to hear." He motioned for Darlene to come sit closer to him. She unbuckled her seat belt and slid nearer to him. He put his right arm around her and she rested her head on his shoulder. A single tear rolled down her cheek.

"You don't have to say it," he said. "I already know. You'd have to be blind not to see what's been happening between you and Roland. Remember, I'm a psychologist. I see things a lot of other folks might miss. It's okay, Darlene. I understand. It's not like we were in a committed relationship or anything." Green hugged Darlene, squinted his eyes in anguish, and kissed her gently on top of her head. She looked up at him and felt guilty that he was letting her off the hook so easily.

"I'm sorry," she said at last. "I do care about you and I'm not sure what to do. I don't want to continue a relationship with you and always wonder if I made the right choice."

"You're in a dilemma. If you choose a relationship with Roland, then you may wonder what we might have been as well. I don't envy you. In fact, I've been right where you are now. There are no easy answers. All I can tell you is that I care deeply for you, and that I understand. You and Roland have a past, a connection that I can't and won't compete with. I must tell you, though, that it's a bewildering past. I just hope that you're not confusing guilt, sorrow, and fear with love. It's easy to do. Even for a psychologist."

Darlene listened carefully to his words. They continued driving through the desert night under the beautiful black Arizona sky. The stars hung so close Darlene thought she could just reach up and touch them. She was indeed tormented over the decisions she was making, and was worried that the Colonel might be right in his warning.

"Hey, don't worry," the Colonel said, breaking the silence. "I'm not going anywhere. You go and figure out what you need to with Roland. Believe it or not, I really like him. He's a good investigator. And if things don't work out between you two, maybe we can try again sometime." Darlene looked up at him and they exchanged smiles. "Hey, stranger things have happened."

"Sir, you're a class act. I'm probably making one of the biggest mistakes in my life."

"Darlene, can I make one last request?" he asked as they pulled up to her apartment.

"Sure," she replied.

"Can I have one last kiss?" She shut her eyes as he gave her a long, passionate kiss that took her breath away. When he finished kissing her, her eyes remained shut for a few seconds. She was mesmerized by his kiss. Green looked at her and smiled. "Just store that away for future reference," he said. He watched her go up to her apartment door, then slowly drove away.

At ten the next morning, Green, O'Leary, Darlene, and Roland met with Stephen Biggs, Special Agent, U.S. Customs, Office of Internal Affairs (IA). Biggs was an attractive, slender young man of twenty-six, who wore wire-rimmed glasses beneath a shock of strawberry blonde hair. He was a shy, soft-spoken, almost geeky guy, who seemed uncomfortable with himself despite his keen intellect and good looks. The task force team briefed Biggs on what they had done so far. He took notes as he listened. When they had filled him in, Green made a very direct point.

"Now, Biggs, we're trusting you to keep this all very close to your vest. There's obviously a—how should I put it—a weak link in your agency. We only want to deal directly with you from now on, and we expect you to fully honor our request to keep everything we say to yourself." Green took note of Biggs' intimidated demeanor, smiled, and added:

"Son, you look like a deer caught in the headlights. Have we totally overwhelmed you with this information or what?"

"Sir," Biggs replied, "this is all a little overwhelming. However, I'll do my level best to get you all the information you need without tipping off the wrong people."

Darlene leaned forward at the conference table. "So you already suspect who these wrong people are, don't you Biggs?"

Biggs looked nervously around the table. Everyone was staring at him. "Yes, I have a pretty good idea, and I've been working on this since I got here six months ago."

Biggs was becoming more uncomfortable. "This keeping information close to the vest, this works both ways, right?" The group assured him it did.

"Steve," Colonel Green said, "I can assure you that the only people who will know about this information are the people sitting here at this table."

"We're not going to burn you," Darlene said. "I can see you're scared to death. Why are you so scared?"

Biggs cleared his throat. "I'm not quite sure yet what I'm dealing with. I don't know who's who, or who I can trust in my own agency." He dropped his head in confusion. "They moved me down here from Washington state, and I'm like a fish out of water here. I could really use some help."

"Hey, man," Roland said, "don't worry. You got us now."

"You know what might make this easier," Colonel Green offered, "is if I pull some strings and get you officially assigned to this task force. Sometimes the best way to be covert is to be right out in the open."

"That's a great idea," O'Leary added. "Then nobody will question why he's meeting with us and working with us. We won't have to worry about cover for him."

"Can you do this, Colonel?" Darlene asked.

"Oh ye of little faith," he said.

"Then why can't we use Steve here to stack Federal smuggling charges on these rats?" Darlene wondered. "Maybe if they're looking at some serious Federal time on top of the state charges, at least one of them might roll (cooperate and turn over evidence against others)."

Green smiled. "That's just what I had in mind."

Steve Biggs relaxed as he got to know the group, and warmed to the idea of being on the task force with them. During the course of conversation, it also came out that Darlene and Roland had again been put on the duty roster. Green saw the dread on their faces at the thought.

"No, you're not," he said calmly.

"What do you mean we're not?" Roland inquired.

"You're going to be taken off the duty roster for the next couple of weeks. It's been arranged."

"Why'd you do that?" Roland replied.

"Because I need you guys too much right now. Your plate's already full, and we need to clear what we got. I can't afford for you to catch another death investigation. Besides, take a good look at yourselves. You two are really tired. No offense, but you look like hell. I need to help you get in shape for what lies ahead."

"Yeah Roland," O'Leary added. "The guy's doing you a favor. You two need a break and quite frankly I do too. Every time the jinx hits you guys I get sucked into it too. We could all use a little break and quite frankly, you two aren't the only investigators on the post. Shoot, the next accident I respond to will be you two if you keep this up."

Instead of being happy about this, Darlene and Roland looked glum. "I guess we should thank you," she told the Colonel.

"I don't get it," he replied. "I thought you'd welcome the chance for a break from duty."

"It's not that, Sir," Roland said. "We're just afraid that nothing's going to happen on those days when someone else is taking our duty."

"How's that, again?" O'Leary asked. "What do you mean?"

"Don't you get it? If nothing happens, then they'll think the jinx is true—that terrible things only happen when we pull duty, and therefore the jinx is true."

"What jinx?" Biggs asked nervously.

As he had done so many times before, O'Leary explained what the jinx was.

By the time he was finished, everyone except Biggs was yawning. Biggs turned to Darlene and Roland and spoke earnestly.

"Don't feel lonely, guys," the young agent sad. "I've been cursed from the first day I got here."

Biggs' expression was so pitiful that Darlene and Roland burst out laughing. "Well, if misery loves company, Steve," Roland said, "then you've joined the right team."

The following morning, the arrested members of Posse Comitatus were arraigned on state charges, with the notification to the court that Federal weapons and smuggling charges would follow. The arrestees made bail and were released upon their own recognizance. Wayne Gilbert, the alleged ringleader, immediately disappeared and became a fugitive from justice.

10

Lost

*"No calamity so touches the common heart of humanity as does the
straying of a little child."*
O. Henry (William Sydney Porter)

Over the next couple of weeks, Task Force Thunder was busy processing evidence and preparing the case against the alleged terrorist and fugitive from justice Wayne Gilbert. Even though Gilbert was a fugitive, the case needed to be prepared in case he was caught. The team was also putting the evidence together against Captain Nedaheiger. Other soldiers had taken over Darlene and Roland's post duty assignment three times and there hadn't been any incidents of note, so in its own way the jinx was still on. Roland and Darlene would be back on post duty in just two days, and both were dreading that something bad would happen as soon as they were back. During this time, their relationship had grown deeper and was no longer a secret.

As Roland's time at Fort Huachuca grew short, they deeply regretted his hasty knee-jerk decision to transfer to Germany. The annual New Year's bash at the Officers Club was approaching, and the post commander expected all officers to attend. Roland wore his dress blue formal uniform and Darlene looked terrific in a burgundy velvet gown with green trim. But the happy couple weren't as happy as they looked. Between the fatigue of long hours of investigative work, the stress of coming back onto post duty, and Roland's impending departure the couple was under considerable strain.

As Darlene and Roland entered the brightly decorated club, she couldn't help but notice Colonel Green staring at her from across the room.

O'Leary, who was sitting by him at the table Green had reserved for his team, also saw the Colonel's expression. "Life's a bitch, ain't it, Colonel," he said, trying to cheer him up.

Green was embarrassed that he had stared at Darlene so obviously. "O'Leary, my friend," he said, "you need to buy me a very strong drink." As Roland and

Darlene approached their table, O'Leary stood and gave them a subtle bow of welcome.

"What would you lovely folks like from the bar?" he asked.

"Man, get me a jack and coke," Roland replied, "and make it a double."

"That will be a coke without the jack," Darlene asserted. Roland gave her a disapproving look and laughed incredulously.

"Make it a triple," Roland said defiantly. "In fact, wait a minute and I'll go with you."

He and O'Leary went off to the bar, leaving Darlene feeling disappointed and a little abandoned. When they returned, O'Leary and Roland were carrying several shot glasses, two whole bottles of Jack Daniels and two bottles of Scotch.

Roland handed Darlene a coke. "Your drink, madam," he said with a phony British accent. The rest of the table giggled at him.

The newest member of the team, Stephen Biggs of U.S. Customs, looked at all the liquor and was impressed. "Damn! You guys really know how to party!" Roland smiled and placed two shot glasses in front of the young agent and two in front of himself. He filled one glass up with Scotch and the other with Jack Daniels and did the same for Biggs.

Then Roland quickly downed both his shots and gave Biggs a defiant look.

"You Feds," he told Biggs, "can't hold a candle to the real investigators in the Army.

Biggs looked around the table as all were staring at him. Then he downed the shot glass full of Jack Daniels. He choked a bit, and as Roland began to laugh, he downed the shot of Scotch. Almost immediately, the young agent lowered his head onto his hands on the table as Roland patted him on the back in congratulations and acceptance. Colonel Green was watching as Darlene glared at Roland and leaned over and grabbed him by the ear and pulled him close to her.

"Leave Biggs alone and stop picking on him," she whispered to Roland. "You're making an ass of yourself." Roland just laughed defiantly and poured out two more shots.

Darlene stared sadly out at the dance floor as Roland settled in to his drinking and talking shop with the others at the table. Colonel Green saw she was unhappy. He tapped Roland on the shoulder.

"Do you mind if I ask Darlene to dance?" he asked.

Roland paused for a moment, looked at Darlene, and said: "Yeah, sure, Colonel, no problem." He then went back to cop talk with the others, which only made Darlene feel worse that he had shrugged her off so easily. As Darlene and the Colonel walked out onto the dance floor, the fast tune the band had been playing ended and a slow one began.

Green held Darlene tight as they danced together.

After a few seconds, Roland stopped talking and looked at Darlene and the Colonel. He felt a pang of regret seeing them together.

"Roland," O'Leary asked, "does the word `goat' come immediately to mind?"

"I'm screwing up again, aren't I," Roland said stupidly to O'Leary.

"Big time, boy! Big time!" O'Leary downed another shot of Jack. A second slow song began, and Roland rose from his seat and walked out to Darlene and the Colonel. He tapped Green on the shoulder.

"Sir," Roland asked, "may I cut in?" The Colonel smiled at them both, kissed Darlene's hand then grabbed Roland's hands and began dancing with him as the club was filled with laughter at his antics. Then he placed Roland's hands on Darlene's and went back to his table. Roland gave Darlene a sheepish expression as he carefully began to dance with her. "I'm sorry I'm such a jerk," he told her as he gently kissed her cheek. She placed her arms around him in forgiveness and he buried his face in her neck. "I'll slow down," he told her. "No more shots. I'll be a good boy for the rest of the night, I promise," he said, giving her his killer smile.

Darlene melted beneath his charm. "I love you Roland," she told him, "and no matter what happens on Monday when we go back on duty, at least we don't have to face it alone." Roland stopped dancing and stared at her with devoted, loving eyes, then again scooped her up into his arms.

When five o'clock on Monday morning came, Darlene and Roland were jogging up Black Tail Canyon. The cold air stung their cheeks red and burned their lungs. Suddenly both their pagers went off at the same time. They looked at their pagers and then at each other, filled with foreboding. Then they sprinted back to their vehicle and called the Desk Sergeant who had paged them.

"I can't believe this, Darlene," Roland said sadly as he waited for the Desk Sergeant to answer his call. "I just can't believe this."

"Don't jump to conclusions," Darlene replied. She started the car and turned on the heater. "It may not be that bad."

The Desk Sergeant's voice sounded anxious as it came through the car's radio-phone. "Were you two jogging up Black Tail Canyon?"

"Yeah," Roland answered. "We were just starting up the trail when you paged us. What's up?"

"Sir, we have a missing little girl, thirteen years old, last seen in her bedroom at 2200 hours (10 pm) last night. The girl had a fight with her parents over a horse at the stables on post. Her dad noticed her missing about thirty minutes ago. Her bedroom window was open and her coat was gone."

"A fight?" Darlene inquired. "What kind of fight?"

"The parents told the girl they were going to have to sell the horse. I got troops with the parents already heading for the stables to see if that horse is gone."

"Okay," Roland said, let's get the calling roster for the mounted search teams started and hopefully we won't have to use them." The search team consisted of volunteers who owned and boarded horses on the post who had training in mounted searches. Most of them were members of the fire department, MP's, and local police officers. At least a couple of times a year, either a child or a tourist would find themselves lost in the treacherous terrain of the Huachuca Mountains. This could be particularly dangerous due to several uncleared ranges that might have unexploded ordnance."

"In this cold," Darlene added, "a kid will go into a hypothermic state real quick, horse or no horse."

"Let's get changed and get to the stables," Roland said. In less than an hour, about twenty mounted volunteers were gathered. "Okay folks," he continued, "thanks for coming out today. We got a thirteen year old girl missing, along with her horse, since 0500 this morning. We don't know which direction she went end after she left these stables. She's wearing a black winter coat with fur around the hood, blue jeans and cowboy boots. The horse is a bay mare with white stockings on the front feet and was recently shoed. You've all been given your search areas, compasses and radios. As soon as you find her, remember to pop a smoke flare as well as getting on the radio. Our radios sometimes don't transmit so well in some of these canyons. Captain Fitzgerald and I will take Black Tail Canyon. Are there any questions?" There weren't and the search began.

As Darlene and Roland searched Black Tail Canyon, she began to sneeze. Roland turned to her. "Did you take your allergy medicine?" he asked.

"Yes I did. That's why I'm so spaced out. I hate that feeling. I wish I weren't allergic to horses."

"Could be worse, Darlene. You could be allergic to me." Darlene smiled at him. She knew that Roland's jokes were the equivalent of a child whistling in the dark. They were both worried about the jinx and the outcome of this search. Hours passed without any word from the others. As darkness descended, Roland began to worry about Darlene's health.

He had seen her shivering for quite a while, and backed his horse over next to hers.

"Darlene, are you all right?"

"I'm cold, but I'll live."

"No, I don't think you are all right. Let me see your fingers." Roland grabbed Darlene's hand and peeled back her glove. He frowned. "Your fingers and lips are purple. You've been shivering since the sun went down. We're going back."

"I told you I'm fine," Darlene said defiantly. She kicked her horse and trotted on ahead on him. Roland sat for a moment and shook his head in anger. Then he caught up with her.

"Damn it, girl," he said as it began to sleet. They had lost radio contact and visibility was about ten feet in the darkness and sleet. Their horses began to slip on the icy rocks.

"We're not going to find this girl, are we, Roland?" Darlene said. They were both crestfallen and cold. They stopped their horses and Roland took her hand.

"Let's go home, babe," he said sadly. "Please, let's go home. You're freezing and it's dark and cold." He took out his Lynsatic compass and tried to get a reading as to where they were. Darlene looked over and saw his compass needle spinning wildly. She took out her compass and its needle also spun around uselessly. "We must be near some sort of magnetic field interference," he said. "It could be something left in the rocks from all the ordnance they exploded around here. It's okay. I think I know the way home." He took off his poncho and insisted Darlene wear it over hers for extra warmth.

They rode for nearly another hour when suddenly, through a thicket, they could see a horse standing about thirty yards away. Roland stopped.

"Darlene, do you see what I see?" She nodded yes and kicked her horse into a gallop after they horse they had spotted. Roland followed. The trail became very narrow along side of a steep cliff. Roland yelled for her to stop, fearing their horses might lose their footing and plunge over the side. As they gained on the horse, they saw something else.

Now the animal they had been chasing had a rider. They got a little closer, thinking it must be another member of the search party. The rider they had followed stopped, turned toward them for a moment, then galloped off into the darkness. Darlene and Roland stopped their horses dead in their tracks. Roland stared at her in shock and disbelief.

"Tell me I didn't just see that," he said.

Darlene shivered and mumbled her reply: "Buffalo Soldier."

Roland's shock at what they had seen turned to fear when he got closer to Darlene.

He pulled his horse up parallel to hers and slid over onto it, riding behind her. "You need my body heat," he said softly. She didn't protest, realizing she may be going into hypothermia. They rode that way in the darkness together. After almost another hour in the freezing cold, they saw a parachute flare. Roland tried his radio and finally got good reception. Over the radio came the welcome news that the missing little girl had been found. Getting his bearings, Roland knew they weren't far from the stables where the flare had been launched. The voice of the Desk Sergeant boomed out of the radio.

"Sir, where have you been? We were about to send the search parties back out for you guys. Everyone else has been in for hours." Roland gave him their location and direction, then told Darlene to hold on tight and kicked the horse into a gallop. In just a few minutes they had made it back to the stables. Roland walked the horses inside, then pulled Darlene down to him, wrapped her in a blanket, and sat her down. Two MP's joined them and took care of their horses. Roland ran to his vehicle, started it, and turned on the heater full blast. By the time he got back to Darlene, she was smothering, coughing, and shivering.

"Sir," said one of the MP's, "you should take her to the E.R."

"That's where I'm headed, guys," Roland answered. He grabbed Darlene in his arms, put her into his car, and raced to the post Emergency Room. Roland carried her into the hospital admitting area. A doctor approached them. "She's going into hypothermia," Roland yelled in panic. The doctor was joined by a nurse and they rolled a Gurney over to Roland who had already picked up Darlene and placed her on it. He held her hand as they wheeled her to a room. There they hooked up a "bear hugger" warmer and draped it around her. The doctor then told Roland to step outside as they examined her.

He waited nervously in the hallway, until at last the door opened and the doctor came out. "Is she all right?" Roland asked.

"She's in a serious hypothermic state, but I'd say she's good, although her chest is badly congested. We're sending her to X-ray to see if there's anything on her lungs. They didn't sound very clear." The doctor paused for a moment, and then asked: "Are you the two searchers who were looking for that kid everyone was worried about?" Roland nodded yes. "They found that kid hours ago. She's fine. She came back to the stables on her own and I guess they couldn't get a hold of you. Where were you, anyway?"

"Black Tail Canyon," Roland answered.

"Wow," the doctor said. "You must have been way back in there. It's supposed to be haunted you know, some sort of old Indian burial ground or something. No wonder your radio wouldn't work." Roland sat down on a chair in the hallway. "Hey man, are you all right?"

Roland gave the doctor a weak smile and nodded that he was okay. "Well, then," the doctor said, "I'll go back and check on our patient." The doctor wandered off to the X-ray lab and Roland sat in the chair in the hallway for over an hour, finally dozing off. He was nudged awake by Colonel Green.

"Are you okay?" Green asked.

"Yeah, I'm good, Sir. Just tired."

"How's Darlene doing? One of the MP's called me and I came right over."

"She's going to be okay. The doc said that had she stayed out there any longer it could have been real bad." A few moments later they were joined by O'Leary and the doctor, who briefed them.

"I got to tell you, it was a close call, guys," the doctor said. "She's going to be fine but we'll keep her overnight. She's got a touch of pneumonia, but you can come and see her now."

They all gathered around Darlene's hospital bed. Roland took her hand and gave her a gentle kiss. The men began calling her a popsicle and making other little jokes to cheer her up. Then the doctor said they have to go. Only Roland stayed behind, wrapping her gently in his arms.

"Roland," Darlene asked, "you didn't say anything to them about what we saw, did you?"

"No, Darlene. They'd think we were crazy. Hell, maybe we are crazy. That's the way I feel, anyway."

"Look on the bright side," Darlene said, cheering him up. "Nobody died today."

The next morning at 1000 hours, Roland arrived back at the hospital. He went straight to Darlene's room, where she was preparing to go home. He entered her room with a bouquet of flowers and a Get Well card. They hugged and kissed and then he helped her with the out-processing procedure. He also carried some flowers she had received from other well-wishers. When they got into his car, Darlene sensed that something was wrong, and turned to him.

"Okay, Roland, what is it?"

"You're not going to like it."

"Just tell me!"

"JAG is going to accept a plea on Nedaheiger. They're taking a BCD (Bad Conduct Discharge) and no time."

"You've got to be kidding me!"

"No, they think that it's enough that his career is destroyed, and they're afraid they don't have enough to get him hard time."

Darlene fumed. "You know, if that little rat bastard was an NCO (Non-Commissioned Officer) or PFC (Private First Class), they'd fry his ass! You know it and I know it! What a bunch of junk this is! Does Rockwell know about this?"

"I don't know. I just got the news a little bit ago and you're right. I agree with you that if Knee High was a peon he'd fry."

"Well they don't call it Criminal justice for nothing," she said, emphasizing the word "criminal." "Take me home so I can change and go over there. I got to stop this!"

"No you're not," Roland said firmly. "You're going to go home and take all this medication they gave you and you're going straight to bed. Colonel Rockwell said if he saw you on the post in under a week he was going to write you up!" Darlene was so mad she couldn't talk. "Don't be mad at me," Roland added. "I'm just a messenger boy. Besides, I took a week off. Thought we'd spend some quality time together before, uh, you know, before I have to go." Darlene looked at Roland, and her anger immediately turned to anguish as she remembered that he would be leaving for Europe soon. They drove home in silence, and Roland tucked her into bed.

As they snuggled together, Roland said: "What say we take off for Tucson tomorrow if you feel better. We'll take in a movie, go to a nice restaurant, then rent a room with a Jacuzzi. We can even get one of those massages you always talk about." Darlene curled up in his arms, nodded yes, and fell fast asleep.

At 0800 the next morning, Roland got a page. He returned the call to his office and when he hung up said: "Hey girly, I have to go in for a short while. I'm behind on some reports and I just need to catch up. I should be back by noon and if you feel up to it, we'll take off for Tucson." Darlene hugged him and he jumped into the shower.

About an hour after Roland left for the office, somebody knocked on Darlene's door.

It was Customs Internal Affairs Agent Stephen Biggs. He had flowers and a Get Well card in his hands, and an embarrassed smile on his face as Darlene opened her door. When they made eye contact, Biggs quickly looked down at the floor and blushed.

"Stephen, you didn't have to do this," Darlene said as she motioned him inside.

"I heard about what happened, and I'm glad you're okay." He handed her his coat.

Darlene giggled to herself at his shyness as she hung up the coat. Instead of coming in, though, Biggs just stood at her doorway. "Come in, Stephen. I won't bite."

Biggs smiled and blushed and Darlene had to grab his arm and literally pull him inside.

She took the flowers he had brought and put them in a vase with some water. Then she turned to her guest. "So Stephen, tell me, how's the Customs business?"

"I don't know," he answered nervously. "Not so good, I guess."

"You look like you're really worried about this stuff." Darlene looked at Stephen as he had a nervous smile on his face. She realized something was bothering him and became more attentive. "Would you like a cup of coffee, tea, hot chocolate, or something?"

"If you're having something, I would."

"How about a nice cup of cocoa. I make it with milk and it tastes better."

"With the little marshmallows?" he asked, sounding more like a kid than a Customs Agent. Darlene showed him a bag of little colored marshmallows.

"Colored, no less," she said. Stephen smiled and sat back in his chair, looking more contented than before. Darlene was tickled by his reaction. "Gee, it doesn't take much to make you happy." Darlene continued as she made the cocoa. "So Stephen, what's wrong? Is there something I can help you with?"

"What are you doing after this?" he asked. "I mean, after the Army? I mean, what are your plans after you're discharged—if you're getting out, I mean, well—?"

"Why do you ask?" Darlene said as she stirred the cocoa in the pan on the stove.

Biggs sat playing nervously with his hands as he sat at the table. "Well, I was just wondering if maybe you might be interested in, you know, becoming a Special Agent with me. I mean with us, you know—working for the Department of Treasury."

Darlene stared at Biggs and smiled. "Dude, were you always this nervous, or did the Department of Treasury do this to you?"

"No, I wish that I could blame this on Customs, but I've always been intimidated by, uh, girls." His face turned beet red as he surprised himself with the candor of his answer.

Darlene poured out their chocolate drinks and handed him a spoon. "So what's the deal here? Are you recruiting me into your agency or what, Biggs?"

Stephen nodded yes as he drank. Then he put his cup down and wrapped his cold hands around it for warmth. "My agency's a mess," he said softly. "We don't have enough people in it like you, Darlene."

Now it was Darlene's turn for an embarrassed look. "Gosh, Stephen, thanks for the compliment. Look, now you're making me blush. It's contagious!" They both giggled.

"No, seriously," he said, "I think our agency's at a turning point and we really need good agents. I want you to think about it." Darlene sipped her cocoa and stared at Stephen in contemplation of his remarks. "You know," he continued, "we really do more than just waive large illegal arms shipments across the border."

"That was good," Darlene said with a laugh. "You have a clever sense of humor."

"Thanks for the compliment."

"What made you think I'd be interested in leaving the Army? I mean, maybe I'm a Lifer for all you know."

Biggs stared at her, took a deep breath, and thought carefully about how to answer. "Just intuition, I guess. I just get this feeling that you're looking for something else. Like there's something missing for you. Also, O'Leary told me about what you said about processing death for a living. I just don't know exactly how you do that. I couldn't do it. I have nightmares enough with what I do as it is."

"O'Leary. It figures," Darlene replied. "There's three forms of rapid communication around here: telephone, FAX, and tell O'Leary." Darlene stood up slowly, took her half-empty cup to the sink, poured out the remainder, filled the cup with water and sat it in the sink. Her mood became serious. With her back to Biggs, she stared at the wall over her sink for a moment and then asked: "So do you think chasing down drug smugglers would lighten my heart any?" She turned around and faced him, awaiting his answer.

"Look," he said, "despite our agency's internal problems, chasing high-level money launderers and Cartel members is a blast. You don't have to work for IA (Internal Affairs). I loved Customs before I came to work for IA. You get to work the cream of the crop narcotics cases at the highest levels. As soon as I finish my mandatory one year commitment with IA, I'm going back to general smuggling and money laundering investigations."

"Why did you volunteer for IA if you're so miserable now?"

"It's a quick way to get your GS 13 (pay grade). I had no idea they'd ship me to this hell hole with a bunch of cutthroat, corrupt managers. It was one of those bad decisions that, you know, seemed like a good idea at the time".

Darlene nodded in agreement and poured him some more cocoa. She sprinkled a few colored marshmallows on top. "I know exactly what you mean," she said sadly. "I'm kind of in the middle of one of those good idea at the time decisions in my personal life. I think that I came to a crossroads and maybe went the wrong way. The only thing waiting for me at the end of this road is another painful experience."

"Why do we do that?" Biggs asked. "Why do we see things and choose the wrong road anyway? You know that old saying that hindsight's 20-20? Well, when I look back on all my really dumb decisions, I can tell you that the red flags were all there before I made them. They were staring at me as plain as day, and yet I chose to ignore them."

"I know exactly what you're saying," Darlene agreed. "I've done the same damn thing and it's catching up to me right now." Biggs smiled sadly, held up his cup in a mock toast, and took a sip of his drink. A long and awkward silence followed.

"Are you talking about Roland?" Biggs suddenly blurted out. Then he blushed and fidgeted nervously with his napkin, regretting his question. "No, never mind. That's none of my business. I'm sorry I said that."

Darlene was crestfallen. She walked out to her living room couch and sat down on it, curling her legs under her and pulling a blanket around her shoulders. Biggs watched her with sad eyes.

"I'm sorry," he said again. "I had no right to ask that. You're sick and I'm making you sicker. I told you, I'm a real klutz with girls. I never say the right thing." Darlene looked at him once again with amusement at his shyness and motioned for him to sit down with her in the living room. He carefully sat down in the chair adjacent to the couch. "Maybe I should go."

"Stephen, it's okay. You didn't do anything wrong. In fact, you're right on target about a lot of things. Maybe you're clairvoyant or something." They sat for a moment staring at the fire. "You know that Roland's leaving here soon for a tour of duty in Germany." Biggs nodded his head yes as he stared at the fire. "So what about you, Biggs? Have you entered any relationships lately that were just headed for disaster?"

Biggs smiled, even as his face turned red. "No, not lately. I'm more the cowardly type who lets relationships with terrific girls slip through my fingers as I watch them go off with my colleagues. Like I said, I'm not much good with women. I know I'm too geeky and they'll just say no."

"Why would you think that?" Darlene wondered. "Don't be so self-conscious. You're a real cutie! Any girl would be glad to have you ask them out." Biggs just shook his head shyly in disbelief. "I'm not kidding, Stephen. You're an attractive guy, and the fact you don't know it makes you even more charming. You're not conceited like most good-looking guys who girls meet. You probably don't realize this, but you're probably disappointing pretty girls every day by not having the courage to ask them out. You're underestimating yourself."

"Thanks," Biggs said, "but my timing's always off. When I do see someone that I'm attracted to and might have the courage to talk to them, they are usually always taken. I don't get the opportunity to meet many interesting girls in my line of work anyway."

Another long silence followed. They were both becoming uncomfortable at the direction the conversation was taking. Finally, Biggs stood up and looked at his watch.

"Wow, look at the time. I gotta get going!" As Darlene started to rise, Stephen stopped her. "No, no, don't get up. You're sick and you need to stay right there." He took his cup out to the kitchen sink, poured water in it, and returned. "Please. Just think about what I said about coming aboard with our agency. I know you're due for a re-up (re-enlistment) with the Army in eight months. You could go anywhere you wanted with Customs. We have ports all over the country, and attaches all over the world. I think you'd be great." He turned and walked to the door, putting on his coat as he went. "Thanks for the hot chocolate, Darlene, and I hope you get well soon."

"Hold on a minute," Darlene said, getting up and walking over to him. "Thanks again for the flowers and the card. And thanks for the company today. I will think about what you said." She gave him a quick hug and he responded clumsily, smiled and left.

Darlene went back to her couch and sat down. She shivered, and it reminded her of how she got pneumonia in the first place. Wrapping herself in a blanket, she stared into her fireplace and began dreaming with her eyes open. It was as though a movie had begun in her head. She thought back to her days as a child, when her father had encouraged her to follow her chosen path in spite of any obstacles people might throw across it. She sadly remembered Nathan and what they had and lost. She thought about Roland, and the rocky road they had traveled together. She thought about all of the death she had processed, the lives cut short through violence or accidents. She relived seeing the head of the headless tank man and the crime scene resulting from SP4 Washington's madness. On they came, the images of all the grisly accounts she had written up, the autopsies and the casual coroner eating his sandwich as he recorded his horrific findings.

Then the face of Captain Nedaheiger appeared, and he was laughing at her for thinking there was equality of justice in the military. His sneering smile reminded her that a lowly PFC would have been hung out to dry for what Knee High was being allowed to walk away from because he was an officer. She sensed how empty her life would become when Roland went to Germany. Then there was Colonel Green and his Task Force Thunder, trying to plug the huge holes in our national security. And finally, she saw young Customs IA Agent Biggs, asking her again to consider starting over at U.S. Customs. Through it all she heard the sound of pagers beeping, sirens wailing, victims screaming and their families crying. How long would she continue down this road of murder and mayhem? Was this really all she wanted to do?

Darlene was awakened by the sound of her own voice: "I'm not going to re-up (re-enlist)," she said aloud to no one. "I'm going to change my life before all this death kills me." She shivered again. There was a knock at her door, and it brought her out of her daydream. It was Roland. Did she want to go to Tucson?

11

About Face

*"To every thing there is a season, and a time to every purpose
under the heaven."*
Ecclesiastes

Darlene soon recovered and the time passed by quickly. Task Force Thunder
continued preparing the cases to be brought against members of Posse Comitatus. The good news was that the U.S. Attorney's Office in Tucson agreed to file
federal charges against the alleged terrorists in Wayne Gilbert's organization.
Another good thing was that the jinx that had plagued Roland and Darlene for so
long seemed to have lifted, as several duty shifts had come and gone without incident. The bad news was that ringleader Gilbert still eluded capture as a fugitive.
Worse yet, only a week remained before Roland was to leave on his tour of duty
in Germany.

All of these conflicting events left Darlene in a kind of limbo. As she sat in her
office one afternoon with her feet up on her desk and aiming a paper airplane at a
photo of a Buffalo Soldier, she suddenly saw Colonel Green and Stephen Biggs
standing in her doorway.

"Must be nice to be able to sit at your desk all day and play with paper air-
planes," the Colonel said to Biggs, who laughed in response.

"Well look who's here—it's Laurel and Hardy," Darlene said. Green and
Biggs smiled and entered her office and the Colonel shut the door behind them as
they took seats by her desk. Darlene sat up and leaned towards them. "Ooooh,"
she cooed, "the dreaded shutting of the door. This must be serious, and I hope
it's not bad news. If it is, I'm more than willing to be kept in the dark, guys."
Green and Biggs laughed at her sarcasm.

"Hey," she continued, "I'm serious. I'm about to climb up in a tower and start
hurting people."

"Well, unfortunately you can't be kept in the dark about this," Colonel Green
said, his tone suddenly becoming serious as he nodded at Biggs to continue.

Biggs nervously cleared his throat, crossed his legs, and began pulling at his sock.

"The A.U.S.A. (Assistant US Attorney/Federal Prosecutor) has accepted a plea for two of Gilbert's men." Biggs looked nervously at Darlene, waiting for her to explode at the news. She didn't. He continued. "The A.U.S.A. doesn't want to chance a trial since the plea was for some pretty good time anyway." Again Biggs paused, awaiting an outburst that didn't come. "There's more. Colonel Green has gotten word that there will be future funding problems for the task force from NSA." Darlene remained uncharacteristically quiet as all this was being offered.

"There's been a Congressional committee convened for the purpose of looking at the NSA," Colonel Green added, "and at some of our practices. It seems there's been an accusation leveled at my boss, Colonel Oliver North, that he has engaged in an illegal arms deal with Iran in order to assist the Contras in their civil war. All operational funding has been virtually frozen and everything is being scrutinized. I had no choice but to brief the A.U.S.A. on this. I'm sure this all weighed into the decision to accept the plea on Gilbert's group and will probably have an effect on his case—if he's ever caught."

Darlene just stared blankly at the wall behind the two men. Green waved his hand up and down in front of her face. "Hello in there," he said, "is anybody home?"

"Is there anything else?" Darlene replied in a flat, monotonous tone of voice.

"Darlene, are you all right?" Green asked.

"Yeah, I'm fine. Why?"

"I don't know," Green said. "You're just not your normal self. We thought you'd be yelling at us and throwing a fit about all of this."

"Oh well," Darlene replied, "sorry to disappoint you. How much time did Gilbert's guys get?"

"Three years," Biggs said nervously.

Darlene stood up, straightened her sweater, and turned to look out her window as she spoke. "Well, three years is better than no years." Her intercom buzzed and she pressed the key. "Yes?"

"Ma'am, Colonel Rockwell wants to see you in his office."

"Thanks." Turning to her guests, Darlene asked: "Guys, do you want to go with me to break this fine news to the Colonel?" Everybody made their way to Rockwell's office. Roland joined them. Darlene sat quietly as the others briefed Rockwell on these developments. When the briefing was done, the men commenced with small talk, but soon became aware of Darlene's detached silence.

"What's with her?" Green asked Roland as if she wasn't there.

"Darlene's got a lot on her mind, Sir," Roland said. "I'm leaving in a couple of days and she's told me that she's at a crossroads in her life right now, with a lot of things to decide. Certain people," he said, staring at Biggs, "have been putting a lot of strange ideas into her head."

Biggs spoke up nervously. "She's a good investigator. We need good investigators. I told her all about our agency and she's interested, I think. I hope she is."

"Son," Colonel Rockwell said, "did it ever occur to you that the Army also needs good leaders?"

Biggs face turned bright red as he replied: "No. I mean, yes, I'm sure they do. I just wanted to offer her something. I was just trying to help. I'm sorry. I didn't mean to offend anyone."

"It's okay, kid," Rockwell said, patting Biggs on the back. "Don't worry. We all do incredibly stupid things sometimes, and they always have a way of working themselves out." Biggs slowly smiled as he realized the Colonel was pulling his leg. "It's just that she's like a daughter to me, and I don't want to see her throw away a promising career in the Army to go off chasing border rats. I mean, it's nothing personal, Biggs, but you understand."

"Yes sir," Biggs replied. They all sat back in silence.

Darlene spoke at last. "Are you all through talking about me to my face?"

Colonel Rockwell quickly changed the subject. "So, Colonel Green, just how serious is this stuff with your boss?"

"It looks like pretty serious stuff," Green said sadly. "I'm flying back to Washington in two days for a mandatory meeting. Everyone's pretty worried. I fear that North's going to be used as a scapegoat. This will put a choke hold on the agency that we don't need right now. I'll be there for a couple of weeks trying to shake loose some purse strings to keep this task force and others like it up and running. We've identified what is a clear and present danger to our national security. These homegrown terrorist organizations are getting more and more powerful, not to mention the Middle Eastern organizations that make Posse Comitatus look like a bunch of Brownies. I fear that political agendas will smokescreen the real issues identified by Colonel North which will destine us for certain disaster." The room sat in astonishment as Green continued. "I hate politicians. Not one of them has a clue as to what is happening on the front lines of national security. Our borders are wide open and the politicians are more worried about the smooth flow of commerce than they are about security."

"And that," Biggs interjected, "is exactly why we need good agents like Darlene."

Colonels Green and Rockwell shot Biggs a disapproving glance, and he smiled sheepishly and became quiet. The meeting broke up right after this.

A few days later, Darlene and Roland drove in silence to the Phoenix International Airport. After a long period, Roland spoke. "This is kind of anticlimactic, isn't it?" Darlene remained silent. "I mean, after everything we've been through. I just never thought it would end like this—with me just leaving and all. Maybe our lives will mellow out some now. You could probably use a break from me. Who knows, maybe I'll run into our favorite neighborhood fugitive Gilbert over there."

Darlene continued staring out of her window. Roland tapped his fingers on the steering wheel to the music, not knowing what else to say or do to reduce the agonizing tension between them. They pulled into the airport parking lot. Darlene couldn't help but notice how much warmer it was in Phoenix than back in the Huachuca mountains. As they walked slowly to the airport shuttle, Roland stopped, dropped his bags, and drew Darlene into his arms. Tears streamed down their faces as they both realized that they would probably never see each other again.

Colonel Kenny Green died of cancer in the mid 1990's, after working tirelessly to bring to the forefront what his boss Oliver North had identified in the 1980's: that the key to our national security lies in strengthening our illusive borders. This was long before Timothy McVeigh bombed the Murtagh Building in Oklahoma City and well before the events of September 11, 2001.

Detective O'Leary finished twenty-five years with the Arizona Department of Public Safety. Colonel Rockwell eventually retired from military service and moved to Scottsdale, Arizona. Captain Nedaheiger was dishonorably discharged from the Army, escaping full responsibility for the murderous consequences of his inaction. Knee High now runs his own security company. Jack Roland completed his tour of duty in Europe and is now retired from the CIA. His relationship with Darlene developed into a lifelong friendship.

When her enlistment ended and as she had told herself while recovering from pneumonia, Darlene did not re-up. Instead she joined the Treasury Department and went to work for U.S. Customs as a Federal Agent. She left the Army disappointed at what she felt was a double standard applied to enlisted men as opposed to officers. It would not be the last time a double standard played a huge role in her life. In fact, what happened when she became a U.S. Customs Agent had an even greater effect on her than being in the Army did. When she made the career move she chose, she had no way of knowing how profound the changes would be, nor how much higher were the stakes in this new game.

12

Johnnie's Angels

"Conviction is worthless unless it is converted into conduct"
Thomas Carlyle

Darlene's last days in the Army were like a dream she was walking through. With her long time partner Jack Roland overseas on his tour in Germany and Operation Thunder up in the air as Colonel Green scrambled in Washington for the money to keep it going, the end of her Army career just seemed to fade away. The send-off party for her was an odd affair, with an ironic, bittersweet feeling cutting through the forced gaiety.

In 1986, for the first time since getting her masters degree at the University of Arizona, Darlene was out of a job. This lull didn't last long, though. She soon found herself heading up security and investigations at a huge complex of resort/retirement communities in the Phoenix/Scottsdale Arizona area. But chasing after burglars, petty thieves, corporate cheaters, con artists and vandals didn't have quite the attraction for her that going after murderers and terrorists had. It wasn't long before Darlene found herself yearning for something bigger to do.

She began thinking back to all that she and Roland and O'Leary and Colonel Green and Biggs and all the other good people she had worked with had accomplished. Their mission seemed so much more important than what she was currently doing. It wasn't that providing security and ferreting out petty criminals wasn't important. It was more that having done some really big things, she felt like she was now sitting on the sidelines. Many people would have taken the very good money she was making as sufficient cause for staying in the private sector, but it just wasn't scratching the itch Darlene had to get back into the big leagues, where the pay might be smaller but the stakes were much higher. Darlene is first and foremost a cop. It is her true calling, and she likes to go after the biggest of the bad guys. So it was that after a year or so, Darlene ended up following Stephen Biggs' advice and joining U.S. Customs. Had she known then what she knows now she might not have made that move. Experience can be a cruel teacher, as she would discover.

The Federal Law Enforcement Training Academy is located in the middle of a swamp just outside the little town of Glynco, Georgia. You won't find Glynco on any map. It is too small. That's what makes it the perfect place to conceal the Academy Darlene now attended. It is near the Georgia coast, and the closest city is Brunswick. This Academy, like the training facility and "Spook School" at Fort Huachuca, Arizona, is a low-profile, out-of-the-way institution the government would just as soon folks not know about. To the north and well up the coast is Savannah. To the south, and well down the coast, is Jacksonville, Florida. To say that Glynco is "out of the way" would be an understatement, but it is here that future Customs Agents receive some of their training.

For four months, Darlene learned the in's and out's of becoming a U.S. Customs Agent. As a seasoned criminal investigator from the Army, there was a lot she already knew. The mechanics of police tactics in an armed encounter with bad guys were familiar to her. She already knew how to move, shoot, and communicate in a crisis situation. The basic procedures involved in search and seizure of evidence, protecting a crime scene, and handling captured suspects were already known to her. What was new were the laws under which the Treasury Department's Customs Agents operated and the many different methods of surveillance they employed.

Darlene found the study of law particularly interesting, a fascination that would eventually assume great significance later on in her life. What you are allowed to do with troops under your command working under the Uniform Code of Military Justice is quite different from the rules Customs operates under. When the object of your pursuit is a civilian, the tools at you disposal are actually far broader in their scope than those in effect in the military. Ironically, the physical requirements of agents weren't as stringent as those required of Army personnel. Darlene had to resist the temptation to let herself get out of the peak physical condition she had maintained at Fort Huachuca.

What she learned the most about that she didn't know before were the intricacies of surveillance work on a big scale. As a Customs Agent, Darlene would spend a great deal of time surveilling crooks via vehicles, aircraft, cameras and wiretaps. She hadn't done much of that in the Army. In addition, the training on the vast amount of paperwork required to do these jobs efficiently and within the law required considerable study. Darlene learned how to navigate the details surrounding court orders and affidavits for search warrants—sworn statements in writing made under oath or affirmation before an authorized magistrate or officer. This training was intense and important. If you're not there legally it doesn't matter what you seize. If you didn't get your evidence lawfully it will not be admissible and you stand to jeopardize your whole case. Ironically, another way of looking at it is that protecting the civil rights of crooks and criminals will in turn protect your case.

Probably the most important tool the Customs Agent has is the confidential informant, known by the initials C.I. The C.I. is the lynchpin upon which most successful prosecutions is based. This had not been the case in the Army. As Darlene's new boss Johnnie Watkins once put it: "Agents don't make cases—informants do. I can put anyone—even a monkey—on the street with money and they can buy dope. Money buys dope, not agents. But it takes an informant to take a street level case up a notch to a big case."

After he told his people this, they pitched in and bought him a large, stuffed toy orangutan, which he kept in his office, sitting on his couch, until the day he retired. That seemingly casual piece of advice was to become the single most important thing that Darlene ever learned. She went on to meet and cultivate many high-level informants who in turn provided her with her biggest successes against the criminals she fought.

There were several female agents in Johnnie Watkins small satellite office located in Riverside, California. In fact, women made up half the team. This was unusual, since nationally women account for less than five percent of all U.S. Customs Agents. It didn't take long for the Riverside office to earn the name "Johnnie's Angels." Johnnie Watkins was a gifted leader, and those who served under him felt privileged to do so. He was a fair and decent man who treated all his people equally, whether they were men or women. Darlene didn't realize it at first, but an unbiased, fair-minded leader like Johnnie was rare.

Unfortunately, his even-handedness toward women and minorities proved to be the exception and not the rule in U.S. Customs, but Darlene had no way of knowing this at first.

After Darlene had married and become pregnant with her son, Johnnie let her continue with her duties right up until the moment of her child's delivery. He never condescended toward her or made her feel like an invalid. It was this utter fairness and consideration for each agent's individual rights that so endeared Johnnie to his subordinates.

Darlene was actually on surveillance duty at the time she went into labor, so she never had to feel guilty that she was letting the team down because of her pregnancy in particular or her sex in general. She also got the feeling that this was how Customs operated in general. She would soon find out otherwise.

After graduating from the Academy and getting into the business of being a Customs Agent, Darlene was able to achieve great success. It wasn't long before she had completed several big cases which resulted in big seizures of illegal goods and the capture of some big-time criminals. In one of those cases, Darlene seized seventy-two million dollars worth of methamphetamine boxed laboratories. There were twenty-two such boxed labs, and the glasswork alone was worth ten thousand dollars in each case. This amount of illegal contraband was a state record at the time. Along with the labs in that case, she also seized several vehicles with hidden compartments, property, real estate, and an entire arsenal of weapons.

This case piggy-backed onto a huge money-laundering operation entitled "Green Bullion." Without the informants inside the operation which Johnnie had warned were the essential ingredients in a successful prosecution, it took months and months of painstaking detail work to close it down. Darlene and her team had to "go up" on three Title 3 wiretaps, which means that a lot of legal work had to be planned and executed before the investigation could go forward. Doing what is called "building a wall away from the wiretaps" led to several different "rips" of money transfers totaling over two million dollars. The extensive training combined with Johnnie Watkins' dynamic leadership began reaping huge rewards for Darlene. She felt that she was making good progress, not only in her war against criminals and corruption, but also in advancing her own career as a Customs Agent.

In Customs, as elsewhere, the evaluations and write-up's one receives play a major role in promotion. The activities of each agent are closely monitored by supervisors and managers, whose job it is to help those under them learn the ropes and get ahead even as they become more effective cops in the war against crime. At least, this is how the system is supposed to work. Having first had a good boss like Johnnie Watkins, who treated each of his people in a fair and straightforward manner, is both a blessing and a curse. After a time, it is easy for an agent to assume that everybody in management works in an honest, above-board manner.

But when such a manager retires or is transferred, the changes which result in management style are often concealed from those "further down the food chain" like Darlene. It is only when one begins to see other, less-qualified agents with no or fewer successful operations under their belt promoted over and above more effective agents that reds flags are raised. This is what began happening to Darlene, and what makes it all the worse is that she didn't even know it was going on for a long time after it began. She had witnessed first-hand the double standard which had been applied against her Customs partner, Special Agent (SA) Ruben Sandoval. Because Ruben was Hispanic, he was treated differently than his white male counterparts at U.S. Customs.

An excellent agent with a solid police background, Sandoval was exactly the kind of person Customs needs if it is to be effective in fighting the huge Latin American cartels which control the importation and distribution of narcotics into the United States. Before joining U.S. Customs, Sandoval had spent seven years with the Secret Service. Prior to that, he had worked for another seven years as a dog handler with the Fontana Police Department. If ever there was an agent who knew the ropes and could infiltrate criminal operations and develop productive informants it was Ruben. But he was guilty of the "crime" of being "Hispanic on a sunny day," and he was going to pay a terrible price for that.

It is a price Darlene also had to pay for being a woman who happened to be a very good cop. She and Ruben were going to discover that they were in an agency with very few men like Johnnie Watkins as managers.

The more typical boss was a man like group supervisor Ivan Winkowsky. It is extremely unfortunate and also a threat to national security that there exists today in U.S. Customs what can only be described as an "old boy network." What this means is that the line former House Speaker Sam Rayburn allegedly told a then-young Lyndon Johnson—"You've got to go along to get along"—is how you advance your career. In addition, there is an unwritten code of silence at work in U.S. Customs, and elsewhere in large Federal and State bureaucracies. This code is similar to the law of "Omerta"—or silence—which is associated with the Mafia and organized crime. If you see wrongdoing and corruption, you may let your supervisor know about it but no one else. If that supervisor brushes the problem under a rug and won't act on it, that's too bad. You are supposed to do nothing about it. This is what those who live by the old boy network call "following the chain of command." It is a chain which often does more to protect wrongdoers than it does to protect and serve the American people. It is how Captain Neda-heiger got off so lightly. When this country is struck on a large scale by terror-ists—and it will be—this is the system which will not just allow that to happen, but in fact necessitate that it happens.

Until this corruption is made plain for all to see and those who perpetuate and profit from it are held to account, there is no way that Americans can ever feel safe. Whether those who conform to this code of silence are themselves corrupt and in some way directly benefit from it or are simply afraid to risk the retaliation and career ruination which follows a "whistleblower," the end result is the same. We have only a veneer of protection at the "imaginary" borders of America. Narcotics, contraband, weapons, illegal immigrants, and even terrorists flow across our borders non-stop in a tidal wave of threats to national security. The situation is so bad that groups of "Minutemen" have formed to do what the Federal government and its hordes of sycophants won't do: patrol our borders and report illegal activities to the Border Patrol and U.S. Customs. These folks are not the "vigilantes" they have been called, even by the President of the United States. Rather, they are doing what decent, loyal Americans have done since 1776: taken it upon themselves to defend their families and their country from both outsiders who mean us grave harm and foreign nationals who want a better economic opportunity than they can get in their own countries. The very departments which should be defending this country, including the Department of Homeland Security and U.S. Customs, are rife with corruption, filled with incompetent or frightened bureaucrats who would rather cover for each other than protect the American people. Are they all like this? Certainly not. But it is a fact that like a variation of the economic principle called "Gresham's Law," the bad folks in law enforcement tend to drive out the good ones. We have, to a significant degree, a phony war on illegal immigration, drugs, and even terrorism. The government desperately wants the American people to feel secure in this country. The effect of this old boy system, however, enables exactly the opposite of adequately protecting our national security. For example, the Al-Qaeda and Taliban terrorists who supervise the growing of the poppy crops from which most of the world's heroin supply is derived are the same folks who attacked us on September 11, 2001. The drug trade is where they get a lot of their money to fund terrorism. More ominous yet, the same methods of narcotics delivery into our country can also bring in weapons of mass destruction, and it is Darlene's darkest fear that this is where the next big attack against America will come from: not from the sky but from railroad tanker cars and cargo container ships.

Infiltrating these terror cells is extremely difficult. The reader must remember that it is the criminal informant (C.I.) who is the backbone of most of what law enforcement can achieve when it comes to safeguarding our borders from the narco-terrorists and their allies. It is the development of these informants, coupled with the knowledge of how to build and follow through a case which will stand up in court that is at the very heart of the national security work performed by Customs and its parents, the Treasury Department and the Department of Homeland Security. If we cannot trust those folks with doing the job and keeping their own house clean of corruption and mis-management, then we are going to pay a terrible price.

One particularly useful informant was developed in another case which Special Agent Darlene Fitzgerald and her associates worked on. This C.I. turned out to be the ex-wife of a criminal "dime-ing out" on her former husband. In exchange for a lighter sentence, which is standard operating procedure in such cases, this woman steered Darlene's team to a seizure of twenty kilos of cocaine, just under a pound of pure tar heroin, and a cache of weapons including fully automatic rifles and sawed-off shotguns.

Darlene also began getting her feet wet as an undercover agent. She went along with a Drug Enforcement Agency (DEA) supervisor on a Colombian cartel case. This took her to a fancy condo in Palm Springs, California, where she spent four days mingling with the crooks involved. Darlene kept her cool even as she sat in hot tubs with these characters and went out for evenings on the town with them. It's not as much fun as it sounds, since an undercover agents risks discovery and death every single moment of the time. Even the finest foods and beverages lose their taste when you're always watching your back.

Darlene and the DEA team eventually traded with the Colombians on four separate occasions. It seems the Colombians were anxious to get into the methamphetamine business. They had discovered they were losing a lot of their cocaine customers to meth. So the cartel was willing to trade cocaine for meth precursors—the stuff you need to manufacture methamphetamine—and not even for finished product. This was a rare event. For the drug consumer, meth provides a bigger bang for the drug buck. The meth "high" lasts longer than a "coke" high does. The bad news for the consumer is that meth also poisons the body more quickly, fully, and dangerously than cocaine does. The health issues and side effects associated with meth are much harsher. But since the drug trade is always about money, the Colombians were eager to get in and Darlene and the other undercover agents involved were only too happy to accommodate them—at least at first.

This "sting" operation netted some pretty heavy hitters in the Colombian cartels, seized about a thousand kilos of cocaine, valuable million-dollar real estate, cash, cars, trucks, and a host of firearms. Over the following years, Darlene worked on many such operations. But it seemed like the story of the little Dutch boy who put his finger in a hole in the dike. Every time one such ring was busted, another immediately popped up to take its place. As the character Gordon Gekko says in the Oliver Stone film "Wall Street": "Greed is good. Greed works!" There's just too much money to be made feeding America's insatiable appetite as the world's number one consumer of illegal drugs.

But for the first few years of her Customs career, and under the fair and watchful eye of a decent man like Johnnie Watkins, Darlene felt again the satisfaction that drives the honest cop to take such risks in the war against crime. All her years of training and service in law enforcement came together as Darlene took her place in the line of agents whose job it is to protect our borders and seize what shouldn't be making its way in or out of the United States, along with the people who profit from trafficking in both contraband and illegal immigration. It was and is a huge undertaking, and represented what Darlene wanted to do with her life. This dedication and sincere belief in the job's importance made what followed all the more painful for Darlene and all the other good cops who got caught up in a system which eventually targeted them, and not the bad guys, as the objects of discrimination and reprisal. How this happened and is still happening is at the heart of why Darlene is telling her story in print.

13

Kill The Messenger

"When a mouse laughs at the cat, there is a hole near by."
Thomas Carlyle

On December 17th, 1990, Jason Fielding was driving his six year old daughter Megan home from her school play in Long Beach, California. Forty-four year old Jason was both a knowledgeable attorney and a seasoned private investigator. For the past half year, he had been on assignment for a special Congressional subcommittee looking into allegations of corruption in the U.S. Customs Service. He had recently returned to California to see his daughter in her first performance in the play.

His wife Anita was a computer programmer who had stayed at Megan's school after the play to help the teachers clean up. She had missed her husband terribly in his long absence, but was grateful that after this assignment he'd be home for good. The Fielding's were a close-knit family, and the long separation which Jason's assignment had necessitated was tough on all of them. Jason's return at this time was the best Christmas present he could have given them.

The drive back home was magical, since Jason was also an adroit amateur magician who enjoyed entertaining Megan with sleight-of-hand tricks. They picked up some take-out food at Burger King and Jason opened his mouth wide while Megan tried to throw french fries into it. She missed more often than not, much to both of their amusement.

On this cool evening, as Jason pulled his car into the driveway, the motion sensors snapped on the lights. Jason helped Megan take off her seat belt, and the two of them grabbed the bags of fast food and headed into the house. His hands full, Jason gently closed the car door with his foot and started up the walkway into the house. He never saw the darkly dressed masked man come out from behind the nearby bushes. His daughter did, however, and she gasped, drawing her father's attention to her.

Jason thought perhaps he'd somehow closed the car door on her hand, and turned toward her to ask if she had been hurt. He never got the question out. The "pfffft" of three muffled shots filled the air. Megan looked on in horror as her daddy dropped like a bag of sand, collapsing to the ground, the life quickly flowing out of him. He looked up at Megan in profound sorrow, as if his last thought was how tragic it was that she had to witness the execution of her father. Megan knelt down beside her dying daddy and cried out in anguish. The perpetrator fled into the darkness.

What exactly had Jason uncovered in his six months of painstaking investigative work? Who was so worried about it that they would have him killed? How would his death affect the ongoing Congressional inquiry? Was organized crime behind this cold-blooded murder, or could it have been someone or something else? History teaches us that the ancient Greeks also killed messengers who brought bad news. What news was Jason Fielding kept from bringing as he died in his little daughter's arms on that cool California evening? Where are his killers now?

14

Basic Instinct

"You must do the thing you think you cannot do."
Eleanor Roosevelt

Nobody can deny that like science and medicine, law enforcement techniques have come a long way. Today's police have the advantage of advanced technology, computers, forensic science, electronic eavesdropping, and a host of things that have come into the field in the time between Sherlock Holmes and James Bond. Yet for all of these, a cop's best friend is still his instinct. To look at a situation and be able to feel that something is wrong, even before you know what that "something" is, may be the most important tool in a crimefighter's kit. As Darlene went through the process of becoming a full-fledged Special Agent of U.S. Customs, she had the feeling—at first just a "hunch"—that something was wrong. A good cop learns to trust their instinct.

Instead of being run on the basis of merit, which is what she had known in the Army (notwithstanding the gentle treatment Nedaheiger had gotten because of his officer status), Customs was something of an "Old Boys Club." White males got ahead while women and minorities were generally left behind. Never mind that the best agents along our vast border with Mexico were Americans of Hispanic descent, folks who could fit right into the criminal culture of drug lords and smugglers. The only minorities who seemed to get ahead were the ones who had learned how to "suck up" to their supervisors. Those who chose to let their performance speak for them usually discovered that nobody was listening.

Flash forward six years to November 11, 1996. By then, Darlene Fitzgerald had been a Special Agent for U.S. Customs for quite some time. She had under her belt many successful operations against those who violate our nation's borders to make an illegal dollar. Sometimes the bad guys preyed upon otherwise innocent people who were seeking a better life in America than what they had at home. Other cases involved bands of criminals who made a career of stealing merchandise or smuggling illegal contraband across America's long and porous national borders.

The only thing standing between the average, decent American and jungle law is the thin blue line of law enforcement officers who work hard every day to protect this country from those who would do it harm. Darlene was a cop, and a good one. She was also honest and not the kind of person who would "suck up" to her superiors. She preferred to let her record of achievement speak for itself. But she had joined an agency in which being a good cop and going by the book was not how you got ahead. She began to see that something had gone terribly wrong. What had started so promisingly for her under Johnnie Watkins had changed into something entirely different. It is said that rust never sleeps. And just like rust, something had begun eating away at her ability to do her job. What that "something" was didn't just affect her, however. It was and continues to be something which puts every American at additional risk, something which, if not corrected, threatens the national security of this country. When honest cops lose, we all lose.

On that sunny day in November, Darlene and Renado Giannini were on surveillance on Mill Street in San Bernardino, California. Darlene was running Operation Black Widow with the San Bernardino Police Department and Special Agents of the Union Pacific and Burlington Northern/Santa Fe Railroads. Acting on a tip provided by an informant—and remember that informants are the backbone of U.S. Customs work—she knew that a band of thugs was hitting boxcars as they entered Redlands and San Bernardino. So far in 1996, these thieves had made off with over eleven million dollars worth of Customs in-bond merchandise. This same ring was also allegedly involved with the manufacture and distribution of "speed," or methamphetamine. Darlene also knew that there was a corrupt Border Patrol Agent in the middle of this mess. She had watched this Agent meet with the bad guys and had built up just about enough probable cause to raid two suspected stash houses.

Darlene was parked in an abandoned warehouse on Norton Air Force Base gazing through binoculars at the crook's house just across the way on Mill Street. Renado was a couple of blocks away with several other officers from his department. While passing the time waiting for something to happen, Darlene remembered that her very first case with Customs had been right down the street. It was where she had met Renado, and it led to the seizure of seventy-two million dollars worth of meth lab equipment and chemical precursors, the stuff you make meth out of.

How different Renado looked back then, all "narc'ed" out in long hair and a gold earring. A muscular guy with red hair and a mustache, Renado was about forty-five years old and handsome in a rugged way. Darlene recalled how effective he was in his undercover look. "Now," she thought to herself, "he's always wearing a suit and tie and I can hardly get the guy out into the field with me." She laughed quietly, but then her mood darkened as she recalled that after that first and many subsequent large seizures of illegal drugs and contraband, she had received no recognition from her superiors for her work. She remembered how hurt she had been that her superior officers never acknowledged the productive work she was doing. At first she thought it was just an oversight. Then, as she succeeded in capturing more criminals and recovering large quantities of contraband, Darlene began to see a pattern emerge in her office.

Recognition wasn't just a pat on the back in Customs. It was how your career advanced. Unless your senior supervisors took notice of what you did and gave you an agency award or some other written form of commendation, you began to get the message that you weren't considered as being "on the team." At the same time, upper management at Darlene's office was lavishing praise and promotion on others whose work didn't measure up to hers. They were sending Darlene a signal: "We will not validate your efforts. You are not going to get the recognition you want and deserve." Without that, Darlene was on a slow boat to nowhere. Why she didn't get credit for the good work she was doing was a mystery that ate away at her all the time. Rust never sleeps.

She was jolted back into the present when a van departed the residence, and she followed it as it made its rounds, dropping off stolen merchandise along the way. A few hours later, Renado had the necessary warrant and the team began kicking doors down. The first place they hit was the main residence of their primary suspect. Renado pounced on the suspect and took him down to the floor. As he handcuffed him, they saw another guy run out the back door. Darlene and another Task Force Officer named Ray took off after him.

Darlene could see that this second suspect was pretty overweight. She decided to let him run a while and tire himself out, figuring that it would make her job of capturing him easier. She had been a runner going back to her climbs up the canyons around Fort Huachuca and from long before, so pacing this suspect was easy. He never made a move to turn around and produce a weapon. Instead, he just got tired out and eventually became so out of breath that he simply fell to the ground. She then pounced on the guy and secured handcuffs on him. Darlene laughed as she told him: "Well, fat boy, you better go on a diet if you want to stay in this line of work! You made this too easy for me!" The search at that location yielded about $500,000 worth of stolen merchandise, including TV sets, designer clothes, VCR's and exercise equipment, all stolen from the railroads.

Her team then proceeded to the second location. It was a large apartment complex in a seedy area of the local ghetto. She and the other officers had to thread their way up a narrow walkway between two windowless walls toward a cast iron gate. As they approached, a large black kid about fifteen years old and wearing an old Army field jacket, opened the gate and walked towards them. The Tactical Force Officer with Darlene's group spoke to the boy. "Hey, partner," the Officer said gently, "would you hold the gate open for us please?"

When the kid saw their raid gear and badges, however, he gave them a dirty look and slammed the gate shut behind him, prohibiting their entrance. Darlene had seen this look a hundred times before, that "I hate you" look of pure resentment and hopelessness. As the youth slammed the gate shut, Darlene and the TFO noticed what appeared to be the end of a rifle sticking out of his jacket sleeve. The TFO yelled "Gun!" and they both grabbed him and shoved him up against a wall.

Renado ran up to them and grabbed the guy, too. The TFO and Renado pinned the guy's shoulders against the wall while Darlene grabbed the object up the young man's sleeve and pulled out a rifle scope. Darlene knew that where there's a scope there's a gun. Just then, the kid tried to jerk away and attempted to reach under his jacket. All of this was going on in a little alleyway with no more than four feet between the walls—a tight situation.

As the TFO and Renado tried to push this young suspect back against the wall and control his arms, Darlene raced to beat him to the gun. Grabbing his jacket, she pulled the bottom of it upwards and felt inside his belt area. Sure enough, there was a pistol sticking halfway out the top of his pants. Renado grabbed one of the guy's arms and tried to wrench it behind him in an effort to stand him up straight so Darlene could grab his gun. But the boy was very strong and lunged forward and bent over, trapping Darlene's hand on the gun in his belt. She could feel the bones in her hand begin to be crushed.

The suspect continued fighting as he tried to reach for his gun. His look told Darlene that if he could get his hands on that weapon he would blow their heads off, no doubt about it. Darlene knew that somehow she would have to get that gun before the suspect did and before he succeeded in breaking her hand. She pressed her feet against the adjacent wall and pushed her shoulder into the suspect's chest in an effort to straighten his torso. As she did so, her heart began racing and, pressing her shoulder and head into him, she could feel the energy begin draining from her body. An instinctive mental defense mechanism caused Darlene's mind to wander in order to block out the excruciating pain she felt. She briefly saw flashes of green grass and could hear children's voices playing.

Renado shouted at her: "Get the gun, Dar! Get the gun!" A sudden rush of adrenaline pounded through her body, and she gave one last powerful push against the wall, pulling the gun out. It went flying, and Darlene jumped to secure it. Then the team wrestled the young man to the ground and cuffed him. Catching their breath, there was a moment of quiet. Then Darlene saw Renado staring at her like the cat who has just eaten the canary.

"What?" Darlene said, breaking the silence.

"You just had to get your hands down a man's pants today somehow, didn't you?"

With that, Darlene got up and pushed Renado off balance, and he fell over laughing. Renado knew that only he and Ruben Sandoval, Darlene's Customs partner, could ever get away with making that kind of joke with her, since she considered both of them like brothers.

As they finished processing the evidence and booking the crooks, Renado said: "So you and Ruben are really going to do this tomorrow, huh?"

Darlene looked at him uncertainly and said "Looks like it."

"Well, Dar, for what it's worth, I think you guys are doing the right thing. It takes a lot of guts to do what you're doing. I know that in most agencies those kind of complaints aren't well received, to say the least." He shook her hand and smiled sadly.

Darlene couldn't sleep at all that night. She was still excited about having fought a fifteen year old gang banger for a gun. She was also, and more importantly, worried about what she and Ruben Sandoval were about to do the next day. Her basic instinct was sending her a distress call, and it was coming in loud and clear.

15

A Gathering Storm

*"An honest man can feel no pleasure in the exercise of power
over his fellow citizens."*
Thomas Jefferson

The next day, Darlene and her partner, Special Agent Ruben Sandoval, went to the World Trade Center in Long Beach, California. There were there to meet with the Equal Employment Opportunity (EEO) counselor on Ruben's EEO complaint. Darlene was Ruben's key witness to the discrimination dealt him for several years by their group supervisor Ivan Winkowsky. As badly as Darlene felt Winkowsky had treated her for being a woman, it wasn't half as bad as what Ivan did to Ruben for the "crime" of being a Latino.

Ruben and Darlene had been partners and office mates for six years. Prior to joining U.S. Customs, Ruben had been a Secret Service Agent for seven years, and before that a dog handler for the Fontana Police Department for another seven years. At forty-one, Ruben was an excellent agent with lots of street savvy and a kind of ESP that had kept the team out of trouble more than once. Darlene couldn't help but notice how nervous and out of character Ruben seemed as they went to meet with the EEO counselor. His streetwise ESP was kicking in, telling him that he was making a mistake. He and Darlene would come to regret ignoring that inner voice of caution. Cops should always pay attention to their basic instincts.

The man they had come to see was a young black agent named Victor Ross. They told him all about the unfairness that was rampant at the RAIC (Resident Agent In Charge) Riverside Office for years. After listening carefully to Ruben and Darlene, the first thing Ross told them was to get an attorney. This surprised Ruben and Darlene, who didn't see at first why this would be necessary. Had they known then what they know now, they would have understood that Ross wasn't just giving them a piece of advice; it was a warning. Mr. Ross also suggested that they consider filing a class action EEO complaint, and sent them on to talk to another EEO counselor.

Mary Conales' office was just down the hall from Ross's, so after that initial interview they went to see her. Conales was a very attractive young Latino woman in her late twenties. Darlene's antennae went up, however, as they told her why they had come over to Long Beach. Instead of being forthright and attentive, Conales' manner struck her as sneaky and a bit coy. Ruben and Darlene told her why they were considering filing a class EEO complaint. They re-iterated what they had told Ross about the rampant unfairness and apparent discrimination they had encountered at RAIC/Riverside. Darlene added that while she, too, had considered filing an individual complaint, she would file a class action if it was more appropriate.

Conales' response was to play ignorant, acting as if she didn't know much about the class complaint system. More red flags popped up in Darlene's mind as she watched Conales closely, trying to figure out why Ross would have sent them to meet with her if she didn't know how the system worked. It just didn't seem right. Conales was a Supervisor, after all, and should certainly have been aware of the mechanisms under her purview. What was going on here? Why would the very person whose advice they needed act like she'd never heard such things before? The last thing Conales told them was that she'd look into it and get back to them. All in all, it had been a very unsatisfying experience.

On November 30, 1996, the SAIC/LA (Special Agent In Charge/Los Angeles) Drake Brinkley spoke at a congratulatory "pizza party" for all those who had recently been promoted. Brinkley headed the Office of Investigations for all of Los Angeles, as well as several RAIC's in Southern California and Nevada. He was a white male about forty-nine years old and appeared rather unassuming and low key. He heaped praise on those promoted—agents who hadn't accomplished nearly what Darlene and Ruben had—while their names were conspicuous by their absence. The honorees had less time in Customs, less experience, and simply didn't measure up to Darlene and Ruben. Yet it was this group of white males who were getting ahead, and not by virtue of what they had done in comparison with Ruben and Darlene. This pattern would be repeated again and again. The message it sent was clear: women and minorities did not fit into the success mold at U.S. Customs.

When he had finished reading the promotion list, Drake turned to another matter.

"Someone at the RAIC/Riverside has filed a grievance," he told the attendees. "Now I have to deal with them." Darlene did not attend this party, but was later told about Drake's not-so-subtle threat. She wondered how Drake had been made aware of the complaint, since it was still at the informal and supposedly anonymous stage and was, by EEO policies, supposed to be confidential. She realized that Conales had told Drake about her and Ruben's visit to Long Beach.

On December 4th of that same year, their Group Supervisor, Ivan Winkowsky, posted an email message from Donald Chin, Assistant Special Agent In Charge (ASAIC), on the bulletin board. Winkowsky fit the mold of success at Customs, and the message he posted read: "For anyone who is experiencing any problems at the RAIC/Riverside, the preferred message of reporting problems is by using the chain of command." Somebody had written the word "One" on the memo, indicating that there was only one person having such problems at RAIC/Riverside. Darlene immediately recognized the handwriting of the word "one" as that of the office "brown-noser": Edwin Easel.

"Easel the Weasel" reminded a lot of folks of the Major Frank Burns character on the old "M*A*S*H" television show. He was a toadying little suck-up who couldn't investigate his way out of a paper bag. It didn't matter to Customs, though. He was in the "Old Boys Club" up to his pointy little ears, and spent a good deal of his time in Winkowsky's office having his cases spoon-fed to him. Easel had no prior law enforcement experience and had not completed a single significant investigation on his own. It didn't matter. He fit the "Customs Crony Club" mold. Darlene and Ruben didn't. Case closed.

Darlene naively thought that she and Ruben could break this cycle of promotion. She was furious when she saw the posted message. Any confidentiality Ruben was supposed to have under the rules had been thrown out the window. When she drew the message to his attention, Ruben was both angry and concerned. He was part of a dying breed of hard core cops. On the job, he was all business and tough as nails. But Darlene had also seen him with his kids, coaching Little League baseball, and doing all the "softy" things good dad's do for their kids. He had been leery at first at having been partnered with a woman, but Darlene had earned his trust through hard work and a steady, professional approach to doing her job. They were a good team which produced great results—and they weren't getting ahead in their careers.

The next day, after Winkowsky had gone to lunch, Darlene noticed that he had left his checkbook on his desk in his office. She took the next check out of his book, then grabbed a quick lunch and awaited his return. She let Bob Mattivi, Acting Group Supervisor, in on the joke she was about to play on Winkowsky. Ivan had often gone around the office complaining about his wife's spending habits. The poor woman always had to either beg him for spending money or sneak an occasional check from his book to buy something. How Winkowsky treated his wife said a lot about his attitude toward women, an attitude he took right along with him onto the job.

Darlene got very angry about this blatant male chauvinism, and as soon as she saw him come back in she went into another office where he couldn't see her. Disguising her voice, she called him up on the phone. She told him she was from his bank and wanted clearance to use his overdraft protection for a check in the amount of $7,000. Darlene suppressed her laughter as she heard Winkowsky frantically grab his checkbook and thumb through it in a state of panic. She gave him the check number and told him it was signed by one Pamela Winkowsky—Ivan's wife. Darlene added that the bank didn't generally make such calls for overdraft protection, but did in this case because of the large amount.

"It just looked suspicious to us, sir," she said in her disguised voice.

"No, no, I'm not authorizing this," Winkowsky replied frantically.

"Well, sir, I'm not here to ascertain if you gave her permission, but only to verify her signature."

"Well, yeah, it is, but I never authorized this amount."

"Sir, it is true that she is on your joint account and doesn't need your authorization. We just wanted to verify that this is her signature."

"Now just hold on a minute," he said, in a state of panic. "I need to put you on hold for a minute."

As Ivan cussed out his wife while dialing her number on the phone, Darlene and Acting Supervisor Bob Mattivi burst out laughing while standing in Ivan's doorway. Darlene was waving the missing check back and forth. Ivan's facial expression went from panic to rage to disbelief.

"Darlene," Mattivi said holding his sides, "that was the funniest thing I've ever seen!" Winkowsky wasn't laughing. Rather, he was furious. He began cussing the two of them out while they collapsed onto his couch laughing. Then, realizing his wife hadn't in fact attempted to write a check for $7000, Ivan relaxed and even began laughing a little himself. That would be the last time Darlene ever shared a laugh with Ivan Winkowsky about anything.

After failing to reach EEO Supervisor Conales directly by phone, Darlene called her secretary and was able to make an appointment for December 7, 1996. She took a day off from work and made the three hour drive to Long Beach to meet with Ms. Conales. Once again, the EEO Supervisor proved evasive and said she still didn't have the necessary information to instruct Darlene on filing a class

EEO complaint. When Darlene showed her the email message Winkowsky had posted she began to squirm.

"How is it," Darlene asked, "that SAIC/LA management found out so quickly about Ruben's complaint being filed?"

"Management must have Victor Ross's travel request for the trip from San Diego to Los Angeles," Conales replied uneasily.

"But Ross's travel request would have been processed through SAIC/San Diego, where he works. There would have been no reason for SAIC/LA to review it," Darlene insisted. Conales had nothing to say about anything, except that she'd get back to Darlene when she had researched filing a class EEO complaint. The truth was that she never intended to help Darlene, and proved it by not returning any of the several telephones calls Darlene placed to her over the days that followed. Darlene was being stonewalled.

16

The "Good Old Boy" System

"You've got to go along to get along."
House Speaker Sam Rayburn

On December 17, 1996, while scanning radio frequencies during an investigation, Ruben happened upon a conversation between SA Edwin Easel and recently promoted Supervisory Special Agent (SSA) Peter Blake. They were wrapping up a surveillance in La Verne, California, and neither wished to travel to RAIC/Riverside to secure some narcotics evidence for the night. As the evidence custodians for the office, they were well aware that this was a major violation of Customs policy which could sacrifice the whole case based on violating the chain of custody rules. Ruben and Darlene had been working in support of the case agent: SA Janet Somers.

On January 9, 1997, SA Somers officially notified Group Supervisor Ivan Winkowsky that she believed the heroin involved in her controlled delivery had been improperly taken home on December 17. It should have been placed in the evidence locker at the office until the following morning. Instead, its value as evidence may have been destroyed by improper storage, so that it couldn't be used at trial.

Winkowsky should have immediately reported this possible violation to the Customs Office of Internal Affairs. He didn't. Instead, he chose to try to cover up this incident, a violation not only of Customs policy but also of federal law. Darlene knew he wouldn't do such a thing for anybody except for his cronies. Now one of those "good old boys" would owe him a favor. This is how it works in U.S. Customs.

On January 29, 1997, SA Janet Somers was asked to fax her entire case file, including her file notes, to Assistant U.S. Attorney (AUSA) Bailey Miller. Somers went to Winkowsky to again voice her concerns about the heroin evidence she felt had been compromised. Her case file included her notes about the misconduct by the evidence custodians—Easel and Blake—and she was sure she would be questioned about this by AUSA Miller. At first, Winkowsky denied ever having heard about this misconduct. When Janet showed him her "9-B Case Chronology and Review Form" dated January 9 and signed by Winkowsky, Ivan suddenly remembered all about it. Yet even after this conversation, Winkowsky again failed to report the matter to Internal Affairs.

Four days later, Darlene's "G-Ride," short for government-issued vehicle, needed to go into the shop. Since Ruben was on leave for a couple of days, Darlene got the keys for his vehicle. When she got behind the wheel, however, Darlene was shocked to discover that his steering was virtually out. Darlene had been training for the 1999 Police Olympics and had extremely good upper body strength, yet she could barely turn the wheel. The brakes on Ruben's car were faulty, too, and although he had repeatedly asked Winkowsky to have the car fixed Ivan had refused.

Darlene went back into Winkowsky's office and got a different set of keys for another vehicle.

"What are you doing?" Ivan asked from behind his desk.

"I'm getting another car," Darlene answered. "That piece of crap you have Ruben driving is dangerous. You're lucky he hasn't been injured in it yet!"

"There's nothing wrong with his car," Winkowsky said, and waved his hand for Darlene to leave his office. Instead, she walked over to his desk and leaned down, placing her face uncomfortably close to his. She slammed the keys to Ruben's car down on the desk, almost hitting Ivan's hand. He was startled and jerked back to create a little distance.

In a low voice cracking with anger Darlene said: "Be careful, Ivan! Be careful!" She then stormed out of Winkowsky's office. From there, she went out to one of Easel's surveillance locations, where she joined Renado and a couple of his officers. She high-fived Renado and then asked: "What are you guys doing here?

"Ah, you know, the usual," Renado said. "Customs can't handle a case without us, Dar, as you well know. Someone's got to watch out for you rookies."

Easel then briefed the assembled team, telling them to watch out for a certain crook to leave the nearby video store. He described the suspect and said they were to follow him when he left. Darlene asked Easel why he didn't have a photograph of the suspect, and he mumbled some weak excuse.

A couple of hours went by. Renado drove up to where Darlene had positioned herself and asked: "Why haven't we seen anybody enter or leave that store? I mean, is it even open?" Darlene got out of her car and walked by the front of the store. There she spied a small sign listing the store's business hours and indicating that the store was closed.

Darlene went back to her car and radioed Acting Supervisor Bob Mattivi, who came out to the site and confirmed that Easel had put everybody onto surveilling a closed store and had not even provided a picture of the suspect. "Where'd you get this guy Easel," Renado asked Mattivi, "the K-Mart School of Investigators?" Renado and Darlene burst out laughing at the ridiculousness of the situation.

"Hey," Mattivi replied, "this isn't my boy. This is one of Winkowsky's protege's."

Darlene stopped laughing. "Bob, old buddy," she said, "do something about this moron. Please. Most of us have real work to do."

Bob shook his head and angrily called Easel over his radio and told him to meet with him. Mattivi was obviously embarrassed at Customs being made fools of in front of Renado and his San Bernardino Police Department officers. As Easel arrived and Bob began asking how such a stupid thing could have happened, Renado drove past and pointed at Easel.

"Hey guys," he told his men, "here's the next Customs G-13." Darlene bristled over the thought that Easel was being promoted above her and Ruben. The upshot of all this infuriated her even more, as Winkowsky once again failed to take any action against his buddy Edwin Easel. This was and is the way Customs works. If you're in with the right people, you can do no wrong. If you're not, you're out of luck.

Near the end of February, 1997, Ruben approached Darlene with a look of extreme concern. "Have you filed anything yet?" he asked.

"Not yet," Darlene replied. "I've banged my head against a wall trying to get EEO Conales to get off her tail and advise me how to move forward."

"I've found out that you have about forty-five days to file your complaint or you won't be eligible. Did you know there was a time limit on this stuff?"

"That's the first I've heard," Darlene said. She could see how worried Ruben was becoming. On March 17th, she filed the following individual EEO complaint with the head of EEO, Lindsey Watts, in Washington, D.C., and sent a copy to EEO Supervisor Conales.

As you will see, the tone of the letter is constructive and hopeful. Darlene, ever the good cop, was only trying to remedy a bad situation—not destroy an agency.

Text of EEO Complaint

"Dear Ms. Watts,
I am filing this Equal Opportunity complaint with great sadness. I feel that I have exhausted all other means to avoid any kind of formal complaint, to include using my chain of command. I feel that these issues could be resolved informally

with proper communication, development of a truly objective/impartial promotion system, and good personnel training for our management.

For the past eight years, my management has treated me very differently from several of my white, male counterparts. This treatment includes management failing to recommend me for awards on successful cases I have completed, when others are consistently submitted for awards for very similar, and sometimes lesser results. In addition to rewards, these same individuals are consistently supported in their cases and assignments. I feel that this biased behavior of our management also had an effect on the recent GS-13 promotions at our RAIC office.

In August, 1996, I talked to our RAIC, James Wilson, about my concerns. As an example of this unfair treatment, I brought to Mr. Wilson's attention one specific case that I put a lot of individual effort into—Operation Truck Stop—where I was left out completely by my supervisor Ivan Winkowsky when awards were presented. Individuals who did much less work on this case than I had were presented awards in front of our entire SAC Office. The case agent, Robert Mattivi, even fully agreed that the way I had been treated was a "real slap in the face." Mr. Wilson agreed that what took place in regards to this case was a mistake, and then he apologized. After my conversation with Mr. Wilson the unfair treatment from management subsided for a while. Mr. Wilson retired in December, 1994. After Mr. Wilson left, the unfair treatment slowly resumed. In November, 1995, another female agent in our office—Millie Landon—complained about very similar issues of gender bias to a member of a Headquarters Inspection Team named Darcy Fields. Millie's supervisor at the time was Allen Casey. As a result of her complaint, she was treated very badly by Mr. Casey.

This blatant retaliation received by my fellow agent, combined with my own concerns about the way I was being treated, prompted me to talk to Mr. Antonio Pulaski. Mr. Pulaski was, at that time, the ASAIC (Assistant Special Agent In Charge) of the RAIC offices in our area. I told Mr. Pulaski of my own concerns and those of others in our office. I provided him with specific examples of unfair treatment where management showed bias in the presentation of awards, schools, and general support on casework. I also warned him that someone would eventually file some type of formal grievance. After my talk with Mr. Pulaski the unfair behavior exhibited by our supervisors stopped. Several months later, when Mr. Pulaski left the U.S. Customs Service, the unfair behavior of our management resumed.

In November, 1996, Special Agent Ruben Sandoval, RAIC/Riverside, filed an EEO complaint regarding many of the same issues and concerns I am presenting to you. Through the course of his EEO investigation, I was interviewed by EEO

Counselor Victor Ross, San Diego region, and by EEO Supervisor Mary Conales, Los Angeles region. I gave Conales and Ross many specific examples of the biased behavior exhibited by our management at RAIC/Riverside.

In addition to many other concerns, I explained to them how my promotion score received by the CAAPS promotion system was much higher than my male counterparts who had been promoted over me. I explained to Mr. Ross and Ms. Conales that during the promotion board convened at the SAC office I had given very clear information to verify that my score was correct. My board consisted of Mr. Donald Chin, Ms. Kelley Lambert, and Mr. Dudley O'Shea. For each case discussed not only did I give them the seizure and arrest information requested, I also provided them with the names of prosecutors, DEA Supervisors, and other agency case agents who would verify all of my work. I had this information written down on a piece of paper next to the correlating case, and I handed the paper to Mr. Chin. Mr. Chin attempted to give this back to me but I told him he could keep it. His lack of interest in verifying my work concerned me greatly.

I further explained to Mr. Ross and Ms. Conales that when the promotion list was released, I phoned every single person—prosecutors, DEA personnel, case agents—to whom I had given it in support of my casework. None of them had been contacted by anyone from Customs regarding my cases. This demonstrated to me a lack of verification of casework.

I gave Conales and Ross many other examples of bias/unfair behavior exhibited by our management. I also gave Ms. Conales a copy of an email message sent to our office for Ivan Winkowsky to post, which he did. The message was from Donald Chin, and directed that any complaints which individuals might have at RAIC/Riverside should be forwarded through the chain of command. This message was in response to Ruben Sandoval's EEO complaint.

I have a real problem with this message. First of all, you will find that no one tried harder to get cooperation from my chain of command regarding these concerns than me. I come from a military background, and I truly believe in the chain of command. This is why I put up with being treated very unfairly for eight years while I continually tried to get help from my chain of command. I wanted very much for this to be resolved informally and made every effort to do so. I went to my supervisor face to face and told him of my concerns. When that didn't work, I talked to my RAIC Mr. Wilson. I subsequently asked for help from ASAIC Mr. Pulaski. That is, BY DEFINITION, using my chain of command!

The combination of my attempting to get help from my chain of command and other individuals complaining to the Inspection Team about management's behavior should have sparked some type of reaction or show of concern from management. This chain of command was probably the most-warned group of people in the history of Customs. Most people in our office could tell you that you could see these complaints coming from a mile away, and that it could have been easily prevented. I am also aware of other offices where similar grievances have been filed (e.g. Calexico, California).

In spite of the above concerns, I am truly proud of being a Customs Agent. It amazes me that when it comes to other programs/systems in our agency (i.e. Customs computer programs, laboratories, fitness programs) Customs literally runs circles around every other agency. We have the "bragging rights" about virtually everything in comparison to our fellow state and federal agencies, except when it comes to systems involving our promotions and awards. When it comes to this, we seem to fall on our face.

This agency deserves to have the absolute best promotions and awards system possible. In light of the recent barrage of complaints involving the recent promotions, the Customs Service should accept the fact that what we have just isn't working. We should view this as a learning experience and as a problem that simply needs to be solved. The CAAPS Scoring System was definitely a step in the right direction, and a good one at that. It just seems to me that in many cases local management simply tossed this scoring system right out of the window, gave it no credence, and reverted back to their old ways.

We do not have to "re-invent the wheel" here to come up with a better system. There are many promotion and awards systems that are excellent models that could easily be tailored to our agency. I DO NOT want this complaint to simply be a part of the problem. I want very much to be a part of the solution. Instead of reacting to the grievances with a "knee jerk" overreaction and/or trying to put a Band-Aid on a great, gaping, oozing hole, let's solve the problem. We can do this. I know we can. Any agency that can come up with amazing systems like our computer system—that other agencies are truly jealous of—can certainly come up with a system of promotions and awards that we can also brag about.

This is the point of my complaint. I'm not asking for people to be punished. Let's train them instead. I am, however, pleading with Customs Service to take a close look at what we have, and come up with better systems of promotions and awards that we can truly be proud of. When it comes to these issues, there is a severe morale problem among our agents. I am confident that if Customs completed a nationwide confidential survey rating its promotional and awards systems we would be very depressed at the results."

That is the letter Darlene submitted. Its tone is hardly that of someone who wants to tear down the agency of which she is proud to be a part. But Darlene was naive in thinking that all she had to do was shine the light on a terrible problem and others interested in fixing it would spring into action.

As Darlene looks back from today's vantage point, she feels like she should have known where all of this would go. EEO Supervisor Conales assigned a counselor to Darlene named Tam Zodo, a Special Agent out of the SAIC/LA office, who in turn worked for Drake Brinkley. SA Zodo had just been promoted under the very system about which Darlene was complaining. Much later, Darlene learned from an attorney that she should never have been assigned an EEO counselor from the same chain of command about which she was complaining.

Several more months went by, and Darlene never heard from SA Zodo. After making dozens of calls, Darlene had only managed to speak with Zodo twice. Both times he told her that he needed to get out to her office so she could sign some paperwork. Zodo never showed up. First EEO Supervisor Conales and now her supposed counselor were stonewalling her. In a final ironic twist, some eight months later Darlene found out that SA Zodo was facing conviction on charges of shoplifting, fraud, violation of federal firearms laws, and money laundering. This was the man whom Drake Brinkley had promoted over Darlene and Ruben Sandoval. With all that illegal activity, it isn't any wonder that Zodo was too busy to lift a finger to help Darlene. The "Old Boys Club" at U.S. Customs operates under rules of its own. The winners are the losers. But the biggest losers of all are the honest cops and the American people they are prevented from protecting. America has not yet felt the full impact of where this poor leadership is taking us. God help us when we do. It'll make "9-11" look like a day at the beach.

17

Wheels and (Worms) Begin To Turn

"When evil men plot—Good men must plan."
Reverend Martin Luther King, Jr.

On September 17, 1997, Darlene and Ruben were again up for promotion. RAIC (Resident Agent In Charge) Lawrence Evantie had given Ivan Winkowsky the assignment to supervise, review, and verify all of the agents' case experience to determine who deserved to be elevated to the level of GS-13. Evantie was the new resident office manager for RAIC/Riverside. The scuttlebutt was that Evantie was another in the Drake Brinkley "good old boy" system, where "brown noser's"—those who shamelessly sucked up to their superiors (and who were usually white males)—got promoted over agents with better track records who made the mistake of being female or non-white.

Darlene had by now serious doubts as to whether she and Ruben and others like them could ever get a fair shake from Winkowsky, especially in light of their pending complaints with the EEO. She wrote a memo to Evantie outlining her concerns, because under the point system in use at Customs, Ivan would decide what was to be forwarded to the Office of Personnel Management. Darlene's request was, of course, denied. You don't crack a corrupt and unfair system easily. So again she and Ruben and others were hammered on their CAAPS (Customs Automated Assistance Promotion System) scores. Even so, they made the Best Qualified List (BQL). It didn't matter.

It may seem to the reader that too great an emphasis is being placed on awards, commendations, and points earned by case agents in U.S. Customs. It is necessary to remember that this system is the sole determinate of how far one can advance in their career at Customs. In the corporate world, such evaluations are often less formally arranged and executed. But in government service, they are the lifeblood of getting ahead. If you do not receive some formal, written, codified expression of acknowledgment for what you achieve in your work, you will be hung out to dry. This is what was happening to Darlene and Ruben, and why this book spends a lot of time on this. What a corrupt system which rewards the less-effective but better-connected employee does is actively root out many of the best and brightest in favor of the more inept and incompetent. If the security of America's borders and what comes across them were not at stake, this would not be of such critical importance. But our security really is at stake.

Darlene's CAAPS score was ten points less under Winkowsky than what she had been given by previous Supervisors as well as two subsequent bosses other than Ivan. Obviously, either all the other Supervisors were way off in their evaluations or Winkowsky was. This unfair treatment continued unabated. On June 3, 1997, Darlene confronted Winkowsky about another example of her second-class status as an agent.

"Can I come in?" she asked, standing in front of Ivan's office. Winkowsky looked up from his desk. A pained expression crossed his face.

"Of course. You're always welcome here," he lied.

"It's about my G-ride," Darlene said in reference to her government car. "It's a real problem. The thing's got over 125,000 miles on it."

"Sounds like it's just getting broken in," Winkowsky said sarcastically.

"Look, Ivan, it overheats and dies on me. The air conditioning doesn't work and I got stuck out in Indio (in the nearby southern Mojave desert) and nearly cooked in the summer heat."

"Yes, it does get hot out there, Darlene."

Darlene tried to control her temper at the way Winkowsky was treating her. "I noticed on this surveillance that (SA) Jerry Johnston was driving a new car."

"Yes, he was," Ivan said, playing with a paper clip on his desk. "It's brand new."

Darlene worked to control her anger. "Jerry's old car only had 94,000 miles on it, wasn't dying or overheating, and his air conditioner worked perfectly. As far as I know, there wasn't anything wrong with his old vehicle. Why was he given a brand new one when mine has been reported over and over to be inadequate and potentially dangerous?"

Winkowsky looked up at Darlene and smiled like the cat who has eaten the canary. "Mr. Brinkley directed that Jerry's truck be turned in and that he be given a new vehicle." With that, Ivan waved Darlene out of his office. At that moment, the desert was not as boiling as Darlene was. Later that day, Darlene bumped into SA Jerry Johnston and asked him about his new G-ride.

"All I know is that Brinkley ordered it, Darlene," he said.

"Look, Jerry," Darlene responded. "Don't get me wrong. I think you're a ter-rific guy and a wonderful agent. You and I are the only two here who come from a military background. I have tremendous respect for what you do, so believe me this isn't personal. It's just that I about got cooked out in the desert yesterday when my G-ride conked out. You and I both believe what the military taught us: the mission comes first, then the men under you, and lastly yourself. I just won-dered what you knew about this, that's all."

"I really am sorry, Darlene," he said sincerely.

"Thanks Jerry. I believe you. This isn't your problem. I'll deal with it," Dar-lene said softly. In time, SA Johnston would also come to learn first hand that the military way of operating was not the way things worked at the Department of Treasury.

Three days later, Winkowsky stopped Darlene in the hall at the Riverside office.

"Hey Darlene, will you come with me into Yolanda's office?" Yolanda Rios was the Office Administrator. She was a dark-skinned, short-haired, very pretty Puerto Rican woman. Her manner was very direct and outspoken, and along with her wonderful sense of humor helped lighten the atmosphere of the troubled RAIC/Riverside office.

There was a slippery quality about Winkowsky's manner which told Darlene something was up. When they were seated, Winkowsky continued. "There's an EEO investigator named Orlando Lopez who's come here to interview people with respect to Ruben Sandoval's case."

"Good," Darlene said. "It's about time." Her reaction upset Winkowsky, but he was uncharacteristaclly humble as he continued.

"Well, I just wanted to let you know that we have a bunch of new cars coming into this office. I haven't forgotten your mentioning to me about the trouble you've been having with your G-ride, and I just wanted to let you know that you'll be getting one of the new cars. I'm sorry it's taken so long, but I'm glad things have worked out for you." He smiled.

Darlene couldn't believe what she was hearing. It was obvious that Ivan was attempting to soften whatever testimony she might give to Investigator Lopez by dangling a new car in front of her. She shook her head in disgust. "Sure, Ivan, sure," she said. Any little vestige of respect she might ever have had for Winkowsky evaporated in that instant. If Ivan had thought that by juxtaposing Lopez's arrival to interrogate witnesses with Darlene's getting a new car, as if that might soften her testimony, he was sadly mistaken. When she was called by EEO

Inspector Lopez to give details, Darlene never pulled any punches—new car or not.

In August of that same year, Darlene finally got through to Mary Conales and told her about the negligence of her "advisor" EEO counselor Zodo. Conales then assigned Darlene a new EEO counselor, Senior Inspector Anna Francisco. So it was that in that month Darlene actually met with an EEO counselor in a timely manner. Ever the background checker, Darlene did a little detective work and discovered that Anna Francisco had a great reputation as a no-nonsense, hands-on counselor and advisor on EEO matters. This became clear at their first meeting, where Francisco explained her rights to Darlene as well as laying out a time-line of deadlines for taking action. She filled out a special EEO form for Darlene that described her EEO rights. Darlene wondered later why Mary Conales hadn't done any of that during their first meeting. By now she was becoming accustomed to the delaying and evasive tactics she would see come to fruition years later in a San Diego courtroom. But let's not get ahead of ourselves.

On December 12, 1997, Darlene gave Senior Inspector Anna Francisco all of the documentation she had supporting her EEO claim. Included in this was a sworn statement by Special Agent Sandy Nunn in support of Darlene and Ruben. Darlene had been friends with Sandy Nunn since they both entered Customs ten years earlier. Nunn is a diminutive blond with a real sparkle about her. She had made a name for herself at the SAIC/LA office cracking what became known as the "L.A. Jewelry Mart Case." That immense money-laundering operation was one of the biggest such cases ever successfully undertaken by U.S. Customs. Details of it had been written up in news magazines like Business Week and Time. Nunn was a first-rate Customs Agent who was herself the victim of the same "old boy network" that was making life miserable for Darlene and Ruben.

When Darlene first read the statement Sandy offered, she was stunned by its directness and candor. She called Sandy to express her concern.

"You're gonna catch hell for this," Darlene told her friend. "You'll probably get transferred to the end of the earth someplace."

"Let the chips fall where they may," Sandy replied. "It's the truth and I stand by it."

"All the same, there will be repercussions, my friend."

"Look, Darlene, if we don't support each other we're going to get screwed. Remember what old Ben Franklin said when he signed the Declaration of Independence, that we'll either hang together or we'll hang separately. If you've got the guts to tackle this corruption, then so do I." Here is the professional, eloquent, and truthful statement written by SA Sandy Nunn:

Since October 1988, I have been employed with the U.S. Customs Service in Los Angeles, California in the capacity of a Special Agent. During this 9-year period, I have been assigned to the Office of the Special Agent in Charge located on Terminal Island. As a long-standing employee in this office, I have had the opportunity to actively observe the overall morale, conduct, general health and well-being of the employee base, daily happenings, politics, and so forth of all personnel assigned to this office. This has afforded me the unique position to draw certain comparisons with regard to each of the five (5) areas outlined above.

When I arrived at the SAIC/LA in October 1988, I observed that employee morale was extremely high. Employees were happy, enthusiastic about their work, motivated, and felt very relaxed in their dealings with upper management. I observed during that time that management appeared to care a great deal about the employees as individuals and that an "open door policy" was encouraged to make it easier for employees to address concerns. This attitude made employees feel more comfortable. Subsequently, for the most part, employee health and well-being appeared to be very optimum since stress levels were low. As a result of a positive work atmosphere, productivity was at an all-time high.

Contrasting that picture with the SAIC/LA today, I observe an office in which employee morale is dangerously low, happiness is non-existent, enthusiasm and motivation has been severely curbed contributing to low productivity levels, and stress has replaced relaxed feelings to the degree that several agents have had to go out on stress leave or have had to resort to taking anti-depressant medications such as Prozac. Further, U.S. Customs is losing experienced agents who feel they have no choice but to leave early either through early retirement or by switching agencies. I have also observed an onslaught of stress-related disorders among my fellow agents consisting of headaches, inability to eat or sleep, feelings of frustration and anger, even suicidal thoughts.

Further exacerbating the problem is what I perceive as a strong tendency on the part of management to micro manage the work of the agents of this office by engaging in lengthy case review meetings, playing definite favorites with certain agent personnel to the exclusion of others with regard to how cases and/or other assignments are to be divided and carried out, and by engaging in favoritism with regard to promotions. Most significant of all is an attitude by management, which I would term "management by threat." There is a definite attitude by management of this office that the way to keep the agents under control is to threaten and intimidate them into submission. This is very common knowledge among everyone in this office and it takes place very openly and to such degree that I have actually witnessed personality changes in agents I have worked with for many years. Further, agents who I know to be highly competent and mature have actually openly expressed feelings of fear toward management. This is due to the fact that there are many examples of productive agents who have been intimidated, threatened, and harassed by upper management over a period of time in this office, as well as throughout the entire Customs Service. Coming from a highly educated background in the field of electronics engineering and having served in the corporate world prior to my employment with U.S. Customs, I find this management style very inappropriate and highly contributory to what is termed under law as a hostile working environment. In point of fact, this behavior is illegal under federal laws and should not be tolerated.

Therefore, I am making this statement of my own free will based upon my observations into these matters. Further, by making this statement and signing my complete name, I am hereby designating myself as a "whistleblower" as defined under the Whistleblower Act with all the protections accorded me under this law.

SANDRA G. NUNN
Special Agent
U.S. Customs Service

When Darlene warned SA Sandy Nunn that by making the written statement presented above she would probably face being transferred, she had no way of knowing that it would happen with such lightning speed. On January 8, 1998, Anna Francisco completed her EEO investigation into Darlene' s complaint. She included in her report Sandy Nunn's statement. She then submitted her report to the very same EEO Supervisor Mary Conales who had stonewalled Darlene for so long. Just four days later, on January 12, 1998, Drake Brinkley signed a memo ordering that SA Sandy Nunn be transferred. Revenge was swift and mean.

On the verge of tears, Sandy called Darlene. "They're sending me to the DEA (Drug Enforcement Agency) Technical Task Force in downtown Los Angeles."

"I'm so sorry, Sandy," Darlene responded. "Everybody in this office calls that place a dumping ground for so-called problem agents."

"Here too. I guess that makes me a problem agent, Darlene," Sandy said sadly.

"Not in my book," Darlene answered. "Look, this fight isn't over. It's just beginning. Keep your chin up. We're all in this together, and believe me, it's worth doing even if they end up making scapegoats of us all." Darlene had no way of knowing that was exactly what U.S. Customs had in mind. Later, when

Sandy Nunn walked out of her supervisor's office, she saw the Customs Task Force Coordinator—Fred Lauder—coming out of the weekly office management meeting.

"Hi," she said to him, "I hear that I'm going to be working for you starting next week."

Lauder stopped dead in his tracks. He was obviously completely surprised by this news. He shouldn't have been. This was not the way transfers worked. Supervisors were always made aware well in advance when personnel changes like this were in the works. But it didn't happen that way this time. Two days after SAIC Brinkley signed the transfer memo for Sandy Nunn, he added insult to injury by signing another one addressed to all agents at the SAIC/LA. This memo stated:

With the expected influx of new personnel in the next 6 months there is a need to place them where they will be the most effective for the Office of Investigations. In an effort to get a better understanding of the background and experience level of current SAIC/LA agents within the immediate commuting distance of Terminal Island, LAX and RAIC/OR, please advise me of the following information for each agent within your chain of command. Please submit this info on all 1811 personnel to Associate SAIC Woody Pillsbury by February 1. Thank you.

1.   Time as a Customs Special Agent?

2.   Time in present group/office?

3.   Time spent in Terminal Island, RAIC/LX, and RAIC/OR?

4.   Investigative disciplines worked?

5.   Office/group in which you would most desire to work within the SAC/LA?

6.   Would you desire a tour in Headquarters?

Drake Brinkley

The content and timing of this memo speaks volumes. It came immediately following Sandy Nunn's transfer, punishment for having written a letter in support of those complaining about unfair treatment in Customs. Brinkley's subsequent memo allowed agents to have real input into the transfer process. But Sandy Nunn was already transferred when this memo was sent. When looking at patterns of discrimination, each little piece of the puzzle is important. How could Brinkley have even learned about Sandy's letter? The only possible source of this information would have been EEO Supervisor Mary Conales, the person to whom Senior Investigator Anna Francisco had submitted her report. If Mary Conales had leaked this information to management, that would have been a clear violation of Sandy's rights under both the Privacy Act and the EEO regulations. If it hadn't been Conales, who else could it have been?

Darlene called Anna Francisco with this news, and Francisco was outraged and upset about what was happening. She went to Conales and expressed her concern. Senior Inspector Francisco was rewarded by being fired from her position as an EEO counselor. Sandy Nunn then filed an EEO retaliation complaint based upon what had happened to Francisco. The web of deceit and payback was growing wider by the day.

On March 2, 1998, Ms. Conales lied in a sworn statement in which she alleged that during Darlene's meeting with her the previous December at her office in Long Beach, Darlene had never requested counseling on the particular issues facing her. Conales also stated that she had made Darlene fully aware of what the EEO process entailed. Based upon that false sworn statement by Conales, Darlene's EEO complaint was denied by the Regional Complaint Center. The reason for the denial was "timeliness." Another piece of the pattern of discrimination fell into place as Darlene realized that she had never heard back from Conales precisely so that her complaint could be denied for failing to fall within mandated time lines about which Darlene knew nothing. It turned out that Conales had pulled similar tactics on Ervin Rios, Ruben Sandoval, Sandy Nunn, and Darlene, among others. For Conales to betray those who came to her for help was like a doctor killing his patients. If you can't trust your mandated advisor, who can you trust?

Three and a half weeks later, Darlene and Sandy met with Jay Rosden, Port Director, at the Hilton Hotel in Lukeville, Arizona. The purpose of the meeting was for Sandy to file an EEO retaliation report after her forced transfer. Rosden listened sympathetically, asking pointed questions and seeming to make a real effort to find out what was going on. After five hours, the meeting was still going on when Darlene received a page from her Acting Group Supervisor David Gray. Darlene returned his call.

"Where are you?" Gray asked. "What are you doing?"

"Didn't you get my voicemail messages?" Darlene replied.

"Yes I did. But (RAIC Lawrence) Evantie wants to know what's going on."

"Look," Darlene said, "I'm in a meeting regarding my EEO issue."

"Well, what issue? I mean, is this something new or what?"

"Why don't you speak to the EEO counselor yourself," Darlene shot back, handing the phone over to Jay Rosden. She felt guilty putting Rosden on the spot that way, but she had felt worse being grilled inappropriately by Gray. Rosden, however, did not look any too pleased at suddenly being thrust into the conversation with Gray. Then it suddenly it became apparent that Rosden was now speaking with RAIC Evantie, who was grilling Rosden on details of the complaint. On Darlene's end of this conversation, SA Arnold Connez, SAIC/LA, happened to walk up to them in the lobby and was an independent witness to the entire exchange. Rosden was starting to squirm, trying to be polite yet evasive about answering Evantie's questions. At that time, neither Sandy nor Darlene had filled out any paperwork for Rosden, nor had they expressed whether or not they wanted to remain anonymous about the issue. All of that seemed beside the point by the time Rosden got off the phone.

The look on Rosden's face was one of disbelief. He told those assembled he was very dissatisfied about the way the whole thing had been handled, very dissatisfied indeed. It was around five o'clock by the time Darlene and Sandy had finished their interviews. Knowing that rush hour traffic back home would be a mess, Darlene went to get something to eat and delayed getting back on the road until seven that evening. As she was driving up to her house at about nine o'clock, she got another page from Gray, who was still at the Riverside office. He tried to put the call on his speakerphone but wasn't able to make it work. Darlene found this somewhat amusing, but she was also put off because Gray hadn't asked her permission to use the speakerphone nor had he identified who else was in the room with him. She figured it was Lawrence Evantie.

"I just wanted to see if you were all right," Gray said. Darlene bit her tongue to keep from calling him a liar. He had never shown the slightest such concern in the past. Gray continued: "Why are you just now getting home? Why did it take so long?"

"I didn't want to get stuck in rush hour traffic, so I ate first. I left at 1900 hours and I just got home."

"Ah, well, Lawrence just wanted to know what was going on, and why you were gone so long." He continued in an official tone of voice, which made Darlene wonder if he wasn't somehow doing this for the benefit of someone else. "The EEO counselor should have contacted Riverside management and made arrangements to conduct the interviews at the RAIC/Riverside Office. The EEO counselor was out of line by not doing so."

"Well," Darlene replied, "I feel that what took place on the phone with Evantie grilling the EEO counselor was very inappropriate."

"Lawrence has every right to know that information, so it wasn't inappropriate," Gray said. Darlene and Gray continued going back and forth on this, as if they both thought someone was watching or recording the conversation.

"You know," Darlene said at last, "there were three people who witnessed the conversation between Evantie and the EEO counselor." This remark was met with a deafening silence. Darlene could sense Gray cringing on the other side of the phone.

"Rosden told Sandy Nunn and me that he was very uncomfortable about the conversation and agreed with me that it was inappropriate."

"He should never have said that," Gray replied. "I can assure you that he would be in very big trouble with his management if they knew he had."

"He didn't have to tell us how uncomfortable with the conversation he was, Gray. We all could see the poor guy was nearly squirming, I mean it was obvious."

"Oh well," Gray said, changing the subject, "I just wanted to make sure that you were okay and had made it home safely."

Sure, Darlene thought to herself right after she hung up, for the first time in eleven years someone at Customs has called to make sure I got home all right. Darlene felt that it was management which was out of line making this call. If they wanted to know what was up, they should have called Rosden and asked. But they called Darlene instead. It was just a fishing expedition to try and find out more about the EEO case Darlene was bringing. Gray didn't care a rat's ass about Darlene. It was his own behind he was looking after, and Evantie's as well.

Then the phone rang again. It was Sandy Nunn. Darlene filled her in on the call she had just received and suggested they call Rosden. On a three-way hook-up, Sandy and Darlene told Rosden what had just happened, including Gray's comment that Rosden might be in very big trouble. Darlene apologized to Rosden if anything she had said or done might have gotten him into difficulty. He assured her it hadn't. When they were done, Darlene went straight to bed. However, she had a hard time falling asleep. Darlene was feeling jumpy and nervous. She was sure something bad was about to happen, but she didn't know what it was. As has been said before, a good cop always trusts their instincts.

18

Puzzle Pieces

"....Life is but a dream."
From the children's song: "Row, Row, Row Your Boat"

On April 7, 1998, Gray called Darlene into his office. "Do you still have your rail project up and running?" he asked.

"Yes. Why?"

"Because I just got a call from our inspectors in Calexico. They said they sent some tanker cars to Union Pacific four days ago and they'll be up next week to check them."

Darlene stiffened. "Next week? We'll lose border search authority if we wait that long! Those idiots don't know what they're doing!"

"Can you handle it? I mean, are you healthy enough to take this on?" Gray asked in a concerned tone. For a moment he was the "old" Gray, the guy Darlene used to know before he went into Internal Affairs. He had been a good agent and even a trusted friend.

Something changed. The sucking up to management and "cover your ass" mentality took hold and changed Gray. He became just another creep in the Drake Brinkley "Old Boys Club." How big this club was—and is—and the destructive influence it has, is at the heart of what Darlene's story as a "whistle-blower" is all about.

"I can handle it," she said.

"I know you've had some kind of bug for a couple of months. Are you okay?"

"I can do this." Darlene knew that Gray was aware of her training for the 1999 Police Olympics. He didn't know that for the past couple of days she had been running a little fever, had some trouble breathing, and was losing her voice. She wasn't going to show weakness to her boss any more than she would suck up to him. She took the detailed note from Gray and walked out.

As she did, Gray made a sound like a train. "Choo-choo," he said with a smile.

It was an old joke. About five years earlier, Darlene had pegged a railroad car as suspicious both because of the way it had been imported into America and subsequent irregularities with its progress from Calexico, California north. Before Darlene could arrange for it to go, this car had gone to Colton, California. Along the way, it had "disappeared" for from nine to twelve hours. Nobody could figure out where it had been. Things happen when railroad cars vanish for a while. Bad things.

Darlene had gotten a call from Ervin Rios about a suspected load of opium coming into Ontario Airport via United Parcel Service (UPS). She was at UPS trying to arrange for a controlled delivery of it to Redding, CA. While there, she got a call from Tom Best of the Union Pacific Rail Police. Tom was an older man who knew more about railroad operations than anybody Darlene had ever known. They had worked together on various rail deals for over six years. "Hey Darlene," Tom asked, "do you know where your rail car is?"

"Why, Best? You gonna tell me that it isn't sitting where it's supposed to be?"

"Nope. It's heeeeere," Best said, singing the word "here" like the little girl in the movie "Poltergeist."

Already busy with the opium seizure, this was another complication Darlene didn't need just then. Making matters worse, it was New Year's Eve, and rounding up a posse was all the more difficult. Darlene ended up making arrangements with the State Bureau of Narcotics Enforcement instead of U.S. Customs.. Ed Saite, head of security with UPS, allowed the opium package to come in on one of his planes.

Darlene had a little time before the opium was to come in, so she raced over to the rail yard and met Tom Best. Sure enough, there was the suspicious car. Best made arrangements for the car to be weighed and placed on a "bad order," which requires it to be routed to a side track, ostensibly for repairs. The idea was to sequester it until the following day. She stayed up all night working on yet another controlled delivery of opium, again put together by Ervin Rios. Rios was a smuggler's nightmare, a brilliant investigator who stacked up seizures of illegal imports one after the other. What Customs Internal Affairs did to Rios was amazing, but let's finish the "Choo-Choo" story first.

Darlene put on a UPS uniform and was flown to Redding where she delivered the opium packaged. She ended up seizing eighteen pounds of the contraband and arresting two bad guys. It made the local papers as a record opium seizure. The next day, Darlene started the logistical nightmare of dealing with the suspicious tanker car. At the Union Pacific police station, she found Best sitting there laughing his head off. This was not a good sign.

"Okay, Tom, where is it now?"

"Well, Darlene, the real question you should be asking is: How did it get there?"

"Get where?"

"Onto an outbound train, about to exit the yard."

"And you caught it?"

"I did," Best said.

"Nice catch." Darlene enlisted the aid of Ervin Rios. Besides being a first-rate agent, Ervin was also a computer whiz. He quickly discovered through the Union Pacific computer system that someone from Customs had released the suspicious car from being held.

Darlene chalked that up to stupidity and laziness. She would never make that mistake again and actually had no idea about what she had stumbled into.

Customs arranged for the car to be moved to the GATX (General American Tanker Car Company) facility about a mile away so that it could be safely entered. Shortly thereafter, they began burning off the excess fuel from the bottom of the car, a process known as "bleeding," in preparation for safely opening the car. As a precaution, the local fire department was notified because before these cars can be opened, a fire team needs to be on hand in case the car has been booby-trapped. This precaution was learned the hard way, and agents had paid in blood for not being careful about opening these cars. Crooks have been known to use explosives with large shipments of narcotics to keep them from being stolen.

Some fool at the fire department had notified the press, and on the day the tanker car was to be opened, the hill overlooking the GATX yard was swarming with reporters and cameras. Everybody wanted to see the big treasure of contraband when the tanker car was opened. As flashbulbs popped and video rolled, the car was opened and—it was empty! This debacle became known as the "Geraldo Rivera Tanker Car Caper," a reference to a TV special in which Rivera opened what was believed to be the secret stash vault of mobster Al Capone. After a lot of fanfare, the vault was opened. It was empty, and Rivera's on-screen embarrassment was echoed in Darlene's empty tanker car case. For weeks after that, Darlene was called "Geraldo" and people made "choo-choo" noises as she walked by. It was not the high point of her career at Customs. It wasn't the low point, either. That would come later.

Darlene laughed at that memory as she drove out to meet Tom Best, who had called her right after she left Gray's office and got the news about the tanker cars coming up from Calexico. As she drove, she called Renado at the San Bernardino

Police Department for some help with a narcotics sniffing dog. As soon as she mentioned a rail car, Renado went "choo-choo." Old failures die hard.

"Ha-ha, Renado. Real funny. Now this time get me a real dog, Einstein, and not some pound puppy." This was in reference to the "Geraldo Tanker Car Caper," where Renado had brought over a dog who just about "alerted" himself to death over an empty tanker car. Darlene arrived at the rail yard and Best was there along with a UP Haz-Mat team.

Dennis Bar (with UP Haz-Mat), Edmundo the foreman from GATX, and Ervin Rios were also there. Darlene climbed atop the tanker car with cutting pliers and removed the Customs seal on the man-way hatch cover. She bagged and tagged the seal for evidence. Edmundo and Dennis lifted the hatch cover exposing the bolts to the hatch port containing the pressure valves.. Darlene immediately noticed that the hatch bolts had been hand-painted white.

"What's with these bolts?" She asked Ervin. He climbed up to take a look. None of them had seen this kind of painting before. It was not consistent with the normal "shop style" paint jobs they routinely saw. This was different. Cops notice when things are "different." Darlene, Ervin, and Best all smiled at seeing this anomaly. "Let's pressure test it," she said to Edmundo and Bar.

At Darlene's request, this car was removed to another location, out of sight of any media. Darlene had done the "Geraldo" bit once. She wasn't about to repeat it if this car was empty. As they began the pressure test, they had another surprise: negative pressure. They opened the valve and heard a distinctive sucking sound, and no air exited or registered on the pressure valve for several minutes. This tanker car had been vacuum-sealed. There was no legitimate commercial purpose for vacuum-sealing a pressurized tanker car. In fact, so doing creates a potential disaster if the tanker is filled with certain volatile substances.

At about this time, Renado pulled up with a dog in tow. Darlene filled him in, and Renado was clearly excited. He had the car checked several times by the narco dog, but the animal failed to "alert." "Another pound puppy, Renado?" Darlene asked. She then put in a call to Gray and advised him on the situation.

"I'll be right out," he replied. When he arrived, Darlene pointed out to him the significance of the bolts being crudely painted white, the car having been manifested as empty, and its shady point of origin. Rios used his computer skills to pull the entries on this particular car. It had been exported back to the U.S. from a company called Grassa, based in Sinnaloa, Mexico.

"Ervin," Darlene asked, "what does 'grassa' mean in Spanish?"

"It means oil," Rios said.

"Tom," Darlene said to Best, "set the car up to be weighed. Hump it at least three times so we're sure to have an accurate measurement." This procedure involves rolling the car downhill, allowing gravity to carry it over a hump containing the scales. It took most of the day to manipulate the tanker car back through the yard, one of the largest rail yards in America, in order to weigh it. While this went on, Darlene could hear Gray on the phone with "the powers that be," pleading for the authorization and funds to pop the car open.

Darlene got on the phone with Assistant United States Attorney (AUSA) Yvette Palazuelos. Yvette had been the federal prosecutor on several of Darlene's Title 3's, which are wire tap investigations, when Darlene had been on the High Intensity Drug Trafficking Area task force designated Group Fifty. Once filled in on the facts at hand, Yvette granted extended border search authority, which only U.S. Customs has. This authorizes searches without a warrant of people, possessions, vehicles, and commodities entering this country.

The suspicious tanker car weighed in at almost 9000 pounds, well over the manufacturer's suggested "lightweight" for this type of pressurized tanker car. Gray gave Darlene authority to have the car moved to the GATX facility while awaiting permission to open it. Everybody sensed that this car—manifested as an "empty" return—was loaded. When Gray returned to the yard along with Evantie, Darlene brought them up to date.

"I would suggest," Darlene said, "that from this point forward we should have the car guarded in order to maintain good border search authority and security."

Gray agreed. "Good. It'll probably not be until tomorrow afternoon before we get the authorization and funding necessary to pop it open."

"It'll take us a few hours to get it over to GATX anyway, sir," Darlene said. Turning to GATX foreman Edmundo, she added: "Keep this car out of sight from both the media and the public."

"No more choo-choo?" Edmundo joked, referring to the Geraldo Caper.

"No more choo-choo," Darlene replied.

That night, Darlene sat in her G-ride watching the tanker car. The hours dragged on. Exhausted from all the activity just passed, she began to doze off and dream. For the umpteenth time, she had the same recurring dream. When she first began having it, she thought it a warning about something and it was scary. After having it several more times, Darlene became less afraid and just more curious about its content. The dream always took her to a different place, while otherwise remaining essentially the same. This time, Darlene found herself in the town she had grown up in—Dayton, Kentucky. She was standing in the street in front of her childhood home. A small boy, about two years old, was stumbling down the street towards her. He was crying, obviously shaken up about something, and was quite dirty. Darlene ran over and picked the boy up. She held him gently as she took him inside her house and began to bathe him. He would not talk.

A beautiful child, he had sparkling blue eyes which seemed to look right through her. As she washed him, Darlene became puzzled because the grime would simply not wash off. The more she scrubbed, the more futile it seemed and the sadder she became. The child just stared at her, begging with his eyes for help that she was unable to provide. As the boy cried softly, Darlene felt like she was dying inside for not being able to separate the child from the filth that covered him. It was a little like Lady MacBeth, endlessly washing her hands to get the blood off them without success. What could this puzzling dream mean?

Just then a loud crash startled Darlene awake, and she instinctively went for her gun. Then she realized the noise was just the rail cars bumping into each other as they were being hooked up. Her rapid breathing began to ease as the adrenaline rush left her body. She holstered her weapon and only then realized that she had the dream yet again. Her concern was: did the dream signify something about to happen or was she just going nuts? With three hours remaining on her shift, Darlene really wanted to go home and rest.

So many times her work had made her so tired she just wanted to resign and do something else. But the trouble was that she didn't think she could do any other kind of work. Being a criminal investigator was all she knew. It was all she had done all her adult life. As a child, she had dreamed of being an undercover cop ever since watching the television show "Charlie's Angels." If she wasn't a federal agent, then who was she? Besides, she really didn't think she could make it doing anything else. Was she the child in her recurring dream? Was the filth that couldn't be washed away the result of rubbing shoulders with the criminals and psychopaths she had spent her life pursuing? All she knew for sure was that she was having the dream more and more. It was haunting her like the ghosts at Fort Huachuca. Her curiosity about dreams was growing, right along with her fears about what dreams might mean.

It took two more days to bleed out the fumes and clear the tanker car with UP Haz-Mat. Along with Haz-Mat's Dennis Bar, David Gray and Ruben Sandoval decided that Darlene should be the one to make the entry. Darlene agreed, and got into the Haz-Mat suit that made her look like an astronaut. Even though she still felt sick, she went ahead, not wanting to appear weak to the rest of the team. When she tasted the oxygen in her mask, she knew at once that the mixture was too rich, but the technician rigging her up paid no attention to her complaints. A tripod was set up on top of the car, and Darlene was lowered by rope inside.

Darlene struggled with holding a flashlight in one hand and a video camera in the other. As she was being lowered through the man-way port, she banged her helmet on the edge, and it came off and tumbled down onto the floor of the tanker car. Somewhat light-headed after breathing the too-rich oxygen, Darlene giggled even as she shone her light down into the blackness searching for her helmet. Then she saw them: huge piles of tightly wrapped packages at both ends of the car's interior.

"Bingo!" she said aloud in satisfaction. She was thrilled to see such a big load. Soon she was at the bottom of the tanker, stepping over lots of marijuana and cocaine. Her light slipped out of her hand as she was videoing the contents, and suddenly she was in total darkness. It was the kind of claustrophobia a coal miner might experience. Trying hard to control her breathing, she knew she was hyperventilating.

"Hey Darlene," Bar was yelling, "are you all right? Are you all right?"

"Yeah, I'm okay, but get me out, will you?" By the time she was pulled out of the tanker car, she was feeling woozy and nauseous. She tore at her face mask to get it off.

"Whoa," Bar said, "take it easy. Calm down. We're getting it off you." Darlene felt like she was on an elevator ride going down fast. She was weak and sleepy. Dennis Bar examined the O2 regulator. "No wonder you were having problems. They set your O2 too rich for your weight."

Darlene glared at the technician who had mis-set her regulator. "You stupid clown," she said angrily, "I told you it was too rich!" The techie looked embarrassed and turned away. Darlene felt physically ill. All she wanted to do was lie down and go to sleep but she saw everybody on the ground below staring up at her, waiting for a report. She gave them a big "thumbs up," and they were ecstatic. When she climbed down unsteadily, there were "high five's" being given all around. Ruben, Ervin, Renado, and Jerry Johnston hugged her happily. "There's a big load of contraband in there," she said. She tried to regain her normal breathing pattern. She certainly didn't want to throw up in front of this happy crew.

One person who did not look pleased was Lawrence Evantie. Deliberately not congratulating her, he said: "Well Darlene, are you just going to sit there, or are you going to arrange for a controlled delivery?" Pointing at his watch, he added: "The clock's ticking."

Darlene glared at him, muttering under her breath: "You S.O.B., you just can't stand this, can you?" But she stood up and said: "I'll see to it, sir," like a good soldier to a bad commander. She went to the GATX bathroom and tried to vomit. Not having eaten anything all day, all she could manage was the dry heaves. Splashing some water on her face, she went back outside and met with AUSA Yvette Palezuelos, setting up the logistics for a controlled delivery to a lumber yard on Mill Street in San Bernardino, CA. SSA Bob Mattivi took over the logistics of the controlled delivery, while Ruben worked with Renado getting bodies for surveillance for the next few days. Gray was bagging and tagging evidence. This was how the team worked, with the exception of Evantie. What was his problem?

Darlene was told to go home and get some rest. After thirty straight hours on the job, she didn't need to be prodded. The seizure ended up being 8000 pounds of pot and 34 kilos of cocaine. Darlene was so burned out, she merely mumbled "Uh-huh" when they told her. To keep awake during her drive home, Darlene guzzled down a large quantity of highly caffeinated Mountain Dew drink on an empty stomach, not the brightest move she could have made. Still, she made it back home okay and, after drinking a little milk to try and settle her stomach, she hit the hay. Her last thought before sleep overtook her was: I am not Geraldo Rivera! I am not Geraldo Rivera! She slept like a baby.

One other piece of the puzzle was what had happened to Ervin Rios. Years earlier, at the time of the "Geraldo Tanker Car Caper," Ervin won a fight against Customs for unlawful firing. He had been off work for over a year and had been financially devastated by it. At the time of his firing, Ervin was working at the Los Angeles International Airport (LAX). He was about to complete a money transport over to the Customs vault. His partner was a woman named Sarah Brooks. As Ervin was pulling out of the LAX parking lot, a carload of Mexican males crashed into him. This accident was clearly not Ervin's fault. Ervin's attempts to get any information on these men was futile. They wouldn't produce any identification, common among illegal aliens. The driver offered Ervin fifty dollars, which he took knowing he would never see these guys again. Fifty was better than nothing.

When Ervin returned to his Customs office, he reported this incident to both his supervisor and Internal Affairs according to agency policy. It was a mistake he would come to regret. This type of thing happens a hundred times a day in Southern California, and numerous times to Customs Agents. A fender bender occurs on a freeway with small damage and some cash is exchanged in order to avoid a hike in insurance rates. It is no big deal. But for some puzzling reason,

Internal Affairs went after Ervin as if he'd robbed a bank. Why? Soon after, Ervin was fired for this accident. Again: why? Nobody who worked with Ervin could believe it. Here was one of the most effective agents at Customs, tossed out over nothing. What possible reason could there be for destroying the career of one of the best and brightest cops working at the Agency?

Both Darlene and Ruben testified on Ervin's behalf, thereby aligning themselves with Ervin "against" Customs. The Department of Treasury's grievance system later declared it a "wrongful firing" and gave Ervin back his job. Still, no one at Customs was ever disciplined for what they had done to Ervin Rios. There was no justice and no consequences for all of the anguish and hardship Ervin had to endure at the hands of U.S. Customs Internal Affairs department. All who knew Ervin were stunned into disbelief by what the poor guy went through. Was his only crime at Customs being "Hispanic on a sunny day?" It sure looked that way to everybody who witnessed it. Scratch up another hollow victory for the Drake Brinkley "Old Boys Club." There was more coming—a lot more. Rust never sleeps. It can take a very long time to put puzzle pieces together. Sometimes it isn't until the last piece falls into place that the whole picture becomes clear. By that time, especially in matters of national security, it can be too late.

19

Sick And Tired

"A lie can travel halfway around the world while the truth
is still putting its shoes on."
Mark Twain

The next morning at six, Darlene's phone rang. It was David Gray. "Can you start on the (federal anticipatory search) warrant?"

"I've already got it written in my head."

"Well, bring your head and your fingers in so you can type this up."

"No problem." Darlene went in to work and wrote up the warrant. She also met with the appropriate authorities at the railroads and at the San Bernardino Police Department.

The office was buzzing with everyone chasing down leads on the case. Then the FBI arrived with their usual song and dance: tell us what information you've got and we'll tell you nothing about what we've got. Such a deal, Darlene thought to herself as she stonewalled the glory hogs from the Bureau. Later, Darlene saw AUSA Yvette Palazuelos and briefed her on the "turf war" with the FBI. Yvette told her not to worry. Unable to seize the case and cop the glory, the FBI left, but not before Darlene let one of them know he ranked just below pond scum in her estimation.

Two days later, Darlene was in her doctor's office. This was her third visit in three months. The ringing in her ears, general feeling of tiredness, and low level fever hadn't subsided. She was referred to an ear, nose, and throat specialist. He gave Darlene a series of tests and blood work and then some bad news.

"I'm not sure of this, but you may have MS," he said blandly.

"Multiple sclerosis?" Darlene gasped.

"Well, it's too early to tell, but a lot of your symptoms match the onset of it."

Upon receiving this bombshell, Darlene's arms, legs, and face went numb and her chest became tight.

The doctor added: "I'm scheduling you for an MRI (magnetic resonance imaging) on Thursday afternoon. We should know for sure after that."

Darlene went back to her office in a total daze. Still contemplating how her life would change if in fact she did have MS, she had barely sat down at her desk when she heard Gray yell for her and Ruben to come into his office.

"Attorney General (Janet) Reno wants a daily briefing on your rail car case. It seems this is the first uncovered use of a tanker car to smuggle in narcotics," he said. "Now look, the FBI has a related case and they're not getting the help they need—"

"My doctor says I may have multiple sclerosis," Darlene interrupted softly.

"I'm sorry about that, but the FBI—" Gray said, before Ruben broke in.

"What happened at the doctor's, Darlene?"

"He says my symptoms match the onset of MS."

Gray insensitively asked Darlene a follow up question on the case, which Ruben answered for her. "Let her answer her own questions!" Gray fired back. "What are you—her attorney?"

Ruben's face turned red and his jaw muscles tightened. Darlene prepared herself to jump between them if things turned uglier, and her facial expression told Ruben to calm down and take it easy. Ruben softened. "Are you all right?" he asked her.

"I'm dealing with it," Darlene said. She turned her head away so that the men could not see her eyes welling up with tears from the strain she was under.

Gray relented. "Hey, I hope things turn out okay on Thursday, Darlene. You can go." Darlene left the office and headed for the bathroom. Ruben stayed behind. As she walked down the hall a few minutes later, Darlene could hear Gray yelling at Ruben. The meeting had moved to her and Ruben's office.

"David," Ruben said, "I'm going to ask you for the last time to stop talking to me like this. I'm not yelling at you!"

Darlene entered her office, where Gray grabbed her by the shoulders and tried to push her outside. "No way, Gray," Ruben cautioned. "I want her to witness this." Gray literally pushed Darlene into the hallway. "I'm not going to put up with this," Ruben continued as he stepped out of the office. Gray followed him but, when he saw Darlene standing there, turned around and went back to his own office.

"Ruben, are you okay?" she asked.

"Did you hear any of that?"

"I heard enough, Ruben. He's just trying to push your buttons to get you to blow up. David Gray is doing Evantie's dirty work for him."

"I know, and I didn't buy into it at all. Weren't you proud of me?"

"Yes. Very. You did a good job of controlling yourself. He's the one who lost it. He sounded like a maniac." The pair walked outside, where Ruben got into his car.

"Hey Dar," he said, "don't worry too much about this MRI stuff. There's no way you have MS. You're in too good shape for that. It's probably just something stupid like AIDS." They both laughed.

As Darlene went back into the building and walked down the hall towards her office, Bob Mattivi motioned her into his. "Evantie's looking for you. The Acting Commissioner of Customs is about to call for a briefing on the tanker car case." Darlene sat down, closed her eyes, and shook her head. "Hey, are you all right. You don't look your gorgeous self at all. What's wrong?"

"Could I see you, Darlene?" Evantie interrupted, sticking his head into Mattivi's office. He led her to a phone where she briefed the Acting Commissioner, Stan Wallace, on what they had so far. Wallace thanked her for the great job she was doing, but he sounded condescending and insincere. Sometimes politicians can be as shallow as teaspoons.

The tanker car in question was now in San Bernardino. It was under surveillance and Darlene's warrant had been written. A couple of days later, she got a call from Ruben. Evidently, Evantie had pulled the surveillance off the car, assuming they had given it enough time. Darlene tried to get it back under surveillance, but to no avail. She knew that crooks would often wait for weeks before attempting to pick up a large load. They'd watch their container until they were sure the coast was clear before retrieving its contents. The bad guys aren't stupid. They know that cops get stingy about footing the large bill full surveillance entails, and they'll just wait it out. Darlene was in AUSA Yvette Palezuelos's office when she got the call.

She knew it was bad news when Ruben first inquired: "Are you sitting down?"

"Yes, Ruben, I am."

"Well, the day after Evantie lifted the surveillance, the bad guys popped the top off the car and made entry."

"What? How the hell did they do that? It's impossible!"

"No it's not, Dar. It's the damnedest thing. They jury-rigged a mechanism with a tripod and a pulley and extracted the hatch-port valve system with a couple of fork lift trucks. As soon as they got inside and saw their load was gone—they split. They even left some of their tools there."

Darlene couldn't believe what she was hearing. Furious, she relayed all this information to Yvette. "If Evantie had left the surveillance team on for just one more day we could have gotten the off-load crew. Now they're gone."

"I can't believe they lifted the watch team," Yvette replied in frustration. "I've had agencies surveill controlled deliveries for weeks."

"This is retaliation against me for siding with Ruben in his complaint against Customs," Darlene concluded. "We're not getting any support here, Yvette." As embarrassed as Darlene was at her agency dropping the ball this way, she was also glad that a federal prosecutor like Yvette was aware of what was going on. How important such awareness by an outsider was would become apparent as time went on.

A few days after this disaster, Evantie called Darlene at home. "Some lady from San Francisco will be coming to the office tomorrow to talk to you about your EEO case."

"I've got an approved sick leave for tomorrow afternoon," she replied.

"If you'll come in the morning, you'll still have plenty of time to make your afternoon appointment."

"Okay," Darlene said. She felt good that maybe someone was finally beginning to take her EEO complaint seriously and investigate it. She should have known better. The next morning, she went into the office and met Lana Janston, Group Supervisor from San Francisco. As Evantie left their meeting, he had this sneaky little smirk on his face. Darlene was thinking about that smirk as Janston began her questioning.

"You are under investigation for wrongful release of information," Janston said. As she began reading Darlene her rights, Darlene interrupted her.

"Evantie told me this meeting was about my EEO complaint."

"Well, it is about your complaint."

"I'm not saying anything until I talk to my attorney," Darlene told her.

"I want you to sign this rights warning."

"I'm on approved sick leave," Darlene said as she walked out of the office. She went back to her own office and placed an emergency page with her lawyer. Ruben was sitting there.

"Hey, what's up, Dar?" Darlene told him what was going on. The phone rang and it was Darlene's attorney. Once he had the facts, he asked to speak with Lana Janston. Ruben was irate. "What a cruel thing to do, knowing about your medical test today. Hang in there. Don't let them get to you." Then Ms. Janston came over the intercom, telling Darlene to pick up the phone.

"It's a witch hunt," Darlene's lawyer told her in a conference call. "They're saying you wrongfully released information contained in your EEO report. Look," he continued, "they are violating your Title 7 and Privacy Act Rights, but you have to participate in this grilling or they can fire you. Now, go to your doctor's office and afterwards you and I will talk more strategy before you go back with Janston, okay?" Darlene agreed and left for her appointment. When it was over, the medical technicians told her the results would probably not be known for another week.

Darlene then spoke with her attorney before returning to her office to continue the "interview" with Lana Janston. "My lawyer has told me to sign the rights warning and to answer your questions to the best of my ability, and that's what I'm here to do."

"The problem arises from the letters of commendation you attached in your EEO complaint."

"Those letters were written by prosecutors and DEA supervisors commending me on my work. It seems like the only people who don't appreciate what I'm doing are in management here at Customs."

"There are improper disclosures in those letters, including case numbers and the names of people under investigation."

"I didn't write those letters. They did. Besides, why don't you go out in the hall and take a look at what's posted on the walls. There are lots of these kind of congratulatory writings. We call them hero letters, because they recognize our best work. You should know that what's on the walls out there is no more a leak than what's in my letters in my complaint file. Everything in the hall can be seen by the clean-up workers and other non-agency personnel."

"What's out there is not important," Janston said, waving Darlene's complaint file. "It's what's in here that matters." She then proceeded to ask Darlene a long series of questions designed to elicit a "yes" or "no" response. Darlene saw through that little game, knowing that if she limited her responses in that way the resultant statement would appear very damaging to her case. So instead she insisted on writing out her explanations.

"I have a plane to catch, you know," Janston said testily.

"I have a career to defend, Ms. Janston. I'll take the time I need to do that." Darlene did the best job she could under these stressful circumstances. It took her five hours to complete her statement. Janston missed her flight back to San Francisco. Darlene wasn't exactly heartbroken about it.

This event perfectly illustrated what Darlene and Ruben and others were citing as their alleged discrimination at U.S. Customs. Its timing is what this was all about. The promotion list for GS-13 (a higher pay grade position) had just been released. Darlene was in the top ten of those awaiting promotion and there were eleven openings, so she should have been assured advancement. The only way somebody else could have been promoted over Darlene was if she had a "red file," signifying that she was under an active, open investigation by Internal Affairs. By policy, no one can be promoted with a red file.

Lacking anything real to get Darlene on, these charges were trumped up at that time precisely for the purpose of denying Darlene the promotion she deserved and merited. While Customs knew these accusations wouldn't hold up, they did serve the intended purpose of making Darlene ineligible for promotion. Darlene's name was removed from the promotion list. Here you have in a nutshell what Darlene, Ruben, and scores of others faced who dared challenge the bias and discrimination rampant in U.S. Customs and its overseer organization today, the Department of Homeland Security. Darlene went to the gym after this ordeal, attempting to swim off her frustration. Evantie's smirking face haunted her like a ghost. She got no sleep that night.

In the next few days, Darlene, Ruben, Jerry, Renado, Mattivi, Gray and others on the team hit both businesses and several houses in San Bernardino in connection with the tanker car full of dope. Then Darlene landed a much bigger fish: a key player in the infamous Arellano-Felix Narcotics Organization. Using her skills as an interrogator, Darlene was able to "flip" this heavyweight, getting him to cooperate. Yvette and Darlene were able to place this CI (Classified Informant) in protective custody, where he provided a lot of valuable information.

"Haven't you gotten OCDETF status on this case and the rail project?" Yvette asked, knowing that Organized Crime Drug Enforcement Task Force projects were entitled to more abundant anti-crime resources."

"Yes I have."

"So where's your back up?"

"You're looking at it—me, myself, and I. Evantie and (SAIC) Brinkley have pulled all my support."

"They can't do that," Yvette said incredulously. "That's undermining a criminal case in order to shut you up." Darlene just stared at Yvette, who then added: "You know, there's a term for this—obstruction of justice."

"Just do me a favor and remember what you're seeing, Yvette," Darlene told her.

The next day, Darlene went for her follow-up medical appointment to learn the results of the MRI and the other examinations and blood testing she'd been through.

"The good news is that you don't have MS," the doctor said to Darlene's immense relief. "The bad news is that you have Epstein-Barr Syndrome, which is commonly called Mono(nucleosis). That's where that ringing in your ears and some of your other symptoms are coming from. Do you swim a lot?"

"Yes."

"You probably picked it up in the pool. I'm afraid it's gone undiagnosed for so long that the ringing in your ears is probably permanent. Your blood pressure is too low and your white blood cell count is too high. Your body fat content is also so low that it's interfering with your regular menstrual cycle and causing a hormonal imbalance. Extended exhaustion, lack of deep REM (rapid eye movement) sleep and too much stress are taking their toll. But other than all that, you're fine."

"Well, doctor, I'd say that you're just a bundle of good news."

"What's going on in your life that's causing all this stress?"

Darlene just smiled, looked down at the floor, shook her head and laughed quietly.

The doctor became very serious. "I'm glad you find all of this amusing, but you won't find it so funny when you end up on a slab in the morgue. I'm going to prescribe some things for you, but above all you need to slow down and get some rest."

"I'll try," Darlene answered, not knowing where this "rest" would come from. That night the dream came again. This time Darlene was back at Fort Huachuca, during her last posting as a Captain in the Army Military Police Corps. She was sitting in her old office, in the chair she knew so well. The dream was so vivid she could smell the wood in the historic old building where she used to work. It seemed like a lifetime ago. She had truly loved being in the Army. She felt in control. Things were simpler back then.

The little two year old toddler appeared in the hallway in front of her. He was filthy and crying and he began walking away. Looking over his shoulder at Darlene, he seemed to call to her with those magically deep blue eyes. Darlene got up from her chair and followed him down the dark stairs. He led her into what used to be the old morgue area.

When he turned to Darlene, he smiled. Darlene felt a strange sensation of peacefulness come over her. As she began walking towards the child, she glanced down and saw that she was wearing her military dress blue uniform. Taking the child's dirty little hand in her clean white glove, Darlene was suddenly jarred awake by her alarm clock. She climbed out of bed, went into her bathroom, and threw up.

20

What's That Smell?

"It is said that power corrupts, but actually it's more true that power attracts the corruptible."
David Brin

On April 22, 1998, Darlene sat in her car by the swimming pool at Costello Park in East Los Angeles. As she waited for the other agents to show up so that they all might serve a search warrant at the house of a suspected bad guy nearby, her mind began to drift. She thought about how this beautiful park came to be. Lou Costello, of the immortal comedy duo "Abbott and Costello," had lost a child. His son had drowned in a terrible accident. Hoping to make something good come from the tragedy, Costello had donated the park and swimming pool to the city in the hope that other children would be taught to swim properly and avoid the fate which befell his little boy. As she waited, Darlene took out her laptop computer and began working on her EEO retaliation.

When the other agents arrived, they briefed each other on the plan, suited up and waited for the tow truck to arrive. The tow truck would be necessary because the house they planned on hitting had a cast iron security gate on the front door and iron bars on all the windows. The idea was to hook the tow truck's hook onto the iron gate and have the truck pull it off after first giving the required "knock notice" to the occupants inside the house.

Darlene was "elected" to be the one to attach the hook to the iron gate. As she approached the house, she began to realize this was not a good plan. The house was old and had a rickety front porch with uneven brick pillars holding up the roof. She did what she was supposed to and retreated. Then Jerry Johnston and a LAPD officer approached and yelled: "Federal agents with a search warrant! Open the door!" No sooner were these words spoken than the driver of the tow truck floored the accelerator. The iron gate was wrenched off and flew into the brick pillars, which in turn fell causing the porch roof to collapse. As the dust settled, Darlene could make out the lone figure of an old black man standing in the doorway with his hand where the doorknob used to be. He was motionless and was in a state of shock. The agents all began laughing at what looked like a scene from an old Mack Sennett Keystone Kops silent film comedy.

After the search was made, Darlene came outside of the house and saw the old black gentleman sitting in a chair on his front lawn, crying as he looked back at the immense damage which the forced entry had wreaked on his home. Suddenly, it was not funny any more. It was this old man's son whom the warrant was directed against, yet it was his home which had received the damage. Immediately Darlene and the others felt guilt and sorrow for what they had done to this old person's home. She thought of her own aging father and what such an experience would have done to him. Here she was, Darlene thought to herself, just another arrogant federal agent swooping down to make this innocent man's life miserable because he happened to have a crook for a son. The raid may have produced some evidence, but it made Darlene feel ashamed all the same.

She went back to her office and struggled with typing up the rest of her EEO complaint. She couldn't seem to shake the image of the crying old guy out of her head.

Why hadn't she tried to console him? How could she and the others have laughed so heartily at what was a disaster for an innocent elderly gent? Darlene remembered the old saying about slapstick comedy: when somebody else slips on a banana peel—that's funny; when You slip on a banana peel—that hurts! She couldn't get the bad taste out of her mouth that the raid had left.

When she finished her EEO complaint work, she faxed it to the EEO office. She was responding to the obvious ploy used by management against her: have Internal Affairs trump up charges they know to be false and unsubstantiatable in order to "red tag" her file and prevent her promotion. Her complaint against this obviously unfair and discriminatory treatment was simply rejected by the Regional Complaint Center on June 26, 1998. There was no reason stated, nor had there been any investigation into the events surrounding her case. The great stonewall continued, and there didn't seem to be a thing she could do about it.

Darlene filed another response to this mistreatment on July 1, 1998, but she never heard back from management on that. So much for the vaunted "chain of command" that she was supposed to use. The simple truth was that U.S. Customs and the "old boy network" that runs it has no place for those who point out the dangerous inequality that permeates the system. It drives out the best agents, leaving mostly those who suck up to their bosses and step on their underlings. To be sure, there are still good agents in Customs and in Homeland Security. But if this way of operating persists, they will also be driven out. You can't run an

agency which needs all kinds of different people to be effective and then discriminate against those who don't fit into your mold. It won't work and it weakens
national security at a time when we are already vulnerable to attack.

Darlene read an article in the San Diego Union-Tribune dated May 16, 1998,
concerning the lawsuit between Ricardo Sandoval and U.S. Customs. Ervin Rios
had kindly forwarded it to her in order to bolster her sagging spirits. Ricardo had
won $200,000 plus $500,000 in attorney's fees plus back pay in his discrimination lawsuit. Ricardo had used the same lawyers that Ruben, Sandy, Ervin, and
Darlene had. She was especially struck by the last page of the newspaper article.
Sandoval had filed a second lawsuit charging that after he had uncovered the
existence of a racist ring in the agency, he had been subjected to a series of internal investigations and was falsely accused of crimes. It was exactly what was happening to Darlene and the others.

Darlene concluded reading the news piece with very mixed feelings. On the
one hand, she was extremely happy that someone who had been getting the same
treatment she had came out a winner in his lawsuit against Customs. On the
other hand, if the powers that be were willing to go after Ricardo, who was
already at the GS-13 job level and was a Special Agent for the Department of
Internal Affairs, what chance did Darlene have against them? Also, having lost
against Ricardo Sandoval, they would really be out for blood next time, and "next
time" meant Darlene's case.

Darlene called her friend Sandy Nunn. "Did you see the news item in the San
Diego paper on Ricardo Sandoval's lawsuit?"

"No," Sandy replied. "Would you read it to me?"

When Darlene finished reading the article, she added: "Did you notice that
Customs used a lawyer from the U.S. Attorney's office instead of from our own
regional council?"

"Yes. What does that tell you?"

"That they don't have much confidence in their own attorneys."

"I agree," Sandy said. "But look on the bright side. Maybe since they lost the
case against Ricardo they'll be less inclined to take on another one with a lot of
the same stuff in the allegations of misconduct and discrimination."

"You know," Darlene said wistfully, "I just wish they'd clean up their act so
we could get on with the business of catching the bad guys."

"You mean the bad guys who aren't in U.S. Customs management," Sandy
added. The two friends shared a sardonic laugh at the thought that Customs
would actually abandon the Drake Brinkley "old boys club" and reward agents
whose work showed merit and initiative.

"You know what stuck in my mind about that article?" Darlene asked.

"What?"

"It was the quote from the juror named Cannon, the person who said that discrimination inside the government is no worse or widespread than in corporate America. But then he added that the government has a lot more power, and that's when it becomes dangerous."

"You think the public is aware of this, Darlene?"

"Nope. I think the public Wants to believe the government is on the job fighting the bad guys. They want to believe that so much they're willing to overlook the facts."

"That's a scary thought," Sandy said.

"I'm bracing for more flak from the agency's dogs at Internal Affairs."

"Me too."

"Hang in there, Sandy. As Yogi Berra once said: It ain't over 'til it's over."

It didn't take long for Darlene's fears about IA to materialize. On June 25, 1998, she was investigated for the second time for wrongful use of Government identification. There had supposedly been an anonymous call to the IA office accusing Darlene of using her Army Reserve ID to gain access to military flights at a reduced or free rate. Darlene was required to make the three hour drive to the Internal Affairs office in Long Beach, California. There, IA Agent Terry Clay escorted her into an interrogation room and read her her rights. As Darlene endured this ordeal, she glanced over to the large glass mirror on the opposite wall, knowing there were people behind it studying her reactions and responses. It was the same position Darlene had put many a witness and defendant in, but she noticed how different it felt to be on the receiving end of such treatment. It made her stomach burn and she sensed the anger rising up into her face.

"Why would you do that?" Clay asked in a patronizing tone about the allegation.

"I didn't. But even if I had, it's common practice to use your military I.D. to "catch a hop" on a space available basis. It's not a violation of any policy. More to the point, if it were a violation it would be the under the jurisdiction of Army CID (Criminal Investigation Division) to check it out, not U.S. Customs."

"What's your point?" Clay asked.

"My point," Darlene replied, trying to control her anger, "is that you're putting me through this crap without ever having checked to see if there was even a violation of Customs rules." With that, she became totally fed up at this harassment and grabbed the written version of the rights statement they had made her sign. "I want a copy of this," she said testily. "This bull—is over!"

"You can't have a copy," Clay said. They argued back and forth and finally a copy of the signed statement was provided to Darlene. It was the only evidence she would ever have that such a meeting even took place. The whole thing was just another trumped-up excuse to harass her and nothing more. Yet again the "red tag" status that this "case" had established was the reason she was excluded from the BQL (Best Qualified List) of those looking to advance to GS-13 status. Darlene knew that the real purpose of this hassling was to get her not to testify on Ruben's upcoming deposition for his federal lawsuit against Customs, and also to "teach her a lesson." Darlene felt like she'd been mugged.

That night, Darlene had the dream again. She was standing in her bedroom as the beautiful toddler appeared. He was filthy and had tears in his eyes. Darlene picked him up and took him into her bathroom sink. She took a washcloth and attempted to clean his filthy hands. Suddenly she and the child were both transported to a lovely pasture, where they stood in deep green grass surrounded by peacefully grazing cattle. As she placed the toddler onto the ground, he motioned for her to follow him.

They walked up to the top of a hill overlooking a pleasant valley. In the distance they could see a farmhouse with construction work in progress. Near that house was a corral complete with cattle chutes where cows are steered in for inoculation. A man was working with some cows in the corral, but Darlene couldn't see who it was since his back was turned. When she tried to get closer she found that she couldn't move. The man in the corral was working with the cows, aided by two dogs who nipped at their heels and kept them moving. He was apparently in his 30's and wore a flannel shirt, blue jeans, and boots. He had a English or Australian accent, probably the latter since he called one of the dogs "Mate," a favorite term of affection in Australia. There was something almost mystical about the man, as if he had an angelic or spiritual aura about him.

Darlene saw a kangaroo hopping around in the distance. There was a pond with ducks swimming across it. Everything about this scene was peaceful and serene. The man's voice was deep and struck Darlene as very comforting, almost as if she knew him. Yet something told her he was a stranger. Near the man she somehow saw two packs of cigarettes on the hood a flatbed truck. One pack was wadded up and the other looked as if it had just been opened. Wildflowers began blooming in the deep green grass. Darlene felt an overwhelming desire to walk over and discover who this man was, but the toddler squeezed her hand and she knew it was time to go. Straining, she took one last look in a vain attempt to glimpse the man's face. She hoped he would turn around and reveal himself. He did not turn around.

When she awoke the following morning, Darlene stayed in bed an extra minute or two, re-playing the dream in her head while it was still fresh. Those short moments above that verdant valley were the most peaceful bits of sleep she'd had in years. Where could this place have been? The kangaroo and the man's accent and calling his dog "Mate" all pointed to Australia. What was that about? Wasn't Australia supposed to be dry, brown, and rocky, kind of like west Texas? Why had the toddler taken her there? Why was the mysterious wrangler's face concealed? Was there some deep meaning underneath all this jangled imagery? Why hadn't the toddler taken her someplace else, like her childhood home in the Appalachian Mountains in Kentucky? Was she losing her mind—cracking under the pressure she felt on the job? None of this made any sense.

Then Darlene remembered what a LAPD narcotics officer had told her once: they were only allowed to work narcotics for three years out of fear of burning out. Darlene had been working major narcotics investigations for eleven years. Was she burning out? She wanted to tell somebody she trusted about these recurring dreams. Yet a voice in her head was telling her to keep it to herself, as if talking about them would betray a confidence. There was also the fear that if she told anybody, she'd end up in a straight jacket in a room with rubber walls.

Darlene filed a second EEO complaint for what she perceived as retaliation with respect to the phony I.D. charge which red-tagged her file and once again killed her chance for promotion. EEO Supervisor Conales never assigned her an investigator for this issue. Darlene knew Conales had received the complaint because she sent it by certified mail and had the signed receipt. Yet Conales continued to stonewall her. June 25,1998, was a very discouraging day for Darlene. That's when she learned that Edwin Easel ("The Weasel") had been promoted to GS-13 despite having a lower CAAPS score than she had. Had Winkowsky followed policy, he would have reported Easel for the incident in which he took home seized heroin, breaking the integrity of the evidence chain. Had that been reported, Easel would automatically have received the mandatory "90 days on the bricks" sentence or even been fired. When Darlene and Ruben confirmed this promotion news, it made them both ill. They left the office early, both to prepare for an evening of "dumpster diving" for evidence and also to have a chance to talk things over.

Darlene got home and tried to take a nap before going out on her night mission. It was no use. She just tossed and turned. Easel's promotion over her and Ruben really stuck in the point that there was blatant discrimination going on. Both she and Ruben were simply much better agents than Easel the Weasel on every level, with their longer service at Customs and prior training in the military and in law enforcement. As an investigator, Easel couldn't find his way to the men's room at Wal-Mart, yet he was now their superior in the chain of command. The inmates were running the asylum and it hurt a lot.

The phone rang. It was Sandy. "I heard the news," she said. "This is so absurd. You and Ruben run circles around that weasel and everybody knows it."

"Uh huh," Darlene responded sadly.

"If this isn't blatant retaliation I don't know what is!" Sandy tried to console Darlene, showing what a good and understanding friend she was, and in fact managed to buck up Darlene's sagging spirits. When their conversation ended, Darlene was ready to go back out into the big bad world and jump into a dumpster looking for evidence in a fraud case. A corrupt businessman in Temecula, California, had bled his business dry of its money and was putting the screws to all the other partners and employees. He had also filed a phony bankruptcy. Having "bled out" the considerable cash in the business, this crook was also involved in laundering the money through some front companies abroad. In wiring this money back and forth, he had committed a host of Customs violations. Darlene went to the dumpster where his business unloaded its trash and prepared to literally dive in looking for documents and other evidence. She was always surprised at the things supposedly smart crooks felt safe in throwing away.

She met Ruben and Jerry Johnston at the dumpster site at about midnight. Although she was on time, they gave her some verbal grief about the late hour. It was obvious everybody was a little grouchy from lack of sleep. Darlene suited up to "dumpster dive" while the other two set up surveillance in an adjacent parking lot. As she prepared to leap into the trash, Darlene smelled something awful—like a skunk. Not able to see anything moving around, she dove into the trash and began searching around. Suddenly she heard a large thud at the bottom of the dumpster and sure enough, out ran a big skunk. She ducked down, held her breath, squinted her eyes, and prepared for the worst. As the skunk scurried up and out of the dumpster, Darlene could hear peals of laughter coming from the adjacent parking lot. Ruben and Jerry had witnessed her encounter with nature's little stinker and found it all quite hilarious. Darlene started laughing in spite of herself.

Although she was lucky that the skunk hadn't sprayed her directly, Darlene still smelled of trash and skunk as she approached Ruben and Jerry. But she had found some great documents and other evidence. Still laughing at her plight, the men were none the less impressed with what she had discovered. Since her car was some distance away, she asked for a lift to her vehicle.

"Hop in the back of my truck here, woman," Jerry said, "'cause you sure as hell ain't riding in my cab."

Darlene turned to Ruben. "Don't look at me," he said, still laughing. "You stink! There's no way you're riding in my car!"

Using some very colorful language concerning her partners' parentage and sexual orientation, Darlene turned and started walking to her car. The men followed her, making "stinky" jokes the whole way and having a wonderful time at her expense. By then, Darlene really didn't care what they said. She was actually quite pleased at what she had uncovered, except for the skunk, of course. Her evidence convicted a crook of fraud and money laundering, and it had been a worthwhile experience. The next day, Darlene briefed her AUSA (Assistant United States Attorney) for fraud—Jim McNarra—on the case and he was very, very pleased. But the events surrounding how Darlene had been cheated out of a promotion stunk worse than the black and white critter Darlene shared a dumpster with. How long this could go on and where it would lead were a very big set of problems, indeed. And the smell was getting worse every day.

21

Dirty Pool

"Winning isn't the main thing; it's the only thing."
Vince Lombardi

In the wonderful spy movie "The Ipcress File," British agent Michael Caine's enemies put him inside a machine designed to wear down his mental resistance to mind control. After just a few hours of this procedure, one of his tormentors comments that during World War 2, it took the Nazis months of beating a prisoner to reduce him to a comparable state. Darlene felt like she was being "tortured" by a management team hell bent on breaking her will to resist the wrongdoing she saw all around her. Rather than confront the problem, U.S. Customs chose instead to attack those who raised issues of discrimination within the agency. Darlene was strong but the "old boy system" was grinding her down.

This pathetic agency response is extremely dangerous on two separate grounds. First, it insures that nothing will be done to correct the problem. Second, it sends a clear message to the entire agency that anyone who acts on perceived grievances will be treated as disloyal and dealt with accordingly. Remember, there is no law protecting federal whistleblowers. Those who could enact such a law choose not to do so for fear that it will come back to bite them. Only a few Senators and Congressmen don't fear legislation which would protect one of their staffers if that underling came forward with evidence of wrongdoing on the politician's part. So unlike in the corporate world, a federal whistleblower is completely isolated and powerless. Without the force of law behind them, a federal whistleblower must rely on the conscience of the system, and you cannot count on something which is often simply not present. The whole purpose of telling Darlene's story is to try and help enable passage of a law to protect federal whistleblowers.

On July 30, 1998, EEO Supervisor Conales lied in a statement regarding the reason for the removal of Darlene's EEO Counselor Anna Francisco. Conales claimed to have spoken several times with Francisco about the time line requirements pertinent to Darlene's case. This lie was to make Francisco look negligent. Darlene called her.

"Anna," she said, "have you read Conales' statement regarding you?"

"What statement?" Anna replied.

Darlene read it to her, and Francisco was appalled. "That's a lie," she said. "Conales never met with me on this and certainly never pointed out what she says she did."

"I just wanted you to know what was going on," Darlene said.

"Conales is a snake."

"Amen to that, sister. Watch your back," Darlene warned.

A couple of days later, Evantie called Darlene into his office. "Why don't you shut the door?" he said.

"I'd rather not, sir," Darlene replied.

Evantie smirked and shook his head in obvious disgust. Then he handed her a letter of disciplinary action for wrongful release of information based on the letters of commendation she had included in the file she sent to Anna Francisco in her EEO complaint. The timing of this meeting with Evantie was a few weeks before Darlene was scheduled to testify in Ruben's federal lawsuit.

Darlene read the letter, then looked up at Evantie. "Is that it?" she asked.

"Well, don't you have any questions or anything to say?"

"No sir, I don't." Darlene turned to leave.

"Wait," Evantie said. "You have to sign this form to acknowledge receipt of the letter. Darlene signed the form. "Hey Dar," Evantie said, "how's that fraud case coming along?"

"The prosecutor says we have enough to get this guy on fraud and money laundering charges."

In the questions that followed, Evantie made it clear that he was trying to undermine the case.

"Hey," Darlene responded, "if you don't like what we're doing, why not go talk to the prosecutor yourself."

"Well I may do just that. You've been on this thing way too long, and I obviously need to move this guy along and get this thing wrapped up."

Controlling her anger, Darlene said: "You do that, Evantie. You do that."

Darlene returned to her office and re-read the letter. A paragraph on the last page caught her eye as being potentially very coercive. It read: "A copy of this letter will be placed in your Official Personnel File for a period not to exceed three (3) years from the date of the letter. The letter may be removed by local management, with my concurrence, should circumstances warrant such an action." Darlene could only interpret this as meaning: "Drop your EEO case and don't testify for Ruben in his and this letter will go away." The letter was signed by Dick Kirkland of the Disciplinary Review Board. Everybody at Customs knew that Kirkland was another of Drake Brinkley's cronies. Now Kirkland was empowering local management, the very same folks cited in the complaints, to make this letter go away if Darlene would play ball.

When Darlene showed Ruben the letter, they left the office to find a place to talk.

"Ruben, you know as well as I do the average fraud case, unlike narcotics cases, takes about three years to develop. I've only been on this one for a year."

"Don't worry. It's just another scare tactic to try and get you to blow up."

"This thing is relentless," Darlene said, showing the signs of strain.

"Yeah, but they're going to come up with stuff like this because they can't get anything real to use against you."

On August 5, Evantie and Darlene met with the federal prosecutor McNarra assigned to the case. McNarra explained the progress made to Evantie. In response, Evantie made a series of remarks designed to undercut Darlene's work. McNarra was puzzled by this and stoutly defended Darlene's work. At the same time, he glanced over at Darlene with a puzzled expression. When the meeting ended and Evantie left the room, McNarra asked: "What the heck's going on here?"

"This is what happens in our agency when you're not a member of the good old boy system." To calm McNarra's doubts, Darlene added: "Don't worry. I'll take care of this and things will be okay." McNarra looked a little calmer as he left. For her part, Darlene waited for another shoe to drop—on her. It didn't take long. On August 7, 1998, she checked her Customs Inbox and found copies of Reports Of Investigations (ROI's) on closed cases. With these were notes from her new Acting Supervisor Dudley O'Shea telling Darlene to modify or explain them. O'Shea, yet another Brinkley crony, was married to the Special Agent In Charge of the L.A. Internal Affairs Office. These ROI's had already been approved by previous supervisors. Darlene had never in her eleven years at Customs seen an agent asked to modify reports on closed cases, which she couldn't do anyway because the computer system didn't let you modify cases once approved.

She asked around and, sure enough, no other agent had been asked to perform such a task. She saw the "old hand" at the office—Bob Mattivi—and asked him about this assignment.

"Never seen the like of it before," he said, shaking his head in disbelief. "Boy, Darlene, O'Shea's only been on the job a couple of days and he's already going after you."

The new GS-13 list had just come out, and sure enough Darlene was on the BQL (Best Qualified List). She had that sinking feeling that she would be investigated yet again on a trumped up charge just to get her file red-tagged and thus be ineligible for advancement. After she had filed a response to her letter of disciplinary action, Darlene got this from Kirkland in a letter: "You expressed very strong concerns in your grievance letter that the letter of reprimand contained language you found coercive in nature. Please be advised that the language in the reprimand states that if you should separate from the Service before this letter is removed from your (OPF) file, it will be removed and destroyed in accordance with applicable regulation."

Darlene thought to herself: How clever of Mr. Kirkland to change the actual wording of the letter and conveniently leave out the part that said: "The letter may be removed by local management, with my concurrence, should circumstances warrant such an action.'"

She read the Kirkland letter to Ruben. When finished she added: "What a moron!"

Later that night, Darlene called Sandy Nunn and read her the letter, too. The two women buoyed each other's spirits. Darlene needed a woman's support, and Sandy was just great at doing that. They were both fighting against a system which was run by and for white males and sometimes all that testosterone could wear them down. When swimming with sharks you should always have a buddy.

On September 3, 1998, Darlene met with AUSA Yvette and filled her in on what was happening. Then she spoke with Arnold Connez, who told her that in the last two staff meetings SAIC Drake Brinkley did something extraordinary.

"He got up in front of all the supervisors and trashed the whole EEO process and those filing EEO complaints," Connez told her.

"Did he mention anybody by name?" Darlene asked.

"Yeah. He said you and Sandy Nunn were a couple of troublemakers."

"Anything else?"

"Oh yeah. He also said you were a hothead."

"Well, I'm getting hotter all the time," Darlene replied. "Thanks for the info."

When she got home that night, Darlene had a conference call with Sandy Nunn and Shannon Getz, a former FBI agent and fellow whistleblower.

"Hey Darlene," Shannon said after hearing the Drake Brinkley story, "Ron James (another Customs Supervisor) told me exactly the same thing. Do you think Ron would testify to that if we got to trial?"

"He's a great guy," Darlene said, "but he hasn't got the guts to buck the big boys."

What was decided was that the three of them would file a Class Action EEO Complaint. They also pitched this idea to Ruben, Ervin Rios, Ricardo Sandoval and Arnold Connez, all of whom came aboard. Darlene was chosen to write up the complaint. Sandy edited it and it was submitted.

Six days later, Darlene got a letter that sent shock waves through her. The envelope had no return address, which should have caught her attention. As a trained investigator in terrorism and letter bombs and such, she should have noticed the lack of a return address right away as a warning signal. The letter didn't blow up, but its contents were explosive just the same. In crude capital letters it read:

"SHUT UP AND RESIGN OR YOUR FLETC PICTURES WILL BE MAILED TO THE TABLOIDS AND YOUR FAMILY WILL BE HUMILI-ATED."

Darlene felt herself go weak at the knees, and she immediately remembered an incident which occurred when she was eight years old. She had witnessed one neighbor shoot another right in front of her. It had happened in her old home town. Vernon Steller had gotten into an argument with a neighborhood weirdo called "Crazy Dave" Jackson. When "Crazy Dave" went to his house, Steller, who was a much smaller man, got a strange look on his face and went back to his own home. Steller's small son Ryan followed him, pulling on his father's coat and shouting "Don't, Dad, please don't!" as if he already knew what was about to happen.

Sitting atop her bicycle, little Darlene watched it all happen like it was a movie. Back out of his house Mr. Steller came, Ryan still tugging on him and pleading. Steller had a gun in his hand, and stood in front of "Crazy Dave's" house yelling "Come on outside! Now's the time! Now's the time!" Darlene was frozen, unable to move, feeling weak and queasy. Finally someone appeared at the door of the Jackson house, only it wasn't "Crazy Dave." It was his brother-in-law Mr. Witherspout. He seemed calm and not mad, and for a moment it looked as though he was coming out to de-fuse the situation.

Darlene felt a glimmer of hope at seeing Witherspout. He seemed like a nice, calm fellow and she hoped he would be able to reason with Mr. Steller. The two men began talking, with little Ryan still begging his father to go back into their house. Because the men were talking and not shouting, it looked for a moment as though it all might blow over. Then, for whatever reason, Steller fired and Witherspout fell to the ground moaning. Ryan started screaming and crying. Darlene could not help but notice Steller's eyes. They looked as dead and numb as she was feeling. Suddenly, a rush of energy came to her, and little Darlene wheeled her bike around and sped back to her house, ran up the front steps, and stood before her startled parents trying to tell them what she had just seen.

Coming back to the present, Darlene held the letter in her hand. Yet she smelled the same smell in the air she had noted as a frightened child. It was the smell of fear, and she remembered that it was a smell she had sensed on another occasion, when as a child she had mis-plugged something into an electrical outlet and a shock ran through her body. She hadn't smelled it in a long time, but she sure was smelling it now.

The "FLETC" the letter referred to was the Federal Law Enforcement Training Center. More than ten years before, Darlene had been trained at this center, which is in Glynco, Georgia. This is where the Department of the Treasury trains most of its federal employees, including federal agents. While there, Darlene did one of the dumbest things in her entire life. She foolishly allowed her husband at the time—a Customs employee—to take nude photo's of her. When Darlene divorced him, he was very angry. This jerk showed these pictures, along with those of a few other women, to some Customs pilots and Air Interdiction Officers, while making some nasty comments about these women.

Several of the men the ex-husband showed the pictures to knew Darlene and at least one of them took offense at this behavior and reported the creep to Internal Affairs. An IA Investigator named Donna Jones told Darlene what was going on. She also said that she had seized the photos and that they would be destroyed after the investigation. The result was that the ex-husband was forced to resign, and ended up working in another agency. As the initial shock wore off, Darlene suddenly realized she was putting her own fingerprints all over the letter and envelope and probably destroying any evidence she might need to catch whoever was doing this to her. She carefully placed the letter and envelope in a plastic bag and sat down to collect herself.

When she had calmed down, Darlene called her most trusted ally: Sandy Nunn. Sandy then paged their attorney and they had a conference call.

"I'm not surprised," the lawyer said. "Customs is capable of anything. I've seen this kind of thing before."

"What should I do?" Darlene asked.

"Well," he replied, "you better prepare yourself for another shock, Darlene."

"Like what?"

"I wouldn't be surprised if Customs turns around and, in order to defend themselves, accuses you of sending the letter to yourself just to bolster your case."

"But I could pass a polygraph test," Darlene protested.

"Inadmissable as evidence in Federal Civil Court."

"Damn," Sandy said. "Damn!"

After this, Darlene and Sandy also contacted Ruben and told him what had happened.

"Would you mind if I talked to a US Attorney I know and get some advice from her?" Ruben asked.

"Not at all, Ruben. Go right ahead." Darlene said. "If they're going to play this kind of dirty pool we'll need all the help we can get."

The next day Darlene was to meet Sandy at the US Attorney's office to sign the EEO Class Action Complaint. Before she left for the meeting, however, Darlene got a call from Ervin Rios that only added to her misery.

"I hope this doesn't upset you," Ervin told her, "but I just got so frustrated about this blackmail attempt that I talked about it to an editor at the L.A. Times."

"You did what?"

"I'm sorry. I know it wasn't too smart."

"It was stupid, Ervin!" Darlene snapped. "Why in hell didn't you ask me first? I'm taking this thing to the US Marshal's Office to pursue it criminally. Don't you think the media will just get in the way? This could generate exactly the wrong kind of publicity for us, which is what whoever sent it wants, anyway."

"I don't know what to say, Darlene. I'm really sorry." Ervin hung up sadly. Darlene felt as though she'd just kicked a puppy, because she liked Ervin and knew he was only acting out of a feeling of helplessness. Then her partner Ruben came in. He told her that his contact at the US Attorney's office had told him that Darlene should put the letter in a safe place—maybe a safe deposit box. Then she said Darlene should contact the Postal Inspectors but not give them the original unless they guaranteed that Customs would in no way be involved in the investigation.

Driving to her meeting with Sandy and their attorney, Darlene could feel herself wanting to cry. The S.O.B.'s were grinding her down, and it was working.

She fought back her tears, gritted her teeth, and pressed on. But during the meeting with the attorneys Darlene just couldn't hold back any more and began to sob. Even as the others present tried to console her, Darlene knew that this breaking down had made them all feel very uncomfortable. It was Darlene who had been the strong one through all this. She had named Drake Brinkley in her earlier EEO filings. She had talked the others into banding together with their complaints and hanging tough. Now she was sobbing like a baby in front of them and it was not the signal they wanted their "quarterback" to be sending. Still, Darlene couldn't stop thinking how her parents, who were both nearing age eighty and were not in good health, would react if all this scandal stuff became public.

While driving home that night, Darlene began nodding off at the wheel. Nothing tires you out like stress does, and the stress she was under was becoming unbearable. She pulled off the I-10 Freeway and found a rest area where she began to doze. In her dream she was at a black tie gala at some place like the Shrine Auditorium in L.A. There, standing beside a large open area, she saw the filthy toddler she could never wash clean.

He passed by her with an angelic smile on his face. She followed him to a staircase overlooking the cavernous theater. Among the hundreds of formally attired visitors, she recognized many celebrities including her personal favorite, the star of the TV series "Policewoman": Angie Dickinson.

Darlene stared down at the toddler and thought, as though the child were capable of reading her mind: "Why have you brought me here? I don't want to be here. I want to go to the beautiful farm where we were before. I want to see who that man is." The toddler looked up at her as if he understood what she was thinking. He nodded in the direction of the edge of the stage. There, standing nearby, was the back of the man she had seen at the farm. He was wearing a black tuxedo and held something in his hand. Darlene descended the steps and walked towards the young man trying to see his face. She had an uncomfortable feeling as she approached him. She didn't enjoy being there.

As she drew closer to the young man, Darlene watched as several of those attending this function came over to the young man and shook his hand or gave him that shallow "air kiss" common among rich Hollywood socialite-types. The man didn't seem comfortable with this phoniness, either, but accepted it graciously. Darlene could tell by his body language that the young man couldn't wait to get out of there. She could hear his accent and raspy voice, and wondered if it had become so deep by his smoking too much for too long. The man shifted his position slightly, allowing Darlene to catch a glimpse of his left eye. It was the same deep blue color as the toddler's. He turned away again, but Darlene had seen enough of his face to know that he was a complete stranger to her.

Darlene felt an odd connection to this young man. It wasn't romantic but was nonetheless rather comforting and even heart-warming. Then she woke up, her mind full of intriguing questions. Why had she been at the Shrine Auditorium? She had worked there once as a designated Secret Service agent protecting Bill and Hillary Clinton during his first Presidential campaign. During such man-power-intense periods, the Secret Service drew upon other specially trained officers from different agencies to supplement their overburdened security force while providing protection to people running for high office.

She had seen some of the very same celebrities as in the dream at various fund raising events in Hollywood and Beverly Hills. The real-life highlight for her during that time had been meeting Angie Dickinson, who shook her hand and asked her how she enjoyed being an agent.

"I like it fine, Ma'am," Darlene had responded shyly.

Angie had looked into Darlene's eyes and complimented her. "My, you're a pretty one," she had said. "You're in the wrong line of work, sweetie." It was one of the most special moments in Darlene's life. When she had been a child, Darlene had pretended to be a policewoman like Angie Dickinson. Upon receiving such praise from her heroine, Darlene had thought quietly to herself that she hoped to look half as good as Angie did at her age.

Thinking back to her recent dream, Darlene wondered if her work with the Secret Service during the presidential campaign had anything to do with it being located at the Shrine Auditorium. She couldn't remember anyone at any of the campaign sites she had worked looking like the mysterious young man. Why was he present at the Shrine when he clearly didn't want to be? She sensed that he really wanted to be back at the beautiful farm in her dream, with his cows, dogs and ducks. Who was he? Darlene struggled to recall his facial features, but all she could visualize were his deep blue eyes. Was he the Angel of Death? Was the toddler her Guardian Angel? Was she losing her mind? Was this threat of blackmail on the level? And if "they" could do this, what else were they capable of?

22

The Beat Goes On

*"Rare is the person who can weigh the faults of others without
his thumb on the scale."*
Byron Langfield.

On September 11, 1998, just three years before that date would live in infamy,
Darlene and her partner Ruben Sandoval met at the shooting range. Darlene shot
her personal best-ever score of 148 out of a possible 150. When they had finished
shooting, Ruben asked Darlene to come over to his house. He also asked Mike
Conner, who was at the range that day, to join them because he had something
he wanted them to witness.

Mike was the IA Agent who had turned in Darlene's ex-boyfriend after he had
inappropriately shown the pictures of Darlene and others he had taken. It's funny
how people's paths may cross again and again, as Mike and Darlene's had. When
they arrived at Ruben's home in Yucaipa, California, Ruben pointed out two
cameras which had been mounted on nearby streetlight poles. The cameras were
aimed in such a way as to cover both entrances to Ruben's home. The group got
out of their cars and photographed the surveillance cameras.

"Whoever put up those cameras should have notified you, Ruben, that they
were watching a crook in your neighborhood," Mike said.

Ruben smiled sadly. "Those cameras are for me," he replied, pointing at his
house. "That's where I live."

Mike was stunned by what he saw. Then Ruben gently filled him in on the
harassment and dirty tricks that had been going on at work. Mike shook his head
sadly and said: "I can't believe it. This is just crazy."

"That's why I wanted you to see it, Mike." Ruben then drove back to the
office and met Darlene there. Needing to use the phone, they both realized that
in all likelihood theirs were now being tapped and recorded. They walked to a
pay phone nearby.

"I feel like they're stealing our privacy and our life," Darlene said as they made their way. From the pay phone, she and Ruben called the Postal Inspector—Alexander Pierce—regarding the threatening letter and what had happened since. They were concerned that Pierce would think they were a couple of paranoid kooks, but he didn't.

As they returned to their office, they both agreed that their home phones were probably tapped as well. Ruben put on a brave front, but Darlene could see the effect this stressful treatment was having on them both. When Darlene got home that night, she searched around her neighborhood for cameras and the like but didn't find any. Then she remembered the old joke: Just because you're paranoid doesn't mean nobody's after you.

A couple of days later, Darlene got a call from Internal Affairs Investigator Terry Clay. He paged her to his private cell phone. Something was odd about the way he spoke. In their prior conversations, Clay had been arrogant and accusatory. Now he sounded meek and sincere. What was going on? More tricks?

"What's up, Terry?"

"This isn't about you, Darlene. I mean, you're not under investigation. I need to meet with you alone."

"My attorney says I shouldn't go along with any more of your witch hunts."

"This is about something you may have heard someone say."

Darlene was getting frustrated at his evasiveness. "Do you think you could be a little more vague, Terry?"

"It's about something someone may have told you."

"Oh, well, now you're really pinning it down for me. Thanks."

"Please, Darlene. I need to see you."

Darlene's curiosity got the better of her and she agreed to meet with Clay.

"Great," he said. "I'll meet you near where you work for lunch at 1pm on Wednesday." They named a restaurant and Clay hung up.

What was unusual was Clay agreeing to drive to Darlene's turf. Before this, all their encounters had been at Clay's office and it had been Darlene who had to make the drive to Long Beach. Now Clay was driving out to Riverside. What was going on? She told Ruben about the call, and he agreed to sit in his car outside the restaurant during the meeting. She also enlisted the aid of her friend and hairdresser Roberta Rossa, who agreed to sit inside the restaurant where she could keep an eye on them. Roberta was a real smart lady whom Darlene thought would have made a wonderful agent. She would be cool and not tip her hand, and there was no way anybody at IA could ever associate her with Darlene. Darlene always thought that there were three types of professionals who have a sixth sense about what to do in stressful situations: cops, shrinks, and hairdressers.

On September 16, 1998, Darlene met IA Agent Terry Clay at a nearby restaurant called Spoons. She saw Roberta, who gave her a nod. Then she spotted Clay sitting at a table facing a window, a technique commonly used by cops who have someone outside keeping an eye on them. Darlene chuckled to herself at the absurdity of her and Clay pretending to meet alone when they both had someone keeping an eye on them.

"Okay, Clay, what's this all about?" Darlene said as she sat down with him.

"I appreciate your meeting with me. My boss and I believe that Internal Affairs is being used by somebody to harm you," he said softly.

Darlene bit her lip and kept from saying what she was thinking, which was: No kidding, Sherlock. I'm dealing with a freaking rocket scientist here. Instead, she just nodded in assent. "Look at this transcript," Clay continued. "It was typed up and then mailed to our office anonymously." The "transcript" purported to be a tape recorded conversation between someone at the Air Unit and Darlene concerning her ex-boyfriend and the pictures he had taken. It bore the signature block of Darlene's Investigative Aide Yolanda Rios, but without her signature. It must have been fabricated by someone who could gain access to Yolanda's signature block and stamp it onto this "document" in the hopes that people would believe it came from Rios.

Darlene read the "transcript" and said in disgust: "This is bogus. This conversation never happened."

"Our office is concerned that someone might be illegally wiretapping your phone because of the way it's written."

"I'd guess this was made up by somebody who knew I had a court order allowing me to record conversations between my ex-boyfriend and me because of the threatening phone calls he had been making. It's also written to make it look like I was recording phone conversations by persons not covered under my court order."

"Could there be any truth to that?"

"I told you it's bogus, Clay, and that's what it is. It's a made-up pack of lies designed to injure me."

"Ah," he said. "I see what you're getting at." Darlene thought to herself: This Bozo is exactly the type of moron they get to work in Internal Affairs—people who couldn't find their own butts with two hands! Serving a term in IA is the only way mediocre agents would ever get promoted.

Darlene expressed her utter frustration about this situation. She spoke of her letters of disciplinary action and quoted the last paragraph of the damning letter which concluded:

"If circumstances change, this letter may be removed (from your personnel file) by local management, with my concurrence, should circumstances warrant such an action."

Rolling his eyes, Clay remarked: "I can't believe someone would be stupid enough to put that type of language into a letter like this."

"Well, they did."

"For whatever reason, Darlene, it's obvious that someone is trying to—"

"Mess with me."

"Yeah. That's it." For once, Clay seemed to exhibit actual sincerity.

"I have a suggestion for you, Clay."

"What's that?"

"Don't meet with me alone anymore."

"Why?"

"Because if you're really not involved in any of this harassment and are just caught in the middle as you say, you should ask to be removed from investigating me anymore. The next time you're asked to investigate Ruben Sandoval, Sandy Nunn or me, just try to get out of it and see what happens." Darlene looked closely at Clay to see if he was getting what she was driving at. He wasn't.

"I don't follow you," he said.

"Think about it, Clay. You'll get it," Darlene said. Obviously, if Clay balked at furthering the EEO witch hunt by Customs, then whoever was behind it might reveal themselves by complaining about IA's lack of cooperation.

On September 16, 1998 all SAIC (Special Agent In Charge), RAIC (Resident Agent In Charge), and Supervisor Personnel from the L.A. and San Diego Customs offices were required to attend a management conference held in Palm Springs, California.

This "class" centered around the topic: "Dealing With Problem Employees." This class was being taught by a private attorney and former employee of the U.S. Customs Office of Regional Counsel. Darlene's good friend Ricardo Sandoval attended this class. When he got back from the conference, Ricardo called Darlene and Sandy. He told them that Evantie had cut Ricardo down in front of the group and that they had exchanged verbal digs. Ricardo's hatred for Evantie and his tactics was evident.

"He's only doing Brinkley's dirty work, Ricardo," Darlene said. "He's trying to smear you by giving the impression that the RAIC/Riverside Office and your office at RAIC/Calexico aren't getting along because of your mishandling things. He's undermining the relationship between the two offices to try and make you look bad."

Darlene thought to herself about just how amazing it is that anybody can so easily alter the perceptions of people when they want to undermine someone. She had heard many stupid rumors about Ricardo Sandoval, the worst one being that he only got his promotion because he filed a lawsuit and that he was really incompetent. She had heard similar negative gossip about (now NY Senator) Hillary Clinton when Bill was first running for President. Literally dozens of men had told her that Hillary was a "real ball buster" and that they had heard from "them" that she was a real bitch to the Secret Service Agents assigned to their protection. The same "they" also said she was nothing more than a political climber.

Of course, these rumors all came from the "Them Zone," where rumors and gossip are spread to fit the agenda of the person spreading it. Darlene was a die-hard Republican whose hero was Ronald Reagan. She believed what she was hearing because it fit her own political beliefs. That changed when she was actually assigned to protect Hillary Clinton as an Adjunct Treasury Agent. She was amazed that after everything she had heard from "them" that what she saw with her own two eyes was so utterly different than the gossip. Darlene had the opportunity to observe Hillary often, both in and out of the public eye. She was nothing like what the malicious rumors had described. From all Darlene saw, which was a lot, Hillary was a very professional, demure, soft-spoken woman who was always warm and friendly toward the Treasury Agents. Never did Darlene see Hillary acting in any way like the "ball busting bitch" she was made out to be by the "They Zone" of gossipers. Instead, Darlene saw her spending a lot of time working very hard on health care issues with her staff. She seemed to Darlene to be very sincere about her work.

Darlene's dad had taught her that people will judge you by the company you keep. In that regard, Darlene had many opportunities to interact with Hillary's staff, most of whom were female. They too were very nice, warm, professional ladies who never came off as overbearing. From her own experience, Darlene could see that Hillary kept very good company. It is the "They Zone" of rumor mongers who use gossip to undermine people they're afraid of. It's a subversive, cowardly tool to advance the perpetrator's agenda, and one that Darlene would always be on guard against.

The three-way telephone conversation among Sandy, Ricardo and Darlene continued. They shared with each other the feelings of how the stress of retaliation was affecting their lives in a profoundly negative way. Ricardo offered that he was going to the gym every night to try and work off the tension that Customs was laying on him.

"That's exactly what I do," Darlene added. "Sometimes I swim until my arms ache so much I could nearly drown."

"Don't give management that satisfaction!" Sandy chimed in.

"How can this be more stressful than what we experience when we've almost been blown up by the bad guys we're trying to catch?" Ricardo wondered.

"Because Customs is our back-up. They're supposed to be on our side," Darlene said.

"Well, I'd sure like to see them start acting like it," Sandy said sadly.

Darlene's thoughts drifted to her recurring dream with the filthy toddler who can't be cleaned. "Look, I don't want to sound crazy but I've been having this same dream over and over. Do you guys believe in guardian angels?"

"I'm amazed you would mention that," Ricardo replied. "Listen to this and tell me what you think. I was working a dope deal undercover in TJ (Tijuana, Mexico). The deal went south (cop slang for a deal going bad) and the crooks thought I was trying to rip them off. They kidnapped me and it was only going to be a matter of time before I got whacked. I was able to convince them that I could get the money they wanted if they'd take me into downtown TJ and let me get my girlfriend to go get it. I was just stalling for time any way I could hoping that my surveillance team could find me. I was wearing a wire and I figured they'd locate me eventually if I lived long enough. So they take me into a shopping mall parking lot and tell me to stay in the car while they went off to call her. All of a sudden this Latino male who was not one of the bad guys gets into the car with me. He says: Hey, Buddy, just calm down. You're going to make it through this, but you got to calm down and clear your head. So then this guy and I talk for several minutes and then the guy got out of the car about thirty seconds before federal agents surrounded it as the crooks returned. But the guy who I sat with had just disappeared. Nobody saw him. He was gone. How he could have gotten past that posse with their guns drawn is still a mystery to me."

"You we're wired," Sandy said. "Did you ever listen to the tape of your conversation?"

"I did," Ricardo said coldly, "and all you can hear is my voice." There was a stunned silence after this. Ricardo is a very sincere, no-nonsense kind of guy. He wouldn't make up a story like this. Darlene wanted to share her recurring dream with them, but she was afraid they'd think she was nuts. Still, hearing him tell this made Darlene feel more comfortable with her toddler dream. Maybe there really are guardian angels. Maybe she wasn't losing her mind after all.

23

Wake Up And Smell The Corruption

"A lie told often enough becomes the truth."
Lenin (1870–1924)

Darlene got a call from Tom Best of the Union Pacific Railroad. He had profiled five tanker cars and was setting them up to be weighed. She quickly passed the word to her new Group Supervisor O'Shea, who seemed enthusiastic about going after them. The same could not be said for her boss Evantie, however. He wanted to pull her off this case but there wasn't anybody else in the office who had the time and expertise to handle it, so he had no choice but to let her take it on.

Along with Best, Darlene and Ervin Rios began the tedious task of pulling all the available info on these suspicious tanker cars. Her enthusiasm was low, however, because Darlene knew that no matter what she did or how much evidence was seized she was not going to get any credit for her work from Evantie and the others in the Drake Brinkley Boys Club. The S.O.B.'s were grinding her down and it was definitely taking a toll. Still, she sucked it up and went ahead with her work, but it wasn't the same.

She got a bit of good news from Chief Inspector Jeremy O'Leary. He had some ideas on how to secure the funding necessary to pay for the opening of the tanker cars. It's an expensive process and by this late date in September the RAIC/Riverside Customs Office was out of money. Darlene told O'Leary to talk it over with Resident Agent In Charge Evantie, and he said he would.

At this same time, the Customs Office held its annual awards ceremony and picnic at a park in Long Beach. Once again, everybody in the office was recognized for their work except for the handful of "troublemakers" that included Darlene. Never mind that her tanker car case seizures were the second biggest of the year by any agent in her office. Never mind that the Acting Commissioner of U.S. Customs had personally called her to congratulate her for her effort. What did it matter that even then Attorney General Janet Reno had been watching what Darlene had achieved? No, none of that mattered to Brinkley, who simply ignored Darlene at the awards portion of the event.

Darlene felt really crushed at this public humiliation, which was exactly what her tormentors wanted. Her attorney told her when he heard about it: "Don't worry. This will only help in our lawsuit." That wasn't much consolation, however, because she realized how far Evantie and Brinkley were willing to go to try and harass her into leaving Customs.

Then word came back from O'Leary that when he met with Evantie about the suspicious tanker cars, Evantie made it clear he wanted Darlene taken off the case and not to be involved in Operation Lite Rail, as it was called.

"What's the deal?" O'Leary asked Evantie point blank. "She's your most effective agent in these things and you're yanking her chain. Why?"

"It's just politics," Evantie answered. He would say no more. He didn't have to. In the corrupt world of U.S. Customs, everything is political. If you're in the "In Crowd" you can do no wrong. If you're not, you're alternately badgered and ignored until at last the frustration of it all simply overwhelms you and you leave. It should be remembered that chasing after drug smugglers and thieves and armed thugs is dangerous work. Agents frequently find themselves in "Kill Zones" where you either get the back-up you need or some bad guys pump you full of hot lead. Like the attorney/investigator Jason Fielding who was gunned down in his driveway while his little daughter looked on helplessly, agents who are being sabotaged by those around them had better keep their backs to the wall and their powder dry. Bad things can happen out there in the field—very bad things.

On October 2, 1998, the U.S. Attorney's Office deposed Darlene with respect to the Ruben Sandoval case. For eight hours she was grilled in an effort to get her to break her stand with whistleblowers like Ruben and Sandy Nunn. Again and again these interrogators tried to get her to change her story or to slip up and contradict something she had said earlier. In a way, they were doing to her in a concentrated form what Drake Brinkley and Lawrence Evantie and the whole "Boys Club" team had been doing against her for years. It didn't work. She stuck to her guns.

Five days later, it was her lawyers in Ruben's case who deposed SAIC Drake Brinkley. Brinkley lied under oath and among other falsehoods denied ever making statements about dealing with complaints from RAIC/Riverside at the November 1996 promotion party. He also lied about having nothing to do with assigning vehicles to agents. Later that day, SSA Peter Blake was also deposed in the same case. He contradicted Brinkley's lie about not discussing the complaints at the promotion party. But then he turned around and lied under oath about him and Edwin Easel taking home heroin evidence overnight and compromising its value in court. It seems like all those who were trying to destroy the careers of the whistleblowers felt they could say whatever the heck they wanted and get away with it. Time would tell.

On October 9, 1998, Darlene and Ruben were loaned out to the RAIC/ Orange County Office to assist in serving a bunch of search warrants. Who should be heading the morning briefing there but Peter Blake, fresh from lying about heroin evidence in his recent deposition. Ruben and Darlene took their seats in a group of about thirty Customs Agents and TFO's (Task Force Officers). They glared at Blake because of what he had said in his deposition. In fact, if looks could kill Blake would have been a goner.

"What a lying little weasel," Darlene muttered to Ruben.

"Shh, you hothead," he replied.

Blake saw them staring daggers at him and immediately looked away with an embarrassed expression.

"Coward," Darlene muttered.

"Take it easy," Ruben urged. "Calm down." Later, after a day spent serving the warrants, Ruben and Darlene found themselves stuck in rush hour traffic.

"Ruben, you realize that little jerk committed perjury and will probably get away with it, don't you?"

"Yeah. Business as usual." By now they were both getting used to such injustices.

"Look, are you still the alternate evidence custodian?"

"Yes I am." Ruben shot her a glance that asked where this was going.

"Think you could get into the evidence locker tonight and take a look at the logs?"

"I'm not supposed to do that without authority from the primary evidence custodian."

"David Gray?"

"The very same."

"Well isn't that convenient," Darlene persisted. "Look, I'm just wondering if maybe they failed to cover their tracks on that heroin botch, that's all."

"I haven't looked, but I doubt they'd be stupid enough to not cover their tracks."

"Never underestimate their stupidity."

After a little more convincing by Darlene, the pair headed out to the RAIC/ Riverside Office and entered the evidence room. The log book told the story.

"Lookee, lookee," Darlene said as they scanned the page with the information on what had happened with the seized heroin in question.

"Jeez," Ruben said in amazement, "this clearly shows that the evidence hadn't gone back to the evidence room until the evening of the following day."

"Bingo," Darlene said exultantly as they exchanged high-five's. They photocopied the incriminating evidence and then Darlene pulled SA Janet Somers' case file on the evidence and found that on her 9-B's (case chronology forms) she had indeed briefed Winkowsky on the heroin evidence bungling and shared her concerns for its implications on the criminal case. They photocopied those too. Then they picked up and contacted the on-call IA duty agent and reported it. Ruben faxed the logs to him and for once they both felt justice in the air. Ruben smiled as they parted. Darlene got a good night's sleep at last.

On October 13, 1998, Darlene and Ruben's attorneys in his federal lawsuit deposed SSA Jerry Johnston and asked him: "Did Supervisor Ivan Winkowsky have a problem with women in law enforcement?"

Before he could answer, the AUSA representing Customs—Tim Deer—took Jerry outside into the hallway. "Don't answer that question," he told Johnston.

He didn't know who he was talking to. Jerry was a former military officer, a fellow Kentuckian with Darlene, and a very honorable agent. He looked at Deer with disbelief, went back into the room where the question was repeated and spoke in a loud and clear voice: "Yes, Winkowsky definitely did have a problem with women in law enforcement."

That same day, AUSA Tim Deer sent a letter which was essentially a gag order to all U.S. Customs employees specifically regarding SA Sandoval's civil litigation against Customs. It went out both by fax and Fed Ex. The memo, which was addressed appropriately to SAIC Drake Brinkley, directed Customs management to "please advise your employees accordingly." There's a term for this. It's called witness tampering.

On the following day, ASAIC (Assistant Special Agent In Charge) Donald Chin was deposed. Under oath, he confirmed that "pre-selection"—an illegal practice which was against OPM regulations—was definitely involved in late 1996 when Ruben and Darlene were passed over for promotion in favor of less-qualified and under-performing agents. Chin worked directly under Drake Brinkley and, to no one's surprise, retired shortly after this deposition was given.

On November 10, 1998, Ruben Sandoval sent a letter to Customs Commissioner Raymond Kelly regarding the lack of an investigation into the mishandling of the heroin evidence and the subsequent cover-up. Ruben and Darlene were sure that Kelly would either ignore it completely or simply sic his Internal Affairs (IA) dogs on them again. However, they wanted to be able to document that he had in fact been informed so he couldn't play ignorant down the road.

A month later, Harrison Wells, who was the Director of the Office of Internal Affairs, notified Sandoval that his office would not be investigating this matter. He stated that IA cannot investigate itself. Instead, the investigation would be turned over to the U.S. Treasury Department's Office of the Inspector General. This office was commonly referred to by agents as "the Black Hole," since everything that went to it disappeared without a trace without any results coming forth. Interestingly, Harrison Wells was himself the target of an investigation by a grand jury on corruption charges which had been brought against him by another whistleblower—RAIC/Calexico Ricardo Sandoval. There were so many whistles blowing that Customs was beginning to sound like San Quentin during a prison break. Speaking of criminals, it was none other than Drake Brinkley who had placed Harrison Wells in the position of Director of Internal Affairs when Brinkley was the Director of Customs Office of Investigations. Perhaps it takes a crook to promote a crook.

On January 17, 1999, Darlene received a call from Tom Best at the Union Pacific Railroad. "I've got five more tanker cars sitting in the yard. They are all manifested as empty but are five to nine tons overweight."

"Sorry, Tom," Darlene replied, "but I've been taken off the case."

"Well, who the hell am I supposed to call then?"

"Isn't there anybody else?"

"Nobody else over there knows about this stuff," Tom said in disgust. "Besides, I don't want to talk to anybody else."

"All right, Tom, what are the numbers?" He gave the tracking numbers to Darlene and she in turn pulled the entries from the Customs computer. Just as she had feared, the Customs general hold she had placed on them had been released. Once again, if it hadn't been for the alertness of Tom Best the suspect cars would not have been brought back to the Colton rail yard. Fighting crooks is tough enough without having to fight cops to do it. It is this reality that drove Darlene and the others to finally become whistleblowers.

Bob Mattivi was the Acting Group Supervisor at this time. Bob was a super agent, and had made some spectacular Customs cases in his distinguished career. He had been Darlene's mentor when she first came on the job. Since she trusted him completely, Darlene showed Bob what they had on these suspicious tanker cars. Then she called Tom Best back and asked him to bring over the routes of these cars. These "routes" were printouts from the Union Pacific computer system which displayed where the rail cars went after they entered the U.S. They looked very suspicious. The tanker cars had been manifested as empty. Railroads invoice their customers by the weight hauled and the distance traveled. Obviously, it is in the shipper's interest to keep the travel distance to the minimum necessary.

These tanker cars had come from Baja, Mexico. They had been sent on to Texas and then to Arizona before making their way back to the rail yard at Colton, California. This made no apparent sense and was not cost effective for either the shipper or the customer in terms of time and expense, unless it was intended to make it hard to follow them. The manifest also had stamped on it: "NO WEIGHT PER WEIGH AGREEMENT." Shippers will often have a standing account set up with the major railroads and are invoiced to their credit lines. These accounts can be set up to pre-pay the routes at the maximum cost, assuming the weight of the cars will be at the maximum. This saves the shipper the expense of having to pay the cost of having the cars shipped to another location to be weighed. When this is the case, the manifest will be stamped "NO WEIGHT PER WEIGH AGREEMENT." This method is not, however, normally done for empty cars. Why would you pre-pay for a full car when that car is empty? And it is never done on pressurized tanker cars. These cars, because of Darlene's Rail Project and Customs holds, have to be shipped to a weigh station anyway. The shipper must bear the cost of the resulting extra distance as part of the price of doing business, thanks to the U.S. Customs Service.

So the way these cars were manifested and routed made no sense. Darlene and Tom Best then briefed Bob Mattivi on what was happening. Mattivi seemed pleased.

"Well, Dar," he said, "it looks like you guys may have gotten yourself another big load. Let me go brief Evantie and—"

"Whoa, Bob," Darlene interrupted. "Before you go up there, there's something you need to know because I don't want you to get blindsided by anything."

"What's up?" Bob asked.

"Evantie pulled me off the rail project and told me flat out to stay away from there."

"You're kidding."

"Do you see me laughing? If you go in there with this, Evantie's going to throw a fit."

Bob looked at her like she was crazy. "Oh come on, Darlene. No he won't. You're just over-sensitive because of all this crap that you and Ruben are going through. Besides, who else am I going to send? Everybody else is in training and you're the only one who knows this stuff." Mattivi smiled at her with that street-wise smile that said to just trust your old mentor and trotted down the hall with the documentation to brief Evantie.

Less than a minute later, Darlene and Tom Best could hear screaming from Evantie's office. Then Mattivi came back to them with a sheepish expression on his face. He tossed the documents on the table by them in disgust. Then he sat down and looked at them with total bewilderment. "I don't know what to say, or what to tell you guys. Evantie wouldn't even entertain the idea of having the tanker cars pressure tested at no cost to the government. This is ridiculous!"

Darlene had been sitting behind the table with her feet propped up on it drinking a bottle of water. As she emptied the bottle, she swung her feet back to the floor and tossed the empty container into a nearby waste basket. "Now do you believe me, Bob?"

"I don't know what to believe. I'm embarrassed to say this, but Darlene, stay away from this." It was obvious from the look of anguish on his face that he was concerned for Darlene, disturbed by Evantie's reaction, and totally stumped about what to do. This was the first time Darlene had ever seen Mattivi at a loss for a quick-witted answer. Bob was an old pro who had never been in a situation like this before. Darlene walked Tom Best out to his car. "What the hell's going on?" Best asked as they stood out in the parking lot. "Is someone corrupt here or what?"

Darlene looked down at the ground as she answered: "Best, you know it ain't me."

"No, I know it isn't you. You and Ruben are the only ones over here I've been able to deal with. But something about this really doesn't look right, Darlene, and you know it."

She looked up into his worried eyes. "And now you know it too, Bob."

After an awkward pause, Tom shook her hand gently. "We'll have to get together and talk about this later. Maybe there's something we're not seeing," he said. But his expression said that in fact they both knew what was going on. Five days later, all of the suspect tanker cars were released without any further examination or inquiry. We will never know what they contained. That's what this story boils down to: five highly suspicious pressurized tanker cars five to nine tons overweight, manifested as empty, shipped in a needlessly long and expensive manner, released against policy so they could reach their final destination, which was a rail yard in downtown Los Angeles. Never mind all the red flags which had been raised and observed by this shipment—they were simply ushered through

Customs. Now why would anybody allow that to happen if there wasn't another, more sinister reason than simple negligence?

Darlene met with Ruben and Renado the day the cars were released and told them what had happened. Renado got a very worried look on his face. "Darlene, this thing is getting dangerous. I'm telling you, this stuff has nothing to do with the EEO crap you guys are dealing with. You've wandered into some serious corruption in your agency, and that guy Brinkley is in it up to his ears—unless—could it be some kind of CIA crap or something?" Renado began looking around in an animated, paranoid fashion, as if he thought somebody was about to get him and said jokingly: "Jeez, I'm gonna get the hell away from you guys. The red dot (of a laser sighted weapon) could appear on your forehead any minute."

They all laughed. Then Darlene spoke: "Yeah, there you go with that 'you guys' stuff. Face it, Renado. You're in this too, dude."

"Oh no I'm not," Renado said. He pulled out his badge. "You see this here? It says San Bernardino Police Department, not U.S. Treasury."

Darlene pulled out her badge, pointed at it, and said: "Oh, you mean U.S. Corruptions." They all burst out laughing, but the laughter was short-lived as the realization that they could be up against something much more sinister crossed their minds. Anyway, Darlene knew Renado was just kidding with that "what do you mean We" stuff. He was a stand-up guy who would never let them down—a man for whom the word "loyalty" really meant something. Men like Renado reminded her of a fellow she had known in the military. Like Renado, he was a man of good judgment and strength of character. Like Renado, he was somebody you could always count on to do the right thing at the right time.

William Watson had served with Darlene in the Army. He had been a Non-Commissioned Officer In Charge (NCOIC). At six foot three and three hundred pounds of pure muscle, Watson was naturally called "Little Willie." When she had been a young lieutenant and the duty officer on one particular evening back at Fort Huachuca in the Arizona desert, Darlene got a call from one of her MP's.

"Hey L.T. (short for lieutenant)," the soldier said in a panicky voice, "you better get out here! We got a wild man! I need help!" Darlene jumped into her G-ride along with Little Willie and the two of them sped out to the west gate of the post in the middle of nowhere. When they arrived, there were two marked units and four MP's surrounding a man who appeared to have gone crazy. One of the MP's dashed over to her and Little Willie, clearly in a panicked state.

"What's going on?" Darlene asked. "What's this guy's problem?"

The out-of-breath MP wore wire rimmed glasses which had been smashed down on his face. "I'm not sure, L.T.," he gasped, "but I think this guy's got rabies."

"Rabies?" Darlene knew there had been a rabies epidemic on post that summer. There had been several rabid skunks, squirrels, and even domestic cats killed by animal control. They had giving out warnings for the past several weeks describing the signs of rabies and suggesting having pets inoculated. Looking at this "crazy" man, she thought he might indeed be carrying the disease. He was foaming at the mouth, swatting at everyone, and growling like a madman. The MP showed her that this man had already broken through two sets of handcuffs and put bite marks in one of the MP's jump boots. Darlene knew that if he was indeed rabid and bit, scratched or even just slobbered on them they would have to receive those god awful rabies shots in the chest with the needle the size of a Louisville Slugger baseball bat—and even those painful injections weren't 100% effective.

Little Willie looked at her and said: "L.T., we can't risk the lives of our men. We may have to shoot this guy."

"Shoot him?" Darlene answered. "You think we have to shoot him?" She was all of twenty-three years young at the time. She knew when she entered law enforcement that this day might come, but this wasn't how she had pictured it happening.

Little Willie saw the terrified look on her face and started to laugh. He turned and walked to the rear of the car and said casually: "Don't worry, L.T. I got you covered."

Then he pulled a tire iron out of the trunk and walked back to the group. "I'll need you two to distract him from the front so I can get a whack at him from the back." Darlene and the MP pulled out their nightsticks and began distracting the crazy man as Willie had instructed. They would poke at him from the front and he would lunge at them while Willie worked his way behind the man. The man lunged at Darlene who fell backwards over a rock. The wild man then ran to her. She looked up into his evil, crazed eyes as he was ready to pounce on her—not a sight she would ever forget. Just as this lunatic got onto her, Willie whacked his skull with the tire iron. As he dropped down, slobber dripped from his mouth onto her uniform. She jumped up in terror, ran to her vehicle, grabbed a cloth lying on the front seat and frantically tried to wipe the slobber off.

The following day, they learned that the man did not have rabies but had been on PCP, a powerful psychoactive drug used to tranquilize elephants, among other beasts. When she heard this news, Darlene's heart dropped. She thought to herself: "Oh my God. I almost ordered this man shot, and he didn't have rabies at all!" Darlene has never forgotten Little Willie's quick thinking and was forever grateful to him for saving her ass. She felt the same kind of warm loyalty to Renado, for he, too, had saved her and Ruben's skin more times than she could count. She was going to need every friend like him she had to face the ordeal that was looming just ahead, and the rabid dogs on her case didn't need any disease to be deadly.

24

Infernal Affairs

"They who give up essential liberty to obtain a little temporary safety, deserve neither liberty or safety."
Benjamin Franklin

On February 8, 1999, Darlene was on surveillance when she got a 911 page from Ruben Sandoval. "What's up?" she asked after calling him back.

"I have to drive to San Diego tomorrow to be interviewed by Internal Affairs." Ruben tried to make his voice sound confident, but Darlene could tell he was nervous and angry at the same time. "Whaddaya say you join me and Renado for lunch?"

"Sure. Okay. Where?"

"The usual place."

"Montezuma's Revenge?"

"We'll see you there at noon."

The place Darlene nicknamed Montezuma's Revenge was a little hole in the wall Mexican restaurant that Ruben and Renado liked. It was off the beaten path and they weren't likely to be seen by anybody from work, most especially agents from Internal Affairs. When she arrived, Darlene was greeted by Renado with his usual bear hug hello. Ruben, on the other hand, looked depressed and worried. Darlene shook his hand and he squeezed hers hard and stared into her eyes as though he wanted her to know he was covering up his fear and pain with a tough exterior.

As she and Ruben updated Renado on what they had been going through, Renado shook his head sadly. "This is about the tanker case," he said a couple of times as they talked. Then he added: "I'm telling you—you were never supposed to find that dope. You've messed up somebody's action. They wouldn't go to these extremes to come after you guys over an EEO complaint. You know it and I know it. This is some serious stuff here. Even your prosecutor Yvette is worried. I'm telling you, you guys are in danger. You guys are in danger."

"Wait a minute," Darlene replied. "What do you mean 'you guys?' I seem to recall that you were out there with us every step of the way and crawling all over those cars. Don't you mean 'We' are in danger, Renado, old amigo?"

"I don't think so, little missy," Renado responded. "There ain't no IA investigations and surveillance on me—at least not yet, anyway." He tried laughing weakly, but the humor quickly drained from his face as he continued. "I'm telling you that what you put together with Rios paints a very scary picture. This isn't just about your EEO fight. You stumbled right into a huge mess. You picked up a rock you weren't supposed to see under."

Darlene's stomach started burning as she listened to Renado go on about the danger they were in. She thought to herself about whether the burn came from the fear of what she had gotten into or the really bad food she had just eaten. Later that evening, she went to the gym and swam a mile in fifty-seven minutes and ran three miles before going home. When she climbed into bed, Darlene couldn't sleep. She was thinking about the recent mass murder in Matamoros, Mexico, where twenty-one men, women, and children were brutally killed by the Arellano-Felix Drug Cartel—the same gang of thugs that all the evidence pointed to with respect to her recent tanker car caper.

The next day, Ruben made the trip to San Diego. He wouldn't let Darlene accompany him. "I can handle this," he said in a less-than-assured tone of voice.

As Darlene entered her office, she passed by the little snake Edwin Easel. Easel had an arrogant smirk on his face, as if to say: "Ha-ha, Ruben's getting his now, isn't he? And you're gonna get yours next!"

Resisting the strong urge to punch him, Darlene said: "Well, Girlie Man, did your kids pick out that wardrobe for you or did they finally settle the Liberace estate?"

"What do you mean?" he asked.

"I mean those are some pretty gay duds you're sporting, there, Edwina."

"Ha-ha. Some joke, Darlene," was the best Easel could come up with.

"Why don't you run into Evantie's office and suck up to him, Weasel. Maybe he'll spoon feed you another case you can screw up."

Fortunately, this unpleasant exchange was interrupted by the office Investigative Aide Yolanda. "Hey, both of you pipe down right now or I'll kick both of your assess." Yolanda was not a person to trifle with—a tough, streetwise New York City Puerto Rican who could definitely make good on her threat. She was also Darlene's good friend, a sharp gal who had her integrity in the right place. Aware of everything that was going on in the office, Yolanda also resented how Darlene and Ruben and others not in the "Old Boys Club" were being treated.

She would also show her spine when she was interviewed by the EEO and IA investigators. That was when she came forward and told the truth at great personal risk to herself. Darlene was thankful for that, and thankful Yolanda had intervened when she did.

Because she hadn't gotten much sleep, Darlene went into the office kitchen and yanked a Mountain Dew from the fridge. Full of caffeine, Mountain Dew is the official "stay awake" beverage of the sleep deprived. When she went back out into the hallway, Darlene was grabbed by Yolanda. "A Mountain Dew this early in the morning and taking on the Weasel?" she asked. "What's up?"

"I'm not sleeping too well, Yolanda," Darlene replied. "I'm worried about some things Renado told Ruben and me yesterday about our stumbling into some high-level corruption here and that our being harassed is more about spoiling somebody's action than about an EEO situation."

Yolanda put a protective arm around Darlene. "Listen, girlfriend, you've got to keep it together. Don't overreact to all this stuff. They're really just trying to get to you. That little episode just now in the hall is just what they want. They know you've got a temper, and they're using Ruben and Sandy to get to you. They ain't got nothin' on you they can come after you with, so they're pushing your buttons."

"So what do your recommend I do?"

"Just chill out, lady. Chill the heck out."

Darlene gave Yolanda a hug for her sound advice. Then she went into her office. The Mountain Dew she drank burned as it went down her throat. It was more like a gulp of whiskey than a soft drink. It made her want to puke. She tried working on some written reports but couldn't focus. She made mistakes in her writing and finally just gave up. Where was this going? She was tired from not sleeping, worried and anxious for not having heard anything from Ruben, and sick to her stomach from stress and Mountain Dew.

She completed packing things up because Customs was moving its office from the northeastern part of the City of Riverside to downtown, closer to the courthouse. The workers had been loading a moving van all day and carrying things over to the new office. Most were sad to be leaving their old digs. They'd had a lot of good times there and there were plenty of pleasant memories, along with some which weren't so pleasant. At lunch time, they all had a little celebration to say goodbye to the old office. There were a couple of bottles of wine involved and a lot of food.

As the afternoon wore on, one of the more decadent and "looser" women agents in the office—Sherry King—was getting plastered along side of David

Gray. Sherry was the kind of female agent who does more damage to the reputation of women in the workplace than most male chauvinists. She'd already had an affair with a former RAIC, the boss of a field office. He was Jim Wilson and everybody couldn't help but notice what was going on. You didn't need to be a keen investigator. They hadn't been discrete in the least. This was doubly troubling, since most everybody knew and liked Jim's wife. Their "infernal affair" had lowered office morale and undermined Wilson's effectiveness as a leader. For her part, Sherry displayed her inappropriate behavior on a silver platter, making it all the easier for the Easel's and Winkowsky's to apply prejudice against women in the work place.

Sherry not only got drunk, but was deposited (with wine in hand) by Gray in his G-ride and taken over to the new office. Everybody saw what was going on, even Lawrence Evantie. But would anybody ever report them for this violation of the rules? Not a chance. What made it worse was that it had been the very same David Gray who had strenuously gone after Ruben for transporting his children in his G-ride when his own car had been in the repair shop. Now Gray was using his official car to haul a drunken female agent and her drink across town.

Darlene observed all of this and the hypocrisy of Gray's behavior just bummed her out. Her phone rang and it was Sandy asking if she'd heard anything from Ruben yet.

"No, Sandy, not a word so far."

"This is just such a pile of crap! The bright side is that these jerks are just proving our point and making one hell of a lawsuit for us. Don't worry, Darlene. Ruben's smart. He'll keep his cool and be all right. I'm sure he'll call us when they're done with him."

Sandy was and is a true and loyal friend to Darlene. She was always there to try and cheer her up when she needed it. Darlene told her about what was happening with Sherry King and David Gray.

"Darlene, you should definitely report it to Internal Affairs just to see if they'd lift a finger to go after one of their fellow goons."

"Yeah, you're right. But Sandy, be cool about everything you do because you don't want to give the SOB's any ammo to come after you. We're all fair game because we don't do the Sherry King thing and because we demand to be treated with respect." There was an awkward pause on the other end, and Darlene knew she'd gone a little overboard with Sandy and she felt bad about. "Hey, I'm sorry to sound the alarm. I know you just called to cheer me up and here I am running you down."

"It's okay, Darlene. I know the pressure you're under. It's a miracle we all haven't lost our minds by now."

"Let's not give them that satisfaction," Darlene replied. When they had hung up, Darlene still felt bad about not being more upbeat for Sandy, who had plenty of problems of her own. It all came down to stress and fatigue. To work off that stress, Darlene went to the gym and swam. She had to stop about half way through, however, and get out of the pool, go to the bathroom, and throw up all the Mountain Dew she had drunk. Then she went back and finished her swim. When she got back to her locker, she saw that Ruben had paged her. She called him and he asked her to meet him and Renado at Montezuma's Revenge. When she arrived there, the fellows were already seated.

"Hey, Dar," Renado said, "I see your hair's wet. How's the training for the Polish Olympics going?"

"It's Police Olympics, you moron, not Polish."

"But you still find time to do an occasional bit of Customs work, don't you?" he continued.

"Are you kidding?" Ruben chimed in. That training is all she does now. I can't get any work out of her anymore. All she does is swim and run." The men laughed.

"Yeah, that's it," Darlene countered, "yuck it up, you turkeys. Okay, enough fun at my expense. Spill it, Ruben. What happened?"

"It's that little turd Weasel," Ruben said, the smile disappearing from his face. "He ratted me out about something that happened six or seven years ago. I had my kids in my G-ride to drop them off at the sitter's. My car was in the shop. I had picked Weasel up before because we had to make a call, so of course he saw this."

"That's it?" Renado said. "That's what the fuss is about?"

"Yeah."

"Unbelievable!" Renado added.

"You know," Darlene said, "if that little turd is just ratting you out on this now, then he should be in trouble for failing to report it when it happened—not years later."

"That's right," Ruben said, smiling at last.

Darlene then told them about what had happened that day with David Gray squiring a drunken bimbo agent around in his G-ride along with her alcoholic beverage, both violations of Customs regulations. "What's more, I'm going to report it to IA and demand that Gray come under the same fire as Ruben.

"Yeah, right," Ruben said sarcastically.

"Like they'll go after their boy, huh?" Renado sneered.

"Look," Darlene fired back, "if Internal Affairs shows an unwillingness to go after Weasel for failure to report and after Gray for driving around in his G-ride with a drunken female agent who's carrying a glass of alcohol, then that shows IA is engaging in selective enforcement of Customs policies. They're proving us right—that IA is the goon squad for Customs' corrupt management." The men nodded at Darlene's point.

Ruben put up a brave front as he told them about his grilling by IA. His voice was detached and without emotion, almost as if he'd been reading his story from a written report, but the stress was right there on his face for all to see. It would ruin him financially if they gave him the maximum punishment of forty-five days off with no pay. Ruben had been through a divorce and had to fight for custody of his kids several times over the past few years. With a new wife and little baby, such a severance would just about break him. The whole thing made Darlene sick to her stomach. She felt nauseous for the second time that day.

By the time she got to bed that night, Darlene had so much on her mind she couldn't sleep. She also knew that lack of sleep was adding to her problems, so she did what her mother had always told her to do for heartburn and the like: she drank some milk and it worked. She finally got a decent night's sleep. The next day, she reported Gray and Sherry King to IA. That was when the office Investigative Aid Yolanda Rios backed up her report and agreed to be a witness, which she relayed to the IA over a speaker-phone. Knowing that she faced retaliation for backing up Darlene's account showed real courage on Yolanda's part.

On February 16, 1999, Darlene got her usual midnight warning phone call from Sector (Customs National Dispatch Center) advising her to be at Thermal, California, airport at six that next morning for a load (controlled delivery of narcotics) from Calexico. When she hung up the phone, she wondered in her sleepy state of mind if the call had been real or if she had dreamt it. She remembered how a couple of years earlier she had dreamt of such a call, jumped into her car and took off for the airport. As she drove, she contacted Sector to confirm and they seemed confused. After much checking and a call to her boss over the radio, she realized that she had only dreamt the call. The following morning when she had gone into the office, Agent Allen Casey had come over the office intercom in a disguised "radio" voice: "Ah, Sector, Sector," he had said, "to 915 (Darlene's call sign). 915, 915—you're dreaming. Click your heels three times and then you can go home." To make matters worse, as Darlene walked down the hall after that fake intercom message, she passed Ruben and Jerry, who walked by her with their arms up as if they were sleepwalking. They giggled as she frowned.

The crowning moment came shortly thereafter, when Bob Mattivi came over the intercom and said: "Everyone involved in tomorrow's escapades please retire to the back for the briefing. Oh, and Earth to Darlene, Earth to Darlene, wake up Darlene—this is a real message."

Darlene then got on the intercom: "Earth to Bob—up yours, good buddy." Then she walked back to the meeting. Everyone there was pretending to be asleep and snoring loudly. But this was a real call, again coming at midnight to alert agents to a six a.m. load.

"Why do they do this?" Darlene thought to herself. "Why don't they just let us sleep until about five and then make the call?" Still, she looked forward to seeing the crew from Calexico. For in spite of Evantie's efforts to undermine the relationship between the RAIC/Riverside Office and Calexico to make Ricardo look bad, everybody saw right through his little ploy. The load came in late, as usual, at about noon. The temperature in the desert town of Thermal was around 115 degrees in the shade. Darlene was tired as was becoming her normal state. When the boys from the Calexico Office pulled up, Carlos Osorio was with them. Carlos was a great agent, a Latino, and a good friend of Darlene's. He was also a member of the ACEC, which stood for the Association of Customs Employees for Change.

When Carlos gave Darlene his usual bear hug greeting, she glanced over at David Gray, who had a condescending sneer on his face. Darlene felt like going over to him, clenching a fist, and wiping the smirk off him. Instead, she just thought to herself: "What a bigot!" The load ended up in a bad part of L.A., where they always seemed to end up. So the little group had to hook up with agents from the SAIC/Los Angeles Office. By that time, Ruben, Darlene and Carlos were looked upon with fear and disgust because of their whistleblowing activities. The L.A. guys treated them like lepers, afraid even to be seen talking to them. It was one more carry-over from the ongoing Internal Affairs assault against them—and it hurt. Darlene had known some of the L.A. agents for years. She had sat on details with them and had been in some pretty dicey situations with them as well. Now, none of them would even make eye contact with her. She concealed her hurt and disappointment by making her usual bad jokes.

The assembled team "briefed up," and not surprisingly, out of thirteen guys, Carlos, Ruben and Darlene were on the entry team. She was sure the L.A. guys saw them as expendable. Carlos would do the "knock and notice," supposedly because of his Spanish language skills. The funny thing was that the team included a L.A.P.D. Officer who also spoke Spanish, but it was Carlos who was to be the first to bust in, followed by Darlene and then Ruben. As she stood waiting for the crooks with the load to arrive, Darlene thought back to the "Surviving Armed Confrontation" course she had recently completed. She remembered the instructors saying that the most dangerous positions in entry teams were the second and third ones in. When the first guy enters, the crooks often don't have time to react. But the second and third persons in are like sitting ducks in the doorway no matter how fast they move.

"Is this a big hint or what?" Darlene said to Carlos and Ruben, who knew exactly what she meant. "Carlos, I'm just going to tuck in behind you, hang onto your shirt, and hope for the best."

"Buena suerte," Carlos said, wishing her "good luck" in Spanish.

By now the time was ten o'clock at night. The bad guys were sure taking their sweet time getting from Thermal to L.A. "Don't they know how tired I am?" Darlene asked Ruben.

"You got that midnight heads-up call too, huh?" he replied. "Why doesn't someone have sense enough to call us the next morning? Why wake us up twice?"

"My thoughts exactly," Darlene replied.

Carlos pulled Darlene and Ruben aside from the main group. "Nice entry team they put together here, huh? Did you notice that the case agent hasn't ascertained whether or not this house has any registered firearms—a real no-brainer for the rest of us poor slobs. Look, we go in fast and low. I'll go right, Dar left, Ruben straight ahead. Remember—low and fast. I don't like the looks of this at all."

"So much for my human barricade," Darlene said softly. When the moment to enter came, they did as Carlos said, going in fast and low. Darlene made a sharp left, into a kitchen where she found two toddlers in highchairs at the kitchen table. As she came around the corner with her gun drawn, the toddlers screamed. She quickly lowered and holstered her weapon, then tried to calm the kids down, hating herself for having traumatized these innocent youngsters. But what else could she have done? The kids were strapped into their chairs. Darlene felt the Cheerios in front of them and they were stale. The kids must have been there for a while, she thought. Then she smelled that their diapers were soiled.

Carlos gave the "all clear" signal. Darlene unstrapped the children and took them into the living room, where she held and comforted them. She gave one her badge and the other her keys to play with. "Where's the mom?" she asked one of the L.A. Agents?

"She's probably one of the crack heads blown out in here," he replied, pointing toward the bedroom, "along with the others—typical Mexicans," he added nastily.

Darlene glanced over to the nearby staircase where she saw Ruben standing there. Unbeknownst to the L.A. Agent, Ruben had heard this racial slur. Darlene could see the pain on his face. When he saw her reading his expression, Ruben turned his head away and went back up the stairs. Darlene couldn't help but think about how many times she had seen this pain, not only on Ruben but on all of the Latino agents she worked with. She thought about smacking the offending L.A. Agent who'd made the remark. Instead, she was able to find some Pampers, change the toddlers, and remind herself that at least they had made it through the door alive. That was worth something, anyway.

The racial slur episode provided an opportunity for Ruben, Carlos and Darlene to have a little chat after the raid was over. They talked about why the ACEC had been formed in the first place, to help bring about change in an agency which was rife with racism and sexism. Carlos was supportive, but there was still some fear on his face. Here was a man who could bust into a completely unknown and dangerous nest of crooks, yet showed concern over what making positive change at Customs might involve. Darlene thought to herself that when the toughest people around you are scared, the world can be a pretty insecure place with nowhere to run and hide.

Darlene got home late that night because the search warrant and suspect booking had taken a very long time. There was no time to get sleep before going to the office, so instead she made herself some strong coffee. When she arrived at work, Ruben was pulling in and they both got paged by Sandy at the same time.

"You too?" Ruben said about the pages. "Boy that Sandy and her 911 calls. You know I love her to death, but you just never know if it's a real 911 or just some juicy info."

"I know, I know," Darlene replied. "I told her to stop doing that and she just doesn't listen." They did a three-way call with Sandy, who came on the line crying.

"Shannon Getz is getting interviewed by IA today and it has something to do with Huge World," Sandy said. Huge World was a technology network-marketing group that Sandy, Ervin Rios and Darlene had all joined. For a nominal entry fee, one became a "distributor" and got tech products at a reduced rate. It worked a little like Avon Cosmetics but for high-tech stuff instead. Darlene had joined because of an Internet course they offered. None of the trio had any intention to sell any products to anyone. They were instead interested in getting tech products at really good rates.

"Look Sandy," Darlene said, "take a tape recorder and a witness and go with her."

"I don't have a tape recorder," Sandy responded sadly.

"Well, stop everything you're doing right now and go get one." Sandy said that she would and they hung up. Darlene could see more pain on Ruben's face.

He said: "They're never going to let up on us, are they Darlene?" He felt a sense of responsibility for what was happening to Sandy and Darlene and others who had been drawn into conflict with Customs by taking his side.

"Ruben, Sandy's tough. When she gets through crying she'll be ticked off and she'll handle this like the pro that she is. She's tough, Ruben. She can handle this."

Sandy called Darlene later that day and gave her the scoop on the interrogation. She sounded a whole lot better. She'd gotten a tape recorder and sure enough, IA turned around and grilled her about Huge World.

"I can't believe they're trying to hang their hats on that," Darlene said. Later, she briefed Ruben on it over lunch with more Mountain Dew's being consumed. By three that afternoon, Darlene had been awake for 36 straight hours. She'd had so much Mountain Dew that her hands were shaking. She thought to herself: "Mountain Dew should do a commercial with Federal Narcotics Agents about how we all use it to stay awake on the job." She wasn't sure if she was shaking from all the Dew, Sandy's ordeal, lack of sleep, or all three. She went to the gym and swam the mile in 52 minutes. She made a mental note to herself: "Before the Police Olympics, get angry and drink a ton of Mountain Dew!"

A ray of good news arrived on March 10, 1999. SA Janet Somers informed Ruben that Easel had admitted to her and to another Agent and also an AUSA that he had, in fact, taken the heroin evidence home with him. This would be instrumental proof that in fact IA did do selective enforcement of regulations on agents, mainly going after whistleblowers and not the "good old boys" network of Drake Brinkley et al. Ruben passed this info along to Darlene, who was preparing to serve a subpoena in Calexico. She asked him to join her on this mission, since it would give them a chance to stop by and tell Carlos about the upcoming meeting of the ACEC (Association of Customs Employees for Change). At last there was something with which the whistleblowers could defend themselves against the relentless onslaught by Internal Affairs.

25

A Tale Of A Tail on Your Tail

"Courage is being scared to death—but saddling up anyway."
John Wayne

When Darlene went back to her office, she signed out for the next day to go to Calexico with Ruben to serve subpoenas. In law enforcement, serving subpoenas is a routine part of the job. An officer just signs out where they'll be and with whom and nobody ever asks any questions. Well, almost never they don't. In this case, however, Evantie had questions as soon as he saw who Darlene would be traveling with.

"Uh, hey Dar," he said after entering her office, "what's this you're going to Calexico for?" Darlene showed him the subpoena she would be serving. "So you have to go to Calexico, then? Can't you just mail this or something?"

Darlene wanted to answer his question by asking him if he'd received his training at the Wal-Mart School of Investigators. Everyone who has ever completed a criminal case knows that subpoenas must be served in person. Instead she replied: "No, Boss, it's been a standing requirement from the U.S. Attorney's Office for quite a few years now that these have to be served in person."

"Oh, yeah, that's right. Okay. I was just wondering what was going on." Evantie then turned and walked out and went down the hall to his office. Darlene picked up her phone and made a call. When she looked up after dialing, there he was again, standing in front of her. Evantie looked impatient. When she didn't immediately hang up and give him her rapt attention he made a little swirling movement with his finger, indicating she should wrap it up so he might speak to her. She told her party she'd call back and hung up.

"What do you need, Boss?" she asked.

"Why do you need to take Ruben with you?" he wondered.

"Boss, it's standard agency policy that due to officer safety concerns no agent is to serve a subpoena alone."

"I know that," Evantie said testily, "but why are you taking Ruben?"

199

"Why not Ruben? I mean, is there some kind of a problem here, sir? Are agents now being told who they can and cannot take with them to serve a subpoena? I've worked here eleven years now, and no one has ever questioned me or any agent I ever heard of about who they can or can't take with them to serve a subpoena." Darlene knew what Evantie's problem was. He didn't want her and Ruben getting together with Ricardo Sandoval because he knew they were developing a strategy for the EEO case that would probably go to trial one day.

"Well," Evantie said as he began squirming, "I was just concerned about whether Ruben was available or not."

"Sir, I wouldn't have put him on the sign out board if I hadn't already cleared it with him." Darlene watched as Evantie stood there, his mind racing to come up with something intelligent to say. She reached for the phone, started dialing, and said: "Why don't I call the AUSA Yvette and let you explain your concerns to her about not wanting me to do my job on this case. I'd really like to hear your explanation to a Federal Prosecutor of why her subpoena is not going to be served."

"No, no," Evantie replied. "That's all right. I just don't understand why you have to take Ruben with you."

"Sir, you still haven't told me why Not Ruben!" With that, Evantie sighed in exasperation and walked away.

The next day, Ruben drove by to pick up Darlene at her home for the trip to Calexico. They talked and decided to take both of their cars to the Interstate 10 Freeway split at the Beaumont exit. There they would leave one vehicle and car pool to Calexico. That would save Ruben from having to make the trip all the way back to Darlene's at the end of the day. Ruben left Darlene's house first to go to his vehicle. Darlene got to her doorway and then went back inside to turn off her tv set. Ruben was already in his car and had begun heading back up the street in his car when Darlene came back outside. As she walked to her car, she immediately spotted a surveillance vehicle whose driver was watching them. This vehicle started down the street straight towards her house, and when the driver realized that Darlene was staring right at him he ducked into a parking space. Darlene thought to herself: "Jeez, I hope I didn't startle the poor sap. What a klutz!" She stood there a moment longer, continuing to give this goofball a solid stare, whereupon he pulled out of his parking space, did a quick U-turn, and sped off.

Darlene got into her car and started to catch up with Ruben, but on the very next block she saw another strange vehicle parked with someone in the driver's seat trying to scrunch down and keep out of sight. A veteran of countless surveillances herself, Darlene had a sixth sense for what was out of place, an instinct all good cops have. She steered her car over to the other side of the street, pulling right up close to the suspect car. At the same time, she heard several long "squelch" sounds come over her radio. She knew from several secret sources, including David "Mr. Internal Affairs" Gray, that when IA is conducting a surveillance on their "secret stealth" radio channel, the IA transmissions came over other Customs agents radios as "squelch" noise. She wanted to alert Ruben, but knew her transmissions would be monitored. Instead, she raced up and caught Ruben's car, then "lit him up," which is cop talk for turning on her police lights. Ruben saw her and waited at the next traffic light. Darlene jumped out of her car, ran up to his, and told him what was going on.

They caravanned up to the freeway and pulled into a Denny's Restaurant parking lot. There, Darlene parked her car and jumped into Ruben's vehicle. Ruben skillfully began conducting counter maneuvers to lose the IA tail they had acquired. Obviously, IA hadn't counted on them taking separate vehicles for the first leg of the trip. It didn't take Ruben long to lose the surveillance vehicle.

"Can you believe this?" Darlene asked.

"It's like the Keystone Kops," Ruben replied. "It's really pretty funny."

"Yeah, so how come I'm not laughing?"

"You've obviously lost your sense of humor, Darlene."

"And you," Darlene said looking over her shoulder, "have obviously lost that poor clown from Internal Affairs."

"How the hell do they train those people?" Ruben asked.

"Well, I hear that just before they get their decoder rings, IA gives each officer a lobotomy."

"Why?"

"So they won't be smarter than their bosses."

"It figures," Ruben said with a smile. Still, the whole sad episode served as a reminder of the fix they had gotten themselves into by becoming whistleblowers. Each seemed lost in their own thoughts as they made the three hour drive to Calexico. When they arrived, Ricardo was happy to see them and took them into his office. It was unlike any government supervisor's office they had ever seen. Ricardo had a beautiful portrait of the Reverend Dr. Martin Luther King on one wall and a huge Mexican flag on another.

"Welcome to Calexico," Ricardo said.

"Looks a lot like Mexico," Darlene replied, pointing at the flag.

"Are you guys hungry?" Ricardo asked. The others nodded and Ricardo took them outside to his car in the parking lot. As they walked, a vehicle passed by them.

"See that," Ricardo said. "That's an IA car—keeping tabs on me." As the trio entered Ricardo's car, the same IA vehicle circled around and passed them two more times. "Can you believe this?" he continued. "These morons have nothing better to do but to nose around us!" Darlene and Ruben told him about their own encounter earlier with IA surveillance vehicles.

"Welcome to the club, amigos. Now you know what my life has been like for a couple of years now. They follow me to work. They follow me home. My life is no longer my own. I have no privacy." The pain and anguish in Ricardo's voice was so thick you could cut it with a knife. His face grew dark as the surveillance vehicle passed by them yet again.

Ricardo drove them to a nearby restaurant where they sat in a booth by the window. Outside they could see the IA car park across the street.

"This is creepy," Darlene said as they gazed at the watcher who was watching them.

Ricardo then told them in great detail about how when he became a whistle-blower years earlier and filed his lawsuit his life was literally ripped away from him. In tale after tale he recounted how Internal Affairs had retaliated against him, making up false accusations and then taking an eternity to investigate what they knew wasn't there.

"It's just harassment. They want to push me out of the Service. This current circus is the twenty-second investigation IA has launched against me. It just about destroyed my family life. All I can do is go to the gym and work off my frustration at the end of the day."

"That's what I've been doing to," Darlene said. Then she looked at how fit Ricardo was. "You're in good shape."

"I should be, after all these years of working out. You know what we "undesirables" used to call where we park our G-rides? The Mexican parking lot."

"Why," Ruben asked.

"Because before Drake Brinkley became the Director for the Office of Investigations, he used to be the ASIC/San Diego (Assistant Special Agent In Charge). He and several other managers had what they called the Mexican parking lot. This is where all the Latino's had to park their beat-up G-rides. We never got good cars. In fact, what we drove were so bad they had a special lot for us away from the front of the building, so visiting bigwigs didn't have to see our lousy cars."

"Man," Ruben said with a sad smile, "I sure can relate to that. It's just what they're doing to me at our office." All this talk only deepened Darlene's hatred for Brinkley. She thought of him as the head of the snake, the leader of the "old boys" club whose poison was infecting the entire U.S. Customs Service. As she drove home that night, she felt like every car was watching her. It was as though she had been stripped naked in front of a bunch of strangers. She also wondered how Ricardo had been able to handle this kind of assault for over two years. It was already getting to her in a big way, just as it was designed to do. Would she have the courage to hang in there the way Ricardo had? Dark thoughts clouded her mind so badly that she almost wrecked her car from being so distracted.

On March 29, 1999, Darlene sent an affidavit and a formal complaint by certified mail to the Director of the Regional EEO Complaint Center regarding the role SAIC/LA and RAIC/Riverside management had played in the Postal Inspector's refusal to investigate the threatening letter and phony telephone transcript she had uncovered. On April 2, she received a response at her home from the Regional Complaint Center regarding these issues. Signed by Luanne Holmes, the Director, and dated March 30,1999, the reply dismissed Darlene's complaint, stating that it was not within the purview of EEO regulations.

Darlene wondered how her formal complaint could have been dismissed on March 30th when it had been received at the Regional Complaint Center on April 1, 1999—the date verified by the certified mail return receipt. Darlene wrote a letter to Ms. Holmes and sent copies of the receipt. "How," she asked in her letter, "could Ms. Holmes have obtained the contents of a complaint and turn it down before she even received it?" Darlene never received an answer to her inquiry. It was enough to drive somebody nuts. The whole campaign of harassment against whistleblowers is designed to do exactly that, and while it may not make its victims crazy, it usually succeeds in getting rid of them. Usually, that is, but not always.

On April 5, 1999, Darlene attended a meeting of the ACEC—the Association of Customs Employees for Change—at the Mission Inn in Riverside, California. Sandy Nunn, Ervin Rios, Ruben Sandoval, Rick Sandoval, and Marissa New were there. So was Justin Pierce, who was the second in command for EEO at the Customs headquarters level. The purpose of the meeting was to establish a united front and an organization to fight the cronyism and corruption which all of the whistleblowers had encountered. They were able to present plenty of evidence to prove their point to Justin Pierce.

"I can assure you," Pierce said after hearing the evidence, "that I can serve as a facilitator between you all and the Customs Commissioner."

"Do you think this guy can be trusted?" Ruben whispered to Darlene.

"Who knows?" Darlene replied. "If he does help us, I'm betting that the Commissioner will just shut him down."

"And if he doesn't help us—" Ruben asked.

"Then he'll probably get promoted."

The meeting of the fledgling whistleblower group ACEC went along smoothly. Darlene read a letter written by Sandy Nunn which outlined the corruption, cronyism, and retaliation that the members had experienced at U.S. Customs. It is important to remember that there are no effective safeguards in place to protect federal whistleblowers.

The entire point of this book is to show why such protections are needed. The letter Sandy wrote ended with a petition-style attachment to which twenty-six brave Customs employees had signed their names. This list included inspectors, agents, supervisors, intelligence analysts, and others. The letter had been sent the day before this meeting to numerous Senators and Congressmen, especially those from California where these employees worked.

The letter also went to Customs Commissioner Raymond Kelly and Customs Commissioner of Internal Affairs Harrison Wells. As she read the letter aloud, Darlene couldn't help but notice "facilitator" Justin Pierce squirming uncomfortably in his seat. The glance he shot at Darlene said: "You're going too far." The look back she gave him said: "I've only just begun." As she continued reading, every emotion she had felt for the past several months struggled to come to the surface, and she worked hard to maintain her focus and control her anger. She felt almost as though she might have a stroke in keeping down the tidal wave of resentment and humiliation she carried in her gut. When she finished reading the letter, she looked up and saw the same roadmap of distress on nearly everybody's face. Then she glanced back at Pierce, and the fear she saw on his face served to convince her that this man was not going to be any help at all to her group or their cause. Darlene's anger turned to hopelessness and she remained quiet for the remainder of the meeting.

During the break in the middle of the meeting, Ricardo handed Darlene a statement by Robert Saitley. Saitley was an ASAIC under SAIC/LA Drake Brinkley. He had been running the largest undercover money laundering operation ever conducted by any U.S. agency—Operation Casablanca. Saitley had read the statement before the House of Representatives Subcommittee on Criminal Justice, Drug Policy, and Human Resources. The following are excerpts from Saitley's statement:

"Beginning in the fall of 1997, Mr. Drake Brinkley leaked information about Operation Casablanca. At a law enforcement conference in Tampa, Florida, Mr. Brinkley provided information about this undercover operation to a network news executive.

Later in the investigation, Mr. Brinkley invited several Congressional staff representatives to Los Angeles to be briefed on a major undercover money laundering investigation. Upon their arrival, he not only paraded them through the undercover offsite, which housed the Alpha Task Force, he took them to the audio and video monitoring station of the undercover storefront, "Golden Empire."

During my meeting with the Commissioner of Customs, I requested an official document which reports the findings of the Internal Affairs investigation related to Mr. Brinkley's false and malicious accusation. To this day, I have received no official response from any Customs Service Officer in regard to any of the topics I discussed with the Commissioner."

As Darlene read Saitley's statement she thought to herself: "Poor man. Now he's going to have the IA goon squad after him just like the rest of us whistleblowers." She didn't know Saitley all that well, but the general consensus was that he was an honorable man and a good manager. She was familiar with a lot of his case work and considered him both impressive and professional. In addition, Saitley was highly experienced, which is a lot more than could be said for Brinkley. Darlene remarked to Ricardo that the whole system seemed hypocritical since she had received a letter of disciplinary action for allegedly releasing confidential information in submitting letters of commendation to EEO. Brinkley, on the other hand, exposes an undercover operation and two undercover sites endangering the lives of undercover agents and confidential sources and walks away "clean." Where are the IA people when it comes to checking out the Customs "Mafia" managers like Brinkley?

"Just watch," Darlene said. "Magically, Robert Saitley will come under some sort of bogus IA investigation."

"He already has, Dar," Ricardo replied, "he already has."

"Of course," Darlene answered, suddenly putting together another piece of the puzzle. "Operation Casablanca was targeting the infamous Arellano-Felix narcotics smuggling cartel. The same bunch that my tanker car investigation is about."

"And the dope you intercepted?" Ricardo asked.

"Same cartel." Darlene's head was nearly spinning with the implications of what they were saying. "Brinkley had made it his personal vendetta to undermine not only my criminal case, but he torpedoed the entire rail project as well. At the same time, Brinkley sabotages Saitley's multi-million dollar money laundering project as well." Darlene paused, as the excitement of this thinking made her heart race and made her breathing rapid as well.

She calmed herself down, and when the meeting ended told Ruben she had to get going. He and others wanted her to stay and help formulate some strategy. "No way," she said firmly. "I've got to get back to the office."

"What's going on?" Ruben wondered.

"I'm not sure yet," Darlene answered, "but I think this house of cards may be a-comin' down." She rushed back to her office and plowed into the Customs automated systems of importation. Her goal was to bring up the entries on the tanker cars she had looked at. When her rail project had begun, she had put what's called a "general hold" for weight on all pressurized tanker cars coming into the United States. This meant that no car should have been cleared by an Customs officer without the car having first been steered to one of the two rail yards that can perform this task: one is in Texas and the other is at Colton, California. There in the computer records she found several releases that were not authorized. Not being very familiar with this end of the Customs computer system, since it had been developed primarily for inspectors, Darlene immediately contacted Ervin Rios and asked him to meet with her.

"I'm getting ready to go on my shift at UPS," Ervin said. "Why don't you meet me at my office?"

"I'm on my way." It didn't take Darlene long to get to Ervin's office, and he sensed something was up as soon as he saw her. "Who has the authority to release a general hold placed by O.I.?" O.I. is Customs term for Office of Investigations, which is the agent's chain of command.

"Only a supervisor with subsequent notice to the agent," Ervin replied.

"Ervin, are you sure about that?"

Leaning closer to Darlene with rising curiosity, Ervin asked: "Why, Dar? What's going on? Whatcha got?"

Darlene removed the printed entries she carried from her jacket pocket, but Ervin's supervisor walked in so she quickly stuffed them back into her jacket. She made up some story to the supervisor about what she was doing there and the man finally left them alone. She again took out the entries and showed Ervin what she had found.

"What's wrong with this picture?" she asked, handing him the entries. Ervin scanned them and immediately noticed something wrong.

"There's a space on the entry where the supervisor releasing the general hold is supposed to put in a special, four digit code number. It's regulation. It's not here."

"You know, the last three tanker cars we were trying to look at had been released three times. Every time, I had to get the railroad to track them down and send them back from central California to be weighed." Every rail car has a distinct eight or nine digit code number for tracking, identification, and billing/invoicing purposes. "Pull up those numbers on your computer." Sure enough, it was Customs personnel and not a bureaucratic blunder by the railroad as Darlene had previously thought which had released the hole on these suspect cars. She showed Ervin the statement by Robert Saitley and he immediately put the pieces of the puzzle together as she had.

He moved over to his desk. As he started to unlock a drawer, Ervin glanced out through the hall window to make sure no one was observing him or coming his way. Darlene noticed how his manner had suddenly changed. He was no longer his usually jolly self, but instead became serious and a bit jittery, which was totally out of character for him.

He pulled out a file he had been carefully maintaining. Inside was a handwritten flow chart which he had created. It stemmed from a cocaine seizure he had made at the airport involving a juvenile and a private jet that had been cleared from a Colombian private airline. Ervin's flow chart tracked the Arellano-Felix cartel to two private aircraft which were conveniently owned by banks in Mexico and Colombia. These banks had been profiled in Robert Saitley's Casablanca Investigation, the undercover money laundering operation. Ervin had also tracked the pilot of the plane from which he had seized the cocaine to a company in Sineloa, Mexico. The name of this company was Grassa, the same name as on the entry documents for the tanker car of Arellano-Felix dope Darlene had seized nearly a year earlier.

"You know, Dar," Ervin said, "when I seized the coke from this kid my supervisor was all over me. He was outraged and he tried to undermine me, all at the direction of the Port Director, Wyndal Nabrowski."

"Wow," Darlene exclaimed as she looked at Ervin's secret file.

"There's more. There's an ex-inspector I talked with named Jeff Weitzman."

"Where have I heard that name before, Ervin?"

"He was the inspector who nailed the famous Hydro truck-trailer load of cocaine at the Otay Mesa Port of Entry."

"Oh yeah. That's right."

"Well, when Weitzman profiled this car, he put a hold on it in ACS for secondary, the place inspectors move vehicles to for inspection and entry. Someone released the hold without authorization and it was just coincidence that Weitzman was working the line and happened to see it coming. He secondaried it anyway, and just as he was about to run his dog on it, his supervisor ordered him to release it. Well, he ran the dog anyway and the dog went crazy. Weitzman defied the orders of his supervisor and popped it open to find one of the largest seizures of cocaine ever. When Weitzman confronted his supervisor about who ordered the car released, the supervisor said it was by order of Port Director Adrian Garcia."

Darlene sat back in her chair and shook her head. "Garcia's been under one corruption investigation after another by the FBI."

"Then you've heard all the rumors?"

"You mean about Garcia being connected to the Arellano-Felix Cartel? We've been hearing that stuff for a long time," she said.

Ervin pulled out a picture from his secret file. It was of Adrian Garcia in his Customs uniform, standing with his arm around another man. "Dar, do you recognize that guy next to Garcia?"

"No. Who is it?"

"That is none other than Carlos Ray Horn, leader of a Mexican smuggling cartel that works hand in glove with the Arellano-Felix organization."

"You've got to be kidding."

"The picture doesn't lie," Ervin said.

"Well let me ask you this, Ervin. Did you know that Adrian Garcia and Drake Brinkley go way back together?" Darlene asked.

"I had heard that, but never was able to confirm it."

"Listen, I also heard that your prior Port Director Wyndal Nabrowski was tight with both Garcia and Brinkley. They all came up together within Customs. Brinkley's been working this southern border for about thirty years."

Hearing this, Ervin rolled his chair up close to Darlene, again glancing at the window that faced the hallway. "Do you remember," he said in almost a whisper, "back in the late 1980's and early 1990's hearing about the `Blue Ribbon Commission Investigation' launched by Congress?"

"I remember it very well, because at that time I was assigned to the Personal Protection Detail of the Commissioner of Customs every time she came to L.A. She spoke quite often about this investigation and about having to report back to Congress."

"Well, I have the entire two thousand page transcript of those proceedings, and you know what? The very same people we're dealing with—Brinkley, Nabrowski, and even Mr. Internal Affairs himself, Harrison Wells—have their names plastered all over that investigation. There was a female OIG investigator named Cherry Rollins and an attorney/private eye named Jason Fielding assigned to the Congressional investigation. Cherry Rollins resigned from the OIG in disgust because of all of the stonewalling she had received from Customs in her efforts to conduct her investigation."

"And the other guy—Jason Fielding—what happened with him?" Darlene asked.

"Jason Fielding was found dead in his driveway in Long Beach with two to the chest and one to the head. It was ruled a botched burglary attempt, but I'm not buying it. Who else shoots like that? Only cops and assassins. This poor guy was gunned down in his driveway in front of his little girl. No doubt he stumbled onto something he shouldn't have."

"Sounds sort of like us, doesn't it?" Darlene said.

"Damn right it does," Ervin agreed, again looking out toward the hallway. "Think of the timing of when I got fired. Think of what we were doing."

Darlene winced as she realized that more pieces of the puzzle were falling into place. "Oh my gosh! That was right after we did the first tanker car, and then we started working in the rail yard."

"That's right," Ervin said. "My supervisor was giving me hell every step of the way. He didn't want me working on the rail project with you at all, Darlene. This isn't a coincidence! They don't want us working these rail cars for a reason. We're not supposed to be over there. And doesn't it kind of make you wonder about your 'Geraldo Rivera' tanker car? Maybe it wasn't so empty after all!"

Darlene's mind was racing. She began to recall how they were all so sure that there was no way anyone could have unloaded that tanker car during the trip up from Calexico in the time frame during which the car was unaccounted for. Now she wasn't so sure.

"We were all so sure," she said excitedly, "that the only way the bad guys could have opened that car and removed the contents was at a specialized facility, like the one in Colton. It never occurred to me that you could just improvise a tripod above the hatch and use pulleys and chains attached to a couple of fork lifts and—"

"And open sesame," Ervin said, finishing her sentence. "How long was that car missing?"

"Between nine and twelve hours," Darlene answered. "That sure as hell would have been enough time for the crooks to track the car off onto a small siding somewhere between Calexico and Colton and access the load."

"We're talking about millions of dollars worth of drugs, so the bad guys certainly have plenty of motivation." Ervin glanced again at the window. Darlene was processing all this information. She sat back in her chair.

"I feel like a fool who just found out they've been had," she said. "I defended my agency to the media when they called that tanker car the Geraldo Car after his Al Capone secret stash fiasco. Now we discover that maybe that car wasn't empty until the bad guys emptied it. Oh man." She sat rigidly in her chair, her mind going back over many other details of many other investigations which had been blocked or had come up empty when a cargo vehicle had slipped off the Customs radar, even for just a short period of time.

Seeing her sitting there blankly, Ervin waved his hand back and forth in front of her eyes. "Earth to Darlene, Earth to Darlene, come in please." He got her attention and continued. "Dar, if we're right about these suspicions and they killed that private investigator Jason Fielding because he found something, just imagine what they'd do to cover up the kind of stuff we've found. Maybe he found out some of these same things. Maybe he even had some concrete evidence or witnesses to back it up. If they've killed once, it won't bother them to kill again. I mean, look at what they've already done, and they don't even know what we've discovered about this rail car business. Think about it. If we're right, then this is a billion dollar thing we're looking to bust up. People have been killed for a whole lot less than this."

Darlene held out Ervin's secret file. "Who else have you shown this stuff to?"

"Nobody. You're the first."

"Good, Ervin. Don't. Not to anybody." She picked up the nearby phone and placed a call to AUSA Yvette Palazuelos. "Yvette, Ervin and I need to meet with you."

"What's it about, Darlene?" Yvette asked.

"I can't tell you over the phone. We need to meet."

"Okay. We'll meet," Yvette replied.

When she hung up the phone, Darlene gave Ervin a long look. "I hope to hell this place ain't bugged, amigo, 'cause if it is—we're toast!"

"I'm pretty sure it isn't," Ervin replied, looking around the room. "Pretty sure."

"Look, do you have any contacts at the LAPD who could pull the file for us on the Jason Fielding murder investigation?"

"You know me, Dar. I have contacts everywhere."

When Darlene left Ervin's office, she could taste the fear in her mouth. Anger had taken a back seat to naked fear. She thought about Jason Fielding being executed in front of his little girl. Had he found something he wasn't supposed to and did it cost him his life? Darlene thought that if she really did have a guardian angel, the message she was getting at that moment was two simple words: Get out!

On April 21, 1999, Darlene got a call from Sandy Nunn.

"Robert Saitley just walked into the SAIC/LA office and turned in his badge and gun," Sandy said excitedly. "He didn't wait for his minimum mandatory retirement or anything."

"I can't believe it," Darlene exclaimed. "Saitley's one of the toughest guys in Customs."

"Well believe it, sister. He just threw in the towel and walked away."

When she hung up the phone, Darlene began to seriously re-consider her options. She was listening to her head, now, and not her ego. Later that day, she got a call from Ricardo. He told her about Cynthia Stone, a woman who used to work for him in Internal Affairs and was still a good friend. Cynthia's husband was a DEA (Drug Enforcement Agency) agent. About a year earlier, Cynthia had to attend some IA training at the Federal Law Enforcement Training Center (FLETC) with David Gray. This was while Gray was still in IA and before he came to the RAIC/Riverside Office. Cynthia said that when she and Gray were at the FLETC, they'd gone to a local bar one night and she had gotten a little tipsy. Ever the gentleman, Gray offered to walk her back to her dorm. When they got there, Gray had attempted to force himself on Cynthia. She ended up screaming as loudly as she could and Gray got scared and took off.

The day after hearing all this, Darlene and Sandy called Cynthia. "Cynthia, did that really happen with David Gray?" they asked.

"Yes," Cynthia replied. "The reason I was afraid to come forward with it was because of the power I knew Gray had at IA. I knew how they used IA to harass and humiliate agents, and I was scared off. But now that I'm no longer working for Customs I'm willing to come forward with this."

"So you want me to forward this to the appropriate agency?" Darlene asked.

"Yes. Yes I do," Cynthia replied.

When she hung up the phone, Darlene turned to Sandy. "What am I, the whistleblower hotline?" she wondered. "Gray only resents me now. When he finds out that I'm reporting this, he'll hate me." Darlene documented her conversation with Cynthia, and she and Ruben reported it both to the Treasury Inspector General's Office and to the FBI.

Two days later, she and Ervin met with AUSA Yvette. As they were going into Yvette's building, Ervin casually remarked: "I checked with my pals at LAPD on the Jason Fielding homicide."

"What did you find out?"

"Not much. The file's disappeared. None of my buddy's can tell me how that happened. I have a theory, though."

"What's that?"

"Our beloved Port Director Wyndal Nabrowski used to work at the LAPD and used to brag about all his contacts over there. So the missing file on Jason is no accident. Somebody pulled that file and has buried it!"

"Another door closes on the truth," Darlene said sadly.

"Not only that, but a couple of my Inspector buddy's told me that they saw (California Senator) Diane Feinstein on the Customs yacht with Drake Brinkley."

"And that's just a couple of weeks after Sandy's letter (alleging corruption and signed by numerous Customs employees) was sent out by certified mail to lots of government folks including her and other Senators and Congressmen."

"Verrrry interesting," Ervin said, mocking Arte Johnson's peeping tom Nazi on the old "Laugh-In" television show.

"I wonder," Darlene said as they stepped into the elevator, "just how far up the chain of command all this corruption goes." They entered Yvette's office and explained to her what they had been piecing together. They showed her the tanker car entries that had been released, as well as the photo of Customs Port Director Adrian Garcia with cartel honcho Carlos Ray Horn. They filled Yvette in on Horn's longstanding relationship with Drake Brinkley and IA's Harrison Wells. In addition, they ran down the connections between the Casablanca money laundering operation and the tanker car case and how they both involved the Arellano-Felix Cartel. Given their suspicions, Ervin and Darlene saw it as not surprising that Brinkley would torpedo both Casablanca and the rail project.

Finally, they told Yvette about the Congressional Blue Ribbon Commission Investigation into corruption in Customs ten years earlier, which involved many of the very same people, and of the murder of Jason Fielding.

"There's just too many coincidences here," Darlene said.

Yvette took it all in, saying finally: "I'll brief the AUSA's on the Casablanca case."

When Darlene and Ervin stepped back outside and into the warm sunshine, neither of them were smiling. Instead, they both instinctively looked up and down the street and sidewalk. At least at that moment, it didn't look like anybody was on their tail.

26

A Demonstration Project

"We have forgotten the history of our country when we have forgotten how to agitate when necessary."
Woodrow Wilson

Darlene didn't fully realize how over five years of harassment had changed her until she got a call from Sandy Nunn. "Hey, Darlene," Sandy said, "we should hold a demonstration about what Customs has been doing to us."

"A demonstration? What put that idea into your head?"

"There's been a series of demonstrations in Riverside against the local police department for shooting a black girl who had allegedly been asleep in her car. The demonstrators say the shooting was racially motivated, and they've gotten their point of view across in the local TV news and in the newspapers. We need to do this."

Darlene listened carefully as Sandy expanded on her reasons for organizing a demonstration. "You know," she finally told Sandy, "five years ago I would have automatically defended the cops, not questioning their actions."

"Yeah, well, that was then and this is now," Sandy replied.

"I'm thinking about this," Darlene said after a short pause. "It just seems like a weird thing to do." Darlene had a similarly troubling experience after the widely televised tape of the beating of the fleeing motorist and ex-convict Rodney G. King by the L.A. cops. While the tape shown by media usually didn't include the lunge King had made for one of the cops' guns, it still seemed like the cops had crossed over the line of appropriate behavior at the very least in their handling of this high-speed chase suspect. Yet when she went to work the following day, Darlene was struck by the uniform defense of the cops' actions by all of her co-workers. She hadn't stood up then for what she really thought at the time, which was that there should have been a thorough and objective examination of the whole sorry affair to get at the truth about what had happened and why. Instead, Darlene kept silent about her doubts in the face of such overwhelming and unquestioning police support by her fellow law enforcers. Now her silence at that time was coming back to haunt her.

"It's not weird to hold a demonstration, Darlene," Sandy told her. "What's weird is what Customs has been doing to those of us who want to root out corruption in our own agency. That's what needs to be put out into the open where people can see it."

"Gee," Darlene replied, "that sounds a lot like what a reporter told me who was trying to get me to go public with all this craziness."

"What did he say?"

"He said that sometimes the best protection you can get is only found when you come into the light."

"That's it, Darlene. That's what we need to do—bring this whole business into the light by staging a demonstration."

"Why not?" Darlene agreed at last. "That just might work. Why don't we ask (their attorney) Tom Allison?" With that, they set up a three-way conference call with attorney Allison.

"Great idea," Tom said about demonstrating. "Your timing is perfect. I just saw where the Customs Commissioner is scheduled to appear before a Congressional committee and tell them he has everything under control. Imagine if somebody interrupts him and says that there are Customs agents demonstrating in front of the RAIC/Riverside Office announcing a huge class action lawsuit for discrimination and retaliation against whistleblowers."

"Can this be done on such short notice?" Darlene wondered.

"You bet it can," Sandy said confidently. And she was right. After that call, the women contacted Ruben, who also agreed it was a great idea. There was just one little matter Ruben wanted to caution them about.

"The thing is," Ruben warned, "we don't want to get into the tanker car corruption business in public. It's too hot and could invite unwelcome consequences. Let's just stay focused on the retaliation against whistleblowers and the class action lawsuit."

"Agreed," Sandy and Darlene replied. After only a couple of days of burning up the phone lines and dealing with a logistical nightmare, the team had put together a nice little demonstration. They had to walk a fine line in organizing this, since they didn't want management to find out about it before it happened and yet needed to spread the word around enough to get a good turnout. They contacted Cathy Harris, a Senior Customs Inspector at the Atlanta office and the author of "Flying While Black: A Whistleblower's Story." This is an important book about racial profiling of black women at airports. For her efforts, Cathy

Harris had received the same retaliatory treatment as the others, and she bravely agreed to fly in for the event.

The Friday before the demonstration, both Ruben and Darlene put in for annual leave for the following Monday. Over that week-end, Tom Allison, Ruben and Darlene met at the Mission Inn Hotel, where they signed the paperwork incorporating the ACEC (Association of Customs Employees for Change). They also worked on their speeches for the upcoming event. Then, on Monday morning, all the key players met for breakfast at the hotel. Darlene finally got to greet many of the people she had only known by phone for so long. They included Mike Connor, Cathy Harris, Tom Allison, John Carman, and Stephen Young. Tom distributed copies of a press release he had prepared, and it read:

"Today, the Association of Customs Employees for Change and the Customs Employees Against Discrimination Association (CEADA) announce their joining of forces to seek a fundamental and important change in how the U.S. Customs Service treats its employees. Tomorrow, the United States Senate will hold hearings on serious problems with the Customs Office of Internal Affairs. Some of these problems have come to light through the efforts of David Kidwell, a reporter for the Miami Herald, and present or former Customs employees who have suffered the denigration of the integrity of the Customs Service.

For too long, the Customs Office of Internal Affairs has been used by unscrupulous management officials to shield themselves and their associates from serious charges of wrongdoing. At the same time these same Customs officials have used Internal Affairs as a sword against those employees who dare challenge their misuse of authority. When employees raise legitimate concerns about management wrongdoing, they are often ignored or subjected to retaliation. Employees who dare to file grievances, report wrongdoing, or claim discrimination are perceived to be disloyal to the agency, and thereafter wrongfully targeted for retaliation.

One of the most effective means available to retaliate against employees is the instigation of an Internal Affairs or administrative investigation against an employee. Internal Affairs and/or administrative investigations are undertaken against these employees for what are often petty, frivolous and false charges of wrongdoing. Subjecting Customs employees to unjustified investigation can, and does, ruin the careers of these employees. Unjustified investigation causes them and their families to suffer greatly.

How could these problems fester to the point that the public, many responsible government officials including the Senate Finance Committee, the Commissioner of Customs, and Customs employees themselves doubt the integrity of the Service?

Because Internal Affairs, hiding under regulations and policies meant to protect legitimate investigations, is allowed to use the same regulations and policies to cover up their blunders and illegal actions. Customs' management reluctance to lift the veil of secrecy has led to the failure of the public trust. So long as the wrongdoers are able to escape public scrutiny for their actions, there will be abuses.

Today, the ACEC and CEADA call for an end to the discriminatory and retaliatory practices of the Customs Service, and those who have, and continue to use the Office of Internal Affairs to discriminate and retaliate against Customs employees. ACEC takes note of, and hope from, the Commissioner of Customs' recent statement acknowledging the past abuses of Internal Affairs. However, we are here today to voice that retaliatory actions are still being undertaken against good and honest employees, and that the Commissioner's efforts to date have been unsuccessful. Unfortunately, the only means available to those who have been wronged is to band together and bring legal action against Customs. ACEC has therefore retained the Washington, D.C. law firm of Davis & Bentzen, P.L.L.C. to seek legal redress on behalf of its members. The firm may be contacted at (phone number)."

Tom's press release pleased the assembled group. It made them feel empowered and confident of receiving the justice they had wanted for so long. It would be the last time they had the luxury of such feelings for a very long time. As Darlene looked around the room at the group having breakfast together, she was impressed with what an able and experienced bunch they were. Tom Allison had been a Customs Supervisor with several record seizures before he left the agency to get his law degree. Sandy Nunn had cracked the "Jewelry Mart" case which had received nationwide attention in Newsweek Magazine and elsewhere. Mike Connor had also been involved in many high-profile seizures and had been interviewed on the ABC News magazine "20-20" about them. Shannon Getz had been an FBI agent and was a survivor of the Oklahoma City bombing by Timothy McVeigh. Ervin Rios was a highly-decorated Senior Customs Inspector. John Carmon and Cathy Harris were highly decorated Customs Inspectors, and Cathy was also a soon-to-be-published author. Ruben and Darlene also had distinguished careers which encompassed record seizures and high profile cases. In short, this was not a rag-tag collection of inept, whining malcontents. Rather, this group represented some of the best and brightest people in Customs and law enforcement.

Among other things discussed as the meeting wore on was a revelation by Mike Connor about the group's nemesis Drake Brinkley. "We worked together for quite a while," Mike said. "I introduced the guy to the woman who would became his wife. Funny thing is, the night I got them together, Brinkley took her bar-hopping in his G-ride."

"Not so funny," Darlene said, "when you consider how Brinkley is trying to stick Ruben for 45 days on the bricks for having his kids in his G-ride."

"There's more," Connor replied. "Stuart Peters, an ex-Internal Affairs investigator, told me he had even better dirt on Brinkley involving the accidental discharge of his weapon which got covered up so as not to mar his record."

After breakfast, the group walked together from the Mission Inn over to the RAIC/Riverside Office where they would demonstrate. As they did, Darlene found herself thinking about how her attitudes had changed over the last couple of years. First there was the end of her reflexive defense of the police amid allegations of brutality. Then came a change in how she saw media and the reporters she encountered. In the past, she had thought of reporters as low-life's who would sell their mother's soul to get a hot story. Now she and the others were quite literally putting their careers and futures into the hands of reporters and their telling of these whistleblowers' stories. It was quite a change, but it had come out of necessity.

Not unsurprisingly, Darlene was chosen as the MC for this event. She introduced Cathy Harris, who gave an excellent account of the abuse she had received at the hands of Customs. Next, the President of the Mexican-American Political Association announced that MAPA was going to file an official complaint with Congress on the demonstrators' behalf. Ruben followed with an impassioned address, after which Tom Allison read the press release noted above. The demonstration ended following a question and answer period. It had gone very well, although as is always the case, it would have been better if more reporters had shown up to cover it.

What was really disappointing was the very scant actual reporting that showed up in the press afterwards. The little notice given was buried in the back pages of newspapers across the country, lost among accounts of dog attacks and UFO sightings. At the demonstration's end, an interesting aside was offered by Shannon Getz to a reporter from the Associated Press. "I've had more stress put upon me at work after filing an EEO complaint, than I experienced when the building I was in was blown up in Oklahoma City." She said this quietly and her voice cracked as her eyes filled with tears. Darlene watched this and Shannon's statement and general demeanor produced an odd reaction in Darlene. While she felt great compassion for Shannon, Darlene also found herself ever after avoiding her. It was as if Darlene feared that by getting close to Shannon, some of that naked fear and fatigue would rub off on her. It was similar to avoiding someone in a wheelchair because you're afraid their infirmity might somehow rub off on you.

Darlene knew that this feeling was wrong, and that it was a kind of prejudice. She burned inside at the thought that they were all out there laying themselves on the line over corruption and discrimination and yet she herself felt a kind of discrimination against Shannon for displaying weakness brought on by stress and fatigue. From then on, she kept herself at a distance from Shannon and was often not there for her when help was most needed. She has regretted this flaw in her character ever since. It cost her a great deal of sleep back then and still gives her pain when she thinks of it today.

The day after the demonstration, Darlene and Ruben had to face their co-workers at the office when they went in to work at RAIC/Riverside. As always, the brave Yolanda Rios was very supportive and even filled them in on the reactions of others at the office. Evantie, of course, had been embarrassed at the sight of the demonstration and was angry. That made Darlene feel better.

Then SA Jerry Johnston came over and gave her a big hug. "You stinker," he said affectionately. "I can't believe you guys did this! What incredible courage you have!" Jerry wasn't the only one at the office who enjoyed seeing Evantie made to squirm. Even the majority—who might agree with their complaint but who didn't support their action—were pleased at seeing Evantie made uncomfortable. But that kind of approval is not the same as standing shoulder to shoulder with the brave few who always seem to make the difference. Very few had the guts to actually take a stand. Much as Darlene loved the feeling of having had some payback against her tormentors, it would have been better if the whistleblowers had gotten some real backup for their position from the others who knew that they were exposing a truly dangerous reality at U.S. Customs but who didn't have the spine to say so. Going along with corruption is what enables it to flourish.

A couple of days later, Darlene's new Group Supervisor Lewis Cohen called her into his office. Darlene thought to herself that another reprisal was coming, but Cohen asked her to bring her tanker case file with her. "I want the whole history of this case and I also want you to bring me up to date on your criminal cases," he said. Still cautious after having been so badly mauled by management over the years, Darlene told Cohen all about her cases, and then expanded the conversation to include her treatment at the hands of Evantie and Brinkley. Cohen seemed surprisingly supportive. Darlene explained the way Evantie and Brinkley had undermined her rail project, but didn't trust Cohen enough to reveal what she and the others had dug up pointing a corruption finger squarely at Brinkley. Cohen might have seemed sympathetic, but he was still management, and was therefore not to be trusted.

"I think you've done a good job on this so far," Lewis Cohen said. "I went up against Brinkley once, and I came out on the short end of the stick. But you've made a good case here, and I think you should have been given more support."

Darlene thought to herself: "What gives with this guy? What is he up to?"

"Darlene," Lewis continued, "you're caught in the middle of a political machine. On the one hand, no one has the extensive knowledge, training or interest in this rail stuff that you have. On the other hand, you've made one hell of a seizure and gained important information on the Arellano-Felix Organization. So I want you to write up your rail project and I'm going to try to ram it through."

"You mean re-write it, don't you?" Darlene asked. "I already had the project written up and running when it was de-railed by Brinkley. We all know what that's about, don't we?"

Cohen laughed. "De-railed. That's a good one, Darlene. But having a spine isn't always popular or politically correct for one's career. Believe me—I know."

Darlene was puzzled by this conversation. Lewis had only been in the office for a couple of weeks. Why would he help Darlene when he had seen what had happened to her and the others? She thought something fishy was going on.

"Look," he said, "take what you've done, update it, and put it in the new project proposal format. I'm not your enemy here. I believe in this project, and I'm going to help you get past the political stumbling blocks that are currently in your way."

"Even if that means going up against Brinkley?" Darlene asked.

"I did it once and I'm not afraid to do it again."

Darlene stared into Cohen's eyes trying to read where he was coming from. Finally, she took a deep breath, got up, and said: "Okay, you got it. First draft will be on your desk by tomorrow morning."

"Hey, whoa!" Lewis said. "I don't expect you to have this done by tomorrow. Take a week, at least."

Darlene responded in her determined "Captain's" tone of voice: "You'll have it on your desk tomorrow, sir."

Lewis started laughing and in a friendly tone of voice said: "Darlene, sit back down here for a minute and talk to me. Let's just talk, okay?" She sat back down as he went on.

"Look, I understand agents like you and Jerry. You're not like the rest of these guys. Your military background and brainwashing is an important part of you. I know. I was a Naval officer. I know how you guys think. Duty and honor above all else. Hell, I admire that in you! But still, you've got to play politics sometimes. Everyone does." There was a long pause after this. Darlene was still trying to figure out why this guy was telling her all this. Then he completely changed the subject. "So how's the Olympic training going? I know you were working hard on cutting your time on your flip turns. Did you ever get Mike to work with you on that?"

"Yeah," she replied. "He showed me a better technique for coming off the wall that not only cut time, but relieved the pressure on my shoulder injury." The conversation continued along this line. Darlene still wondered about why Cohen was working so hard to win her trust.

"Could you put together a meeting with the federal prosecutor," he said, again changing the subject, "the Customs Inspectors and the locals involved in the rail project?"

"That's a good idea," Darlene agreed. "I'll see to it."

The next morning, Darlene placed the draft of the "new, improved" rail project on Lewis' desk along with a note telling him that the meeting would be at the U.S. Attorney's office on Monday morning at nine. Darlene had lunch with Ruben and Renado and briefed them on her warm and fuzzy meeting with Lewis. They weren't sure what to make of it, either. Renado said he'd be at the meeting. "Don't worry, guys. I'll get a fix on this and point this boy Lewis in the right direction."

At the Monday morning meeting, most of the people involved in the rail project were on hand, including Darlene, Lewis, Renado, Ervin, AUSA Yvette and Chief O'Leary.

A bit of small talk was suddenly interrupted by Yvette who asked Lewis point blank:

"So tell us, Lewis, who is torpedoing this project? Do you know who that is?"

To everyone's surprise, Lewis fired back: "Drake Brinkley."

"Why is he doing that?" Yvette continued.

"I don't know," Lewis replied. There was a moment of silence. Then the group began doing some brainstorming over how to proceed. After that, Lewis handed out copies of Darlene's new, second version of the "Operation Lite Rail" proposal. After everyone had read the proposal there was a little more discussion and the meeting broke up. Renado, Ervin, and Darlene stayed behind to have a private talk with Yvette. It was then that they updated the AUSA on the suspicions and information that they'd gathered.

"You want to know what I think?" Renado said to Yvette. "I'll tell you exactly what I think. Darlene has stumbled into one serious case here. She was never supposed to find that loaded tanker car, and they sure as hell don't want her finding another one. You know what else I think? I think that Brinkley guy is crooked as hell and all of you guys are in danger. I'm not kidding."

"What do you mean 'you guys,' Renado?" Darlene asked. "You've been in the middle of this since day one, boy. If they miss me, the bullet will probably hit you." After this little exchange, they all sat silently for a moment, lost in thought. The Brinkley suspicion was now right out on the table in front of an Assistant U.S. Attorney. That was a pretty significant development. There would soon be another.

Former Customs Inspector and well-publicized San Diego whistleblower John Carman had told Darlene and some of the others that there was an FBI agent out of San Diego who was already looking into border corruption issues related to the Hydro tanker car seizure. The FBI Special Agent was a man named William Motts. A meeting was scheduled with him. Ervin Rios, Sandy Nunn, Ruben Sandoval, John Carman, Clark Janice and Darlene all met with him. They told him everything they had assembled on the tanker car case so far and he seemed a bit overwhelmed. They could tell he was hearing a lot more detail on the corruption behind the case than he ever thought he would. His face grew darker and more concerned as the pieces of the jigsaw puzzle were laid out before him. Darlene sensed that FBI man Motts looked upon pursuing the investigation as too much work and a political nightmare.

Ten days after the demonstration, Ruben was called into Evantie's office with Lewis in tow. There Eveantie read Brinkley's proposal to give Ruben 45 days on the bricks, which was administrative time off without pay. Darlene was at the gym working out when she got the page, and she and Renado met Ruben at the usual place. Ruben was both livid with rage and extremely worried at the same time. He knew that this punishment would kill him financially, as he and his wife just had a new little baby boy. Darlene and Renado spent the better part of an hour trying to console him.

The gloom from the night before followed Darlene into the office the next morning. As she passed David Gray in the hall, she looked at him briefly and said: "Hey." He looked back at her with an expression that was pure evil. Darlene knew that Gray's IA thug buddies had already clued him in on the impending attempted rape investigation. Darlene felt a shiver of fear and regretted leaving her gun in the trunk of her G-ride. It had come to this, she thought. Somebody in her own office looked like they would probably kill her if they could get away with it. Darlene sat at her desk, waiting for another shoe to drop. As if on cue, Gray walked by her office and hit the wall with his fist so hard that it knocked one of Darlene's pictures right off the wall. Her partner Ruben wasn't around, and she was becoming more scared and angry by the minute.

A little time passed and Gray pounded on her wall again. She thought he was going to put his fist through it. But her fear quickly turned to rage and she felt her blood begin to boil. She had a tennis racquet next to her desk, and she took it and walked down the hall to Gray's office. She swung the racquet against the metal frame of Gray's door. Now it was his turn to be startled and he almost jumped out of his chair. "Oh, sorry Gray," Darlene said sarcastically. "Did I disturb you?"

Gray looked up briefly, then went back to working on his computer, ignoring her. She regained control of her temper and walked back to her office. Her chest was pounding and her face was flushed, but she felt better. In a little bit, Ruben came in. She told him what had just happened. He walked over to where she sat, squatted down next to her chair, and told her in a firm whisper: "Now, you better listen to me. You had better start carrying your pea shooter. I mean it. I don't want to see you unarmed anymore! That crazy bastard Gray is likely to do anything and I don't want to see you get hurt."

Darlene smiled at him nervously and said: "Don't worry, little man. I have a tennis racquet."

Ruben rose and stood up. "Give me that," he said, snatching away her racquet.

Darlene stuck out her tongue at him. "You're a bad boy, Ruben. I'm telling Daddy on you!"

This broke the tension and they shared a good laugh together. But the point had been made. The game was getting rough, careers were being affected, and anything was possible.

That night, Darlene's recurrent dream came back. She was standing in the Daniel Boone National Forest in South Central Kentucky on a trail overlooking the waterfalls at Cumberland Falls State Park. This was a spot she knew well, since it had been one of her most favorite places when she was growing up. She had used to sit there for hours listening to the relaxing sound the water made as it rolled over the falls. Now she again was feeling the cool rocks on the overhang above her head. The air was fresh, cool, and crisp. The brilliant colors of the fall foliage blazed around her. She was at peace and felt like she could stay in that spot forever. The toddler appeared just down the trail from her. He was still filthy, and stared at her with his deep blue eyes and melted her heart. As she walked towards him he smiled. Sensing he was about to lead her off to someplace else, Darlene said to him: "Please, let us stay here for just a little while." He smiled impishly, and then they were someplace else.

Now she and the toddler were back at the farm in her dreams. From the top of a hill, they could see the farm below. She looked for the corral and there he was—the strange young man she had seen so often before. He was sitting on the back of an old flatbed truck, whose bed and side railings were made of wood. It looked like the truck Darlene's grandfather had used to take feed to the cows and horses. She could only see the young man through the wooden planks. He was dressed the same as before, smoking a cigarette and dangling his legs gently back and forth. On the tailgate next to him sat a Styrofoam cup of tea, with the tag of the tea bag draped over the cup's side. She could again hear him speaking in that strange, soft accent. His voice was deep and he appeared to be talking to the ducks and chickens. He also had something he was feeding them. Now he seemed completely at peace, not at all the way he appeared when she had dreamed of seeing him at the Shrine Auditorium. He was now where he belonged.

Darlene took a deep breath and noticed again how beautiful everything was. She also felt a deep sense of inner peace. Darlene approached the truck in an effort to see the man's face. Something stopped her and she briefly felt frustrated. She could only glimpse the side of his face through the wooden planks. But his eyes again captivated her, with their ocean-blue dreaminess. She tried to yell to get his attention. Instead, she woke up.

As she lay on her bed unable to get back to sleep, Darlene pondered this dream. What did it mean? If the stranger was the Angel of Death, why was he smoking casually and talking to poultry? If there was some kind of message here, why wasn't she getting it? Why was the toddler always dirty and pitiful looking? Why couldn't she ever see the man's face? Why was it that every time she began feeling secure and peaceful the toddler would jerk her into another place or she would wake up? She was more puzzled than ever, but couldn't tell anybody about these dreams for fear that such information would come back to haunt her. The corrupt Customs managers and IA could have had a field day with her dream, saying she was nuts and using it to attack her credibility. She could imagine Evantie, laughing in her face and ridiculing her as he took away her badge and gun. He would have put her on "stress leave" if he knew about the dream. She would never give him that satisfaction.

On May 25, 1999, Darlene got a call from Sandy Nunn. "I just got a letter of disciplinary action," Sandy said. "I'm on the bricks for three days starting today."

"The swine," Darlene said.

"Oh well," Sandy replied, "I guess the way to look at it is that they're only proving our point and making our future litigation easier." Darlene met with Sandy and her mother later that night. It was obvious that all this stress was making Sandy's mother a nervous wreck. It made Darlene glad that she had not told her own parents about what was going on at work. Like a bad cold, stress is not something you want to spread around to others.

27

Somebody Loves You, Somebody Hates You

"Men occasionally stumble over the truth, but most of them pick themselves up and hurry off as if nothing ever happened."
Sir Winston Churchill.

In late May of 1999, Darlene and Sandy Nunn had lunch with ex-Customs Special Agent Ron Bundy. Ron had retired from Customs rather than continue receiving the kind of discrimination and abuse the Customs whistleblowers were getting. He had been a money laundering and fraud expert who had worked large undercover (U.C.) projects with David Gray. When Darlene filled him in on what Gray had been up to, he startled her with his reply. "I'm not surprised," he said.

"Why?" Darlene asked.

"Darlene, don't you get it? David Gray is crazy about you and has been for years."

"What?" Darlene exclaimed in shock. "Where are you getting this from? No way!"

"Don't you remember that Christmas party a few years ago at the U.C. offsite? Remember that someone stole one of your shoes—a red pump?"

"Yes. So?"

"It was Gray. For weeks after that party, all any of us heard from him was about Darlene this and Darlene that, and about how great you looked in your red dress and shoes. That nut carried your shoe around for days. He kept it in his desk. We all thought he was loco!"

Darlene received this information in stunned silence. Then she said: "I had no idea, Ron. None of this makes any sense. Gray's happily married."

225

"I'm telling you, Darlene, married or not this guy's obsessed with you. Remember how he was trying so hard to get you assigned to the U.C. project permanently."

"Yes."

"Well, if he hadn't gotten transferred to IA, with his pull, he would have gotten his way. Why, he even told everyone that was why he was putting in for the RAIC/Riverside office—to work with you, the infamous Darlene."

"Well," Darlene said, "I had been wondering why he made it a point to move into the same office as Ruben and I."

"Exactly," Ron said. "He fully expected that you and he would partner up because of your previous friendship, and that he would worm his way into a relationship with you. Then, when he was sent to do management's dirty work on Ruben, you did the unexpected and stood up for Ruben against Gray."

"I stood up for the truth and defended my partner against discrimination and retaliation," she replied.

"Yeah, well that's not how Gray sees it. You and he go way back before Ruben. He thought that since you were so close, you would naturally side with him against Ruben, and when you didn't he saw that as betrayal."

"You know," Sandy interjected, "all this makes perfect sense. I noticed that Gray always acted like a jilted lover around you."

"Jilted lover?" Darlene said incredulously. "This is ridiculous. We were only friends. The man never even made a serious pass at me. He knew I hated married men who cheat on their wives."

"Trust me," Ron said. "Gray would have picked and chosen his timing carefully. He would have waited until you were vulnerable and wormed his way into your life. He sees Ruben as the man who stole you away from him."

"This is just so nuts!" Darlene responded. "Ruben and I have never even contemplated a relationship. Ruben's a happily married man. This is crazy!"

"No it's not," Ron insisted. "Gray doesn't know the relationship you and Ruben have. He only thinks that you dumped him for Ruben."

Sandy nodded her head in agreement. "I've seen how David Gray looks at you."

"You've seen this too?" Darlene asked.

"He's in love with you," Sandy continued. "He blames Ruben for turning you against him."

"That's it," Ron said. "Face it, Gray has it in for Ruben, and it's more than just doing management's dirty work."

"How the hell did I miss this one?" Darlene said at last. "I'm supposed to be a trained investigator." She stared at her plate, then pushed it away. "I'm sure as hell not hungry anymore. This is kind of revolting when you think about it."

A couple of days later, Darlene got a 911 page from Sandy. When she called her back, Sandy was hysterical. Her father had just died of a heart attack. Sandy was extremely close with her dad Rocky. He had been an Air Force pilot and a twenty year veteran of the Immigration Service. He and Sandy's mom Jean had been married for nearly fifty years.

Ruben, Ervin, Shannon and Darlene all attended Rocky's funeral. He was buried with full military honors and a formal salute from the Border Patrol. Both Sandy and her mother were crushed by Rocky's passing. What was worse was the knowledge that Rocky had been in despair over Sandy's ordeal at Customs. He took personally the retaliation and wicked treatment his daughter was getting at work, but felt powerless to do anything about it. "I'm old and weak," he had told Jean shortly before he died, "and I can't help my daughter." Sandy's cruel and unfair suspension from work had been the straw that broke the camel's back. It literally killed Rocky Nunn.

Ruben and Darlene soon noticed that almost no one from Customs came to this funeral. This was completely out of character for Customs, and all cops. Anytime someone in the service loses a loved one, especially a parent who had served his country for so many years as Rocky had done, it is customary for the entire office to come out. Shannon later told the group that Customs managers had put the word out and everyone feared coming to the funeral. This was about as low as any human can get.

Yet Customs managed to added insult to misery when they chose the day Sandy's father died to initiate another IA investigation. This goes beyond kicking somebody when they're down. This is the kind of harassment and retaliation the Old Boys Club felt empowered to use against whistleblowers. The timing of the IA inquiry could not have been better calculated to cause Sandy pain, which was its sole intention. The allegations were groundless.

Internal Affairs claimed that months earlier, Sandy had inappropriately accessed the TECS computer records in support of her EEO complaint. It was about a case involving Jeff Weissman, a Customs Inspector and dog handler in Nogales, Arizona, which is on the U.S.—Mexican border. After his dog had alerted him, he had flagged a "dirty" tanker truck. His boss told him to let the truck go through and enter the United States. Weissman stuck his neck out by opening the tanker truck up anyway and he found eleven tons of liquid cocaine inside. Customs promptly shut his follow-up operation down, just as they had with Darlene's "Rite Rail" investigation. Weissman eventually got hold of Sandy Nunn, who noted the similarities between what happened to Weissman and Darlene's Rite Rail operation. Customs waited until Sandy was grieving to hit her with the IA inquiry. This is what whistleblowers face when they take on a corrupt management.

That night, Darlene went home after the funeral and called her dad. She told Kelsie how much she loved him and they enjoyed a few laughs together. At about that same time, Sandy Nunn was standing over her father's grave vowing that she would not stop fighting the system until justice was done.

Darlene had been training hard for the Police Olympics, which were held during the first and second weeks of June, 1999, and she had entered three events: a cross-country 10K Run and two swimming events. The 10K took place on the equestrian trails at a park in Pasadena, California. She knew it would be a tough run when she saw a sign posted at the trail's beginning which read: "Advanced Riders Only." It was one of the toughest cross-country courses she had ever run, and reminded her of her days jogging up the canyons back at Fort Huachuca in Arizona. She survived the run, which turned out to be almost as much fun as it was grueling.

The swimming events were being held at the Aquatic Center in Pasadena. The first one was scheduled for a 9 am start. To get there, Darlene had to make the two hour drive from home and get there an hour before the start time in order to check in. She hadn't slept the night before because she was nervous and anxious about what lay ahead. It was cold that morning, and after completing the first event, Darlene stretched out on one of the benches. The sun came out and warmed her up and she fell asleep. Her rest didn't last long, though. She awoke to hear them calling the next event on the loudspeaker system. The other swimmers were already behind their blocks. In an embarrassed rush, Darlene ran over to the sign-in table, only to discover that she had forgotten her event card. She dashed to her locker, got her card, and ran back to the event. The other swimmers glared at her for making them wait.

"Swimmers take your mark," a voice called over the speakers. Darlene jumped up and got into position. "Stand down, stand down," the voice said. "Lane seven, would you remove your sunglasses please?" Darlene glanced about and noticed that all the other swimmers were laughing at her. She suddenly realized that she was wearing her sunglasses, stepped down, put on her goggles and got back into position. She felt like an idiot, of course, and cursed the stress she had been under for making her commit such a boneheaded mistake. Still, she ended up winning two silver medals.

The Monday following the Police Olympics, Drake Brinkley put out a SAIC/ LA office-wide email message congratulating everyone who had won medals at the Police Olympics—everyone except Darlene. "How childish that is," Darlene thought to herself at the omission. She hadn't competed for the glory of U.S. Customs, anyway. But it still hurt. When Ruben came into the office she showed him her medals. He gave her a big hug and told her how proud of her he was. Then Jerry Johnston came in, saw the medals, and gave Darlene a congratulatory high-five. When Darlene told them how she had made a fool of herself with the sunglasses they all enjoyed a good laugh together. Things took a more sober turn when she showed them the email from Brinkley.

Ruben was incredulous. "I can't believe it! That's really low. What a bunch of idiots!"

Darlene tried to conceal her pain but they could tell she was stung by the email and the omission of her name. It was just one more example of the campaign against her and the others. The strange thing about stress is that it is cumulative. As injury is piled atop injury, there is a buildup of frustration, disappointment, and rage which eats away at your soul like rust.

Later that morning there was an office meeting where Jerry congratulated Darlene in front of everyone. Ruben was not pleased and was about to say something about Darlene being left out of Drake Brinkley's email. Darlene gave him a gentle kick under the table and shook her head "no" to make him refrain from commenting. Lewis acted impressed at seeing her medals and others congratulated her as well. Evantie, on the other hand, simply sat in his chair and glared at her with a condescending smirk on his face. Darlene knew that she had a reputation as a "hothead" and rather than give in to the immense anger she felt toward Evantie and the repression he represented, she got up and left the meeting. She knew that her blowing up would give her enemies the excuse to fire her—or worse.

On July 18, 1999, Darlene received a response from Customs Regional EEO Complaint Center on one of the retaliation complaints she'd filed. Inside was a statement from none other than EEO Supervisor Mary Conales stating that it was in fact she who had turned over Darlene's EEO file along with Sandy Nunn's letter to Internal Affairs back in 1997. It had taken two full years for Conales to admit to this breach of regulations. It flew right in the face of the two sworn statements Conales had submitted stating that the treatment Darlene and the others had been getting could not have been retaliation because there was no way management could have known about the EEO complaints. Now it was clear that management had known about the EEO business all along because Mary

Conales had told them all about it. Darlene showed this letter to Ruben and he immediately grasped its significance.

At the time Conales had turned this complaint information over to IA, Internal Affairs was under the command of Elaine Black. Black's second in command was Stella O'Shea, whose husband Dudley O'Shea was a close friend of Drake Brinkley's. Elaine Black later became and was currently the Assistant Agent In Charge under Brinkley. In addition, this illegal leak happened when David Gray was working in IA. So there was the interconnection of all the managers with respect to who was filing complaints, and this made possible their concerted retaliatory actions. The pieces of the puzzle now fit neatly together, and the picture revealed explained exactly how the harassment happened.

When Darlene faxed this to her attorney Tom Allison, he said this information was golden and that Mary Conales was toast.

A couple of days later, as Darlene and Ruben were in the office completing some reports, Lewis appeared in their doorway. "Ruben, Evantie and I need to see you in Evantie's office," he said. Ruben and Darlene exchanged worried glances, knowing that this was going to be Ruben's sentencing to forty-five days suspension without pay.

"I'm not going in there without a witness," Ruben said warily. "Let's go, Dar."

Together, they entered Evantie's office, where he sat behind his desk gazing at a document and wearing a smug expression. Darlene resisted the powerful urge to kick the chair out from under Evantie and wipe that smirk off his face. Her temper was nearly getting the better of her, now. Funny how stress lays your emotions bare.

"Sit down," Evantie beckoned. Ruben and Lewis sat, but Darlene stood defiantly in the doorway in a military "at ease" position. With obvious relish, Evantie began reading Ruben's letter of suspension. His hands tightly gripping the armrests of his chair, Ruben's knuckles turned whiter with each word as Evantie read the letter. Darlene was surprised to see Lewis sitting there with an expression of disgust on his face, even throwing an occasional dirty look Evantie's way. When he finished reading, Evantie said: "Let me have your badge, weapon, and keys."

Ruben handed over his badge and gun. Then he said: "My keys are in my desk drawer."

Evantie glanced over at Darlene. "Can you get them for us, Dar?" She simply glared at Evantie. She thought him to be the most uncompassionate, evil person she had ever met. Evantie was loving every minute of it. "Uh, Dar, the keys?" he repeated.

Darlene took a deep breath and was about to do something that might have gotten her in big trouble when Lewis walked over and placed a hand on her arm. He spoke to Ruben while looking into Darlene's eyes. "Ruben," Lewis said, "I'll show you how to file an appeal on this in my office." Lewis was squeezing Darlene's arm as if to say "Don't do anything. Come with me. We'll handle this." Darlene nodded that she would go with him to his office.

Ruben got up from his seat and walked over to Lewis and told him: "You know this is bullsh—, don't you?"

Lewis nodded his agreement and said: "C'mon guys. Let's go over to my office and talk." For his part, Evantie looked at Lewis with disgust at this apparent betrayal by a fellow manager. They stopped in the hallway by the Sign In/Sign Out sheet and Darlene looked at her partner's face. She felt helpless to do anything about the anguish she saw on Ruben, and it was about to drive her to tears. Before that could happen, she began walking out.

"Where are you going?" Lewis asked.

"I'll catch you later," Darlene answered. "Ruben, I'll be back in a little bit and drive you home." Then she signed out and drove over to the Union Pacific rail yard in Colton.

Darlene sat up on the hill overlooking the yard, watching the tanker cars moving onto the "hump" to be weighed. Her mind was racing. She was now convinced that this tanker car business was what all the trouble was about. Renado had been right from the beginning and she and Ruben hadn't seen it early enough. She felt keenly what this trumped-up punishment was going to do to Ruben financially, just as it was intended to do. This was hardball but nothing like the game her father had taught her to play so many years before. In this game you just didn't get tagged out. The opposition could make sure you never made it off the field. She kept seeing Evantie's evil smirking face and it made her angrier by the moment. To take her mind off things, she drove to a nearby Jack In The Box restaurant.

As she passed by the drive-thru window, she remembered how Ruben had taught her that Jack In The Box was Joaquin En La Caja in Spanish. She didn't want to go back to the office but she did want to drive Ruben home. He would want that and he certainly deserved that loyalty from his long-time partner. She turned the car around and went back to the office.

Pulling into the parking area, she saw Evantie walking to his G-ride. For a moment, she saw herself gunning the engine and just running the guy over. Doing this was to her stamping out something that was pure evil, like killing Hitler or shooting a mad dog. She began to press down on her accelerator when a car nearby honked its horn, snapping her out of her murderous rage. She hit the brake and watched Evantie get into his car.

How had she become a person who contemplated murder? All of this crazy abuse at the hands of Customs was really beginning to warp her mind, turning her into someone she desperately did not want to become. She was like a ticking bomb, and she wasn't sure how to keep from exploding. Then she saw Ruben step out of the office and look around anxiously. This snapped her out of the dark thoughts that had overcome her and she quickly pulled her car up in front of this decent, honest man who had just been hung out to dry by his boss for the crime of being a good U.S. Customs agent.

On the way to Ruben's house, the two partners didn't talk very much. What was there to say? "This will all work out," Darlene spoke at last. "You've got a lot of friends who care for you and who will be loyal to you." It all sounded so hollow, she couldn't even convince herself much less this poor good cop who was about to be strangled financially by wickedly corrupt managers who didn't want him on the force. Darlene cursed herself silently for doing such a lousy job of bolstering Ruben's spirits. She had never been much good at showing the compassion that was truly in her heart. Revealing this soft inner self embarrassed her for some reason, and here she was failing at the attempt she most wanted to succeed. The next forty-five days were some of the toughest Ruben ever had in his life and there wasn't a darn thing Darlene could do to make it better. This was hardball, all right, and she felt like she had just struck out in the bottom of the ninth inning.

Somebody—either Lewis or AUSA Yvette—must have put some pressure on somebody because Darlene suddenly found herself back on the rail project. On August 2, 1999, Darlene put in for the Customs Physical Fitness Specialist School at the Cooper Clinic in Dallas, Texas. Two days later, she got her memo back with Evantie's handwriting on it stating that Brinkley was not sending anyone. When she had submitted her request, she had also sent her memo to the Regional Fitness Director Peter Blake. Blake then called her and told her that there were in fact several funded positions and that he had forwarded her application to headquarters. In the past, Darlene would have been puzzled by this contradictory information. Now it just seemed like it fit into the regular routine of mistreatment by Brinkley and company.

Several days later, Darlene received her school selection packet from headquarters. She showed Lewis the memo from Evantie, the memo from Blake, and the packet from the School. She knew that by doing this she was putting Lewis in a difficult position, but she needed to know if she could trust him or not and this would make a good test. She told Lewis that several years before, his predecessor Ivan Winkowsky had cheated her out of going to this school even though she had been selected "most qualified" not only at the RAIC level, but also for the entire SAIC Office. Lewis seemed sincere when he said: "Dar, I'm going to take care of this. This time you will be going." And in just a couple of hours Lewis stuck his head into her office and said: "Pack your bags. You're going to Dallas."

Later that same day, Yolanda Rios, the office Investigative Assistant, told Darlene she had heard Lewis and Evantie arguing over something concerning Darlene. Darlene felt at last that she really could trust Lewis. It was the first time she had felt that toward a manager in years. The RAIC/Riverside Office was a pretty grim place for Darlene to work in, and now Evantie would see Lewis' defense of Darlene as another betrayal by an underling. Evantie considered Lewis' and Blake's involvement as an end-run for which he would have to get even. It didn't take long. Lewis was soon force-transferred—which is not a transfer one puts in for—to Washington, D.C. He had to sell his recently-purchased house and uproot his kids from school and transfer everything on short notice. The cost to the government for such forced-transfer can be significant but Customs considers retaliation against those who don't "play the game" as worth the expense.

The day before Darlene left for Dallas, there was an office meeting. Lewis mentioned that Darlene was going to be gone for a week at the Fitness School. Evantie arrogantly gazed at Darlene and responded: "Well, I hope you don't come back here thinking you're gonna try to whip us into shape or anything."

Darlene gazed at him and noticed a pack of his cigarettes lying on the table in front of him. Evantie was a chain smoker. She reached forward and slid his pack of smokes toward him. "No, Lawrence," she replied calmly, "I'm gonna come back here and buy you a carton of cigarettes." Everyone laughed except Evantie, who fumed in embarrassment.

It was just a reflex on Darlene's part, and she knew right after she spoke that Evantie would figure out a way to make her pay. She just couldn't help herself. She'd had it with the abuse. Then Evantie said something interesting.

"You all know how hands-on Brinkley is with respect to vehicles," Evantie began. "Well, he has reiterated the agency's policy on vehicles and he's determined to see it followed." What made the remark notable was that Brinkley had testified under oath in Ruben's civil case that he had nothing to do with vehicles and that anything related to them was somebody else's assignment. Evantie had just put the lie to Brinkley's sworn testimony in front of a whole room full of witnesses.

Darlene made a note of what Evantie had just said and filed it away with all the other bits of evidence she was going to need later on. Yet, for a brief moment, Darlene actually was looking forward to her next week of work at the school in Dallas.

28

Twisting The Knife

*"There comes a time when you must take the bull by the tail
and face the situation."*
W.C. Fields

Darlene spent a wonderful week at the Customs Physical Fitness Specialist
School at the Cooper Clinic in Dallas, Texas. It made for a tremendous release of
the pressure and frustration she worked under at RAIC/Riverside. For seven glo-
rious days, she didn't have to suffer at the hands of the Drake Brinkley's,
Lawrence Evantie's or Harrison Wellses. But it was back to the same old grind
when she returned the following Monday to her office.

When she signed on to check her email, there was a message from headquarters congratulating the top three Significant Problem Solving Projects. Operation
Lite Rail—Darlene's rail project—won an award for one of the best projects of
the year. Attached to the email was a list of names of all the Customs employees
who had participated. Each participant was to receive a Commissioner's Citation
and a cash award of $1000. Everyone on the project was on that list. Well, not
quite everyone. Darlene's name was nowhere to be found. This omission would
have been incredible if it were not by now routine. Another missing name was
that of AUSA Yvette. It was as if the whole rail operation had gone forward without the "engineer" and the "conductor."

These omissions and what they represented made Darlene's heart sink. It was
the final blow. She hadn't just been stabbed in the back; management was twisting the knife. She printed out the email message and stormed down to Evantie's
office with it, thinking she just might cram it down the S.O.B.'s throat. Pounding on his door with her fist, Darlene found that Lewis and Yolanda were suddenly standing beside her.

"He's gone. He's gone." Yolanda said.

"What's wrong, Darlene?" Lewis asked. Darlene gave him the email message.

"Where is he?" Darlene demanded. Without waiting for a reply, Darlene rushed over to Yolanda's desk and thumbed through Evantie's appointment book. He had gone on leave for a week. Darlene then rushed back to her office, grabbed her keys, and started for the door determined to take some time off before her rage made something terrible happen.

Lewis tried to talk to her as she was signing out. "Dar, I hope you know I had nothing to do with this." Darlene ignored him and went home where she broke down crying. All of the anger, frustration and helplessness of two years of emotional abuse finally caught up with her in a way she finally could no longer shake off. She'd had enough of watching people she cared about be harassed, humiliated and beaten down. Darlene called in sick the next day and began looking for another job.

On September 1, 1999, Sandy Nunn resigned in disgust from the U.S. Customs Service. The day she resigned, she and Darlene held a celebration. "I feel free—totally free!" Sandy exclaimed, adding: "I feel great about this decision!" Darlene found herself envying Sandy, who had already found a good job in the private sector. This inspired her to do the same. At Sandy's going away luncheon, Darlene presented her with a plaque from the Association of Customs Employees for Change that honored her "for demonstrating courage against insurmountable odds."

Two weeks later, Darlene, too, accepted a job with a good company far away from the corrosive influence of U.S. Customs. The next day, she submitted her letter of resignation along with two weeks notice to her Supervisor Lewis. Remarkably, he seemed in total shock and disbelief. He tried to talk her out of it, but her mind was made up.

"It only goes downhill from here," she told him. "If I stay on I'll either have a breakdown or somebody's going to set me up to get bumped off." Ruben waited for her back in their office. He knew her plan, inasmuch as they had discussed it thoroughly before she went ahead with it. Sadly, he read her letter of resignation. As he did, Jerry Johnston walked in.

"What's going on, folks?" Jerry asked innocently. Ruben handed Jerry the letter.

As Jerry read it, he actually dropped down into a chair and began to tear up. When he, too, was unable to talk her out of leaving, Jerry gave Darlene a big hug. "I'm really going to miss you," he said sincerely. "Who's going to give me crap and keep me straight around here?"

For her part, Darlene felt like a ship's captain abandoning her loyal crew, as though she was running away from a fight. But she knew she had made the right decision. Sadly, she began taking her pictures and wall decorations down and boxing them up along with her other personal possessions. One of these was a photo from a tanker car investigation which showed Darlene atop a rail car waving at the camera. She presented this picture to Ruben. "Hey paisano," she said, "if you miss me just take a look here and I'll always be giving you a friendly wave." She hung the snapshot on his bulletin board. Ruben was teary-eyed, too, and gave her a big hug.

"God how I wish I was going with you," he said sadly. Darlene thought to herself how scarred and chewed up they had been by Customs. At least and at long last she was leaving—but it hurt.

On September 24,1999, Darlene walked into Evantie's office for the last time. Lewis was with her as she turned in her badge, gun, bulletproof vest, and her keys. Rather than the joy Sandy had felt on leaving, Darlene just felt empty. The badge that had for so many years represented justice and honor now sat on Evantie's desk as a badge of dishonor, tarnished by managers like Drake Brinkley, Lawrence Evantie, and Harrison Wells. Lewis made another valiant try at talking her out of it, but the die was cast.

Ruben and Jerry walked Darlene out of the building and over to Ruben's car for her trip home. Jerry put his hands in his pockets, looked at her in disbelief, and said: "So that's it, huh?"

Darlene smiled at this good man. "That's it," she replied. "Like they say, it all ends not with a bang but a whimper."

"Darlene," Jerry protested, "don't do this. Let's just turn around, walk back upstairs, get your stuff back and go catch bad guys." His eyes filled with tears as Darlene took his hand in hers. He pulled her into a long hug. She thought about all the good friends she was leaving as he continued. "I'm gonna miss you, my Kentucky gal." She and Ruben got into the car and slowly pulled out of the lot. Looking back over her shoulder, Darlene saw Jerry standing there watching her go. He looked so pitiful Darlene again felt as if she'd let him and her other buddies down.

She and Ruben talked about her new job and how lucky she was to be starting a new life far away from the corruption at U.S. Customs. "I'm really happy for you," he said, and his good attitude made the trip home a lot easier. Ruben helped Darlene carry all her stuff back into her home. It was an awkwardly difficult moment for them both. They were two old warriors who each had difficulty expressing emotions other than anger. Like the cowboy pals in old westerns who come to a parting of the trails, they really didn't know how to say good-bye. For seven years they had ridden together through thick and thin, good and bad.

Now, because of relentless management abuses and sheer incompetence, they had come to the trail's end and it was over.

Ruben gave her a quick hug, told her he'd call her soon, jumped into his car and sped away. Darlene knew he was hurting and maybe thinking she'd left him all alone in the ongoing battle against the Evantie's and Brinkley's in the Customs world. She hoped in time he would see that she had to leave in order to survive. It had come down to that. She knew that what she'd miss most about leaving was the people. These included her old mentor and surrogate father figure Bob Mattivi, who had always taken time out from his busy schedule to guide her in the right direction with his good judgement and sparkling wit. She missed Jerry Johnston, her fellow kindred spirit from Kentucky. Jerry was always so gentle and soft-spoken and added calmness to any situation—something a "Type A" personality like Darlene really needed. Jerry had understood Darlene better perhaps than anyone else in the office, since their backgrounds were so similar.

Darlene also keenly missed Yolanda, the Investigative Aide. She had been like a big sister who always watched Darlene's back for her. Darlene thought back about all the laughter she had shared with Bob and Yolanda. Would she ever laugh like that again? Of course, she also missed her partner Ruben, her best friend and "big brother." Renado, too, was hard to leave, with his wonderful sense of humor and unerring street smarts. Most of all, Darlene missed an intangible quality: noble loyalty. It was this above all else that bound together the decent men and women in a big outfit like U.S. Customs, just as it had when Darlene was in the military. Noble loyalty is all the more real because it is intangible.

That night, the recurrent dream came again. Darlene was in her old Customs office where she had first worked on going to Riverside. She was joking with Ruben, Jerry, and Mattivi. She felt secure and loved. When she looked down the hallway, there was the toddler yet again. She barely recognized the child at first, for now he was no longer filthy and crying. This time he was clean and beautiful, healthy, happy, and smiling. She went to him and picked him up. He smelled wonderful with that distinct "baby smell" of talcum powder and innocence. She took a deep breath of him and closed her eyes.

When she opened them again, they were back on the farm. Everything was beautiful and brightly colored. The green grass waved in the wind, and Darlene felt a cool Spring breeze on her face. Putting the toddler down, they walked together to the top of the hill. Below them, the farm lay in a gentle valley with cows grazing in nearby pastures. Then she heard the voice of the mysterious young man with the Australian accent. "G'day mates," he said cheerily.

The young man stood below them next to an old pickup truck. Only this time, he was facing them and actually walked up to them. He had a knowing smile on his face and radiated a peaceful, almost angelic glow. The toddler tugged on Darlene's hand and, glancing toward the approaching young man, nodded his head for her to go to him. As she approached the young man, Darlene felt more and more at peace. It was as though she had known this young man all her life and was drawn to him, not in a romantic or sexual way, but as a trusted friend. For his part, the young man put peace back into Darlene's heart.

He took her hand, looked shyly into her eyes, led her to the back of the pickup truck, and picked her up and gently set her down on the back of the truck bed. Then he jumped up and sat next to her. He was wearing a flannel shirt with a green tee shirt underneath and a pair of cowboy boots. The truck began to move as they dangled their legs over the edge. It rolled gently down the hill toward a pond. Darlene never gave a thought to who was driving because it didn't matter. She felt an implicit trust toward the young man, trust she had nearly lost in the real world at Customs.

The truck stopped at the pond and backed up with the rear of the truck facing the water. The young man looked over the whole scene and said: "Isn't this beautiful?" Darlene nodded and smiled. Ducks swam over as if to greet them. The young man gave Darlene some breadcrumbs to feed them. They sat there in total peace and tranquility for what seemed like hours. The sun shone and the birds sang. The man turned to Darlene and said softly: "Everything's going to be okay, you know." She smiled back and studied his face. She wanted to remember every detail so that when she awoke and if she ever saw him again she would recognize him. He was ruggedly handsome and she placed her hand atop his.

"Thank you," she said at last.

He looked at her and smiled, his deep blue eyes sparkling: "You're going to be all right, mate," he said. "Everything's going to be all right." For the moment, the young man was right. For the first time in years everything really was all right. But there was another storm coming, even if there weren't yet any dark clouds in Darlene's dream.

29

Trial By Ordeal

"Injustice anywhere is a threat to justice everywhere"
Reverend Martin Luther King, Jr.

Flash forward to 2005. It had been eight years since the first complaints were filed against U.S. Customs in this EEO case, six years since Darlene had left Customs, and over three years since the attack on America on September 11, 2001. The lawsuit entitled "Fitzgerald-Nunn versus Department of Homeland Security," which had been filed in federal court years earlier, was snaking its way toward trial. But the judges who were to preside over the case kept changing. The process was like a weird variation of the "Whack-A-Mole" video game. Every time it looked like the case would finally get in front of a jury, the judge would be replaced by another and the whole pre-trial process would begin again.

Darlene had finally left Customs back in 1999. The stress of being a federal whistleblower and operating without any legal protection against retaliation had taken its toll. The case kept dragging expensively on, which was undoubtedly the point. Darlene, Sandy and their whole team were getting their energy and finances eroded by the Chinese Water-Drip Torture courtesy of Uncle Sam's gang. This abuse of the legal process began taking a wider toll. Darlene's phone rang. It was former Customs Officer John Carman.

"Are you sitting down?" he asked.

"Okay, John, I'm sitting. What's up?"

"Gary Webb is dead." Darlene was stunned. Gary Webb had been a friend and an outstanding investigative reporter whose groundbreaking newspaper articles on government corruption had led to the publishing of a book on the subject called "Dark Alliance." In it, Webb skillfully established an unholy relationship between government officials, the CIA and the multi-billion dollar narcotics trade in this country.

"Dead? How? What happened?" she managed to ask.

"They say it was a suicide," Carman said in voice tinged with doubt. "What do you think? Was he depressed the last time you saw him?"

"I didn't think so," Darlene answered. She had first met Webb right after her book "U.S. Customs: Badge of Dishonor" had come out. She'd been on some television shows talking about the book and met Gary at a promotional function. He had been very interested in hearing about her tanker car case—Operation Rite Rail—and about the implication that tanker cars could also be used to deliver weapons of mass destruction by terrorists. "It was weird," Darlene recalled. "After our books came out, we were both swamped with letters, emails, phone calls and stuff from people in the so-called "War On Drugs" who were having similar hassles and experiencing the same kind of retaliation we had. We knew then that this thing was much, much bigger than we had ever thought in our wildest dreams."

"What'd Gary say about how he was feeling?" Carman asked.

"I thought he was excited and upbeat. We both realized we had enough material for another whole book on the cronyism and corruption in several areas of federal law enforcement and on what this might mean with respect to national security. I got the distinct impression he was already working on his next book."

"Another book?"

"Yeah."

"Do people who are excited about writing a new book commit suicide?" John wondered. "I mean, aren't they usually up and enthusiastic?"

"You'd think so," Darlene replied. But over the next several days, Darlene and John got information that made Gary's suicide a more real possibility. After the CIA had publicly denied Gary's thesis, the newspapers simply accepted their denial and that's all she wrote. Gary was isolated and hung out to dry. His friends and associates didn't back him up. That will depress anyone. Darlene knew all too well how Gary could have felt betrayed and that betrayal is one of the most depressing things that can happen to you. People who know and saw important details suddenly can't remember what they saw or heard. Witnesses to abuse and retaliation are intimidated into silence. Job opportunities dry up as former bosses and managers tell your prospective employers bad things so they won't hire you. Even some family members become uncomfortable around you—all for trying to fix something that's broken. The ultimate cost of such courage can be as high as one's life, and there are enough corpses around the illegal drug trade to fill the Arlington National Cemetery.

The deaths of men like Gary Webb by his own hand and attorney/investigator Jason Fielding at the hands of an assassin must be weighed against the background in which they died.

"I'd say Gary's was a constructive suicide, that is if he really did take his life," Darlene told John a few days later. "Just like our resignations were a constructive discharge. Gary was a whistleblower like us in a way, and he suffered for it big time."

"Yes, I can see that," Carman said, "but what a waste of talent."

"Amen to that, brother."

On February 28, 2005, jury selection on Darlene's lawsuit began in San Diego Federal District Court. It didn't take long. There really isn't much in the way of examining potential jurors, what lawyers call Voir Dire, as there is in other jury cases. It's basically the luck of the draw. The attorneys representing Darlene and company were Gastone Bebi and Jack Stennett. The trial lasted three weeks and made history when Superior Court Judge and former AUSA Yvette Palazuelos took the stand and testified against U.S. Customs. That was the first time in history that a Judge had testified against the U.S. Government. Fitzgerald-Nunn vs. Department of Homeland Security was thus a landmark case.

One of the reasons Darlene had been given by Customs management for pulling the plug on her tanker car case was lack of funds. If this was true, how is it that throughout the entire trial the well-paid SAIC/LA (Special Agent In Charge of the L.A. Office) Lisa Black sat with the defense team. If the government could afford to have this high-ranking official earning more than $100,000 per year sit idly for three weeks, don't you think they could have funded a project which had already interdicted a huge amount of drugs and was poised to interdict even more? It made for a peculiar scene. At the defense table were two Assistant U.S. Attorneys—Jester and Thelma Ikel. With them was a Customs Regional Council attorney. And joining them for no apparent reason other than window dressing was Homeland Security's top dog for the entire L.A. region, which runs from Oxnard, a city north of Los Angeles, to Las Vegas to the Arizona border to San Diego. One would think Lisa Black would have more important things to do for Homeland Security than twiddle her thumbs in a San Diego courtroom for three weeks.

Defense attorney Jester's method of defense of Customs was nothing more than a protracted bout of mud slinging. He did everything possible to attack Darlene's character and personal integrity. In trying to attack the threatening letter Darlene had received in 1999, he accused Darlene of having a torrid past. What was the evidence of this? She had foolishly and many years earlier let an ex-husband take nude photographs of her. It was a dumb thing for Darlene to have done, but it hardly qualifies as a torrid past. Further, it took a lot of guts for Darlene not to allow herself to be blackmailed into dropping her case and shutting up. She knew that all she had to do is settle the case, take the money and this would all just go away. But Darlene and Sandy weren't just interested in winning. They wanted the truth to come out—the whole truth! That's what the justice system was supposed to do. This would not be the case.

That was it—Jester's totally lame defense response to the threatening letter someone had mailed to Darlene. It was a dismal performance by Jester, one that didn't seem to generate a very sympathetic response from the jury. Then he switched gears, and while Darlene remained on the witness stand he handed her a "document" which purported that she had nothing to do with Operation Lite Rail, the tanker car case she had worked on for so long. It could have been a real "Aha!" moment from a Perry Mason melodrama—the crucial evidence. Only it wasn't.

When Darlene and Sandy Nunn went to lunch, Sandy had her first opportunity to look the new piece of "evidence" over closely. Sandy had been a former Immigration and Naturalization Agent who had worked extensively on the Fraudulent Documents Task Force. Jester couldn't have picked a worse adversary to spring his surprise on. After a careful examination, Sandy showed Darlene why she was convinced the document wasn't genuine. Lunch over, Darlene again found herself on the stand in court, only this time it was her side's attorney who was asking the questions.

"What's wrong with this document?" Gastone began.

"There are numerous things wrong with it. First, all official government documents are written on letterhead stationery. No exceptions. This one isn't. This is supposed to be the approved proposal for the Think Tank's Light Rail Project. Not only isn't it on letterhead but it doesn't even have a file number."

"Is that unusual?"

"All official documents have file numbers."

"What else?" Gastone asked.

"This document contains a lot of sensitive information. By federal law and Customs regulations, it should therefore also have a FOUO stamp—"

"FOUO?"

"For Official Use Only. Real documents like this always have that stamp. And most of all, there is no approving individual on this document anywhere, no signature block, and no authentication. This thing looks like somebody just typed it up on their home computer. And why are we just suddenly seeing this today?

Discovery (where the defendant and plaintiff must show the evidence they will present in court) on this case was over almost a year ago. Why didn't Mr. Jester produce this in discovery so we could have a chance to authenticate it?"

During her testimony, Darlene could see the presiding Judge Quinterez looking over her shoulder as she pointed out the glaring defects in this trumped-up piece of "evidence." Darlene smiled contemptuously over at Jester and there were some jurors who actually broke out laughing at his clumsy attempt at deception. Two and a half days after she began, Darlene finished on the witness stand. By everybody's reactions she had clearly damaged Jester's defense and he had failed to impeach her credibility.

True to form, Jester tried the same mud-slinging tactics when Sandy Nunn took the stand. Jester told the court that Sandy was "crazy." She had been pulled off duty, he said, and had her gun taken away. The clincher was that during an interview, Sandy was observed taking notes without benefit of paper or pencil. This truth-twisting was straightened out as the jury learned that in fact Sandy had taken sick leave, which was why she turned in her weapon. As to the note-taking example, Jester was unable to produce a single witness or corroboration of any kind to back up that particular lie. In addition, Darlene and Sandy's team proved that when she returned from sick leave, Sandy's gun was returned to her and she got right back into her assignment for Secret Service training, learning how to protect Heads of State and also Presidential candidates in the upcoming 2000 elections. The Secret Service doesn't train crazy people to protect Presidential candidates. But the jury heard the mud.

The other bit of character defamation Jester was able to get before the jury involved Sandy declaring bankruptcy back in the 1980's. This had nothing to do with the case at hand. In fact, the jury subsequently learned that Sandy and several others had been the victims of an embezzler who had taken them for thousands of dollars. It was Sandy's cooperation with the FBI which helped them catch the embezzler and lock him up. But the cumulative effect that Jester hoped for was that the jury would forget the facts and be left with a bad taste in their mouths with respect to Sandy and Darlene. This is what you do when you don't have a case—lawyering at its most under-handed. It has nothing to do with the facts of a case. It's just mud, and lawyers only do this because sometimes it works.

Darlene's old nemesis Lawrence Evantie took the stand next. His first misstep was in admitting under oath that he had in fact stopped Bob Mattivi and Darlene from checking 25 to 40 Tons of contraband in five railroad cars. This was a far cry from his deposition, in which he "couldn't recall" anything about these five cars. Magically his memory had been restored at the trial. But now Evantie cited reasons for shutting the investigation down.

First, he claimed the government didn't have the money. He said that the first tanker car seizure had cost something like ten thousand dollars and he got chewed out for it. Under cross-examination, Evantie revealed that eight thousand pounds of marijuana and thirty-four kilos of pure cocaine were seized. He even admitted that the Acting Commissioner of Customs had actually praised Darlene in Evantie's presence for her outstanding work. That was hardly a condemnation the jury heard.

Veteran Senior Special Agent Bob Mattivi later testified that he had been on many wiretap investigations in which hundreds of thousands of dollars were spent with no results. His testimony in support of Darlene's case was backed up by several other agents. In the face of all this rebuttal, Evantie took another tack. He stated that pressure testing tanker cars wasn't Customs' job, it was the Customs inspectors duty. This, too, was debunked by both Mattivi and Senior Inspector Rios. All the different law enforcement members were already on board the "jump team" which had been assembled as part of Darlene's Operation Lite Rail. Rios went on to testify that it had been Evantie who had interfered with not only the Special Agents, but the inspectors as well when they tried to check these tanker cars.

One of the excuses raised by the defense (Customs) in this EEO case was their application of statistics or "stats" against the plaintiffs (Darlene and Sandy). These stats are listings of the arrests, seizures and indictments an agent has documented in the Treasury Enforcement Computer System (TECS). The defense cited these stats in explaining why they force-transferred Sandy and failed to promote Darlene.

"Mr. Evantie," Gastone said, "there has been a lot of testimony in this case of just how important stats are to agents as far as (obtaining) promotions and assignments. And there has been a lot of evidence that stats are very important to managers and their office, wouldn't you agree?"

"Yes," Evantie replied.

"Now Mr. Evantie, wouldn't a seizure of, oh, say twenty-five to forty tons of marijuana be a stat that would bring a lot of recognition and help for your office?"

"Yes."

"Well, how about twenty-five to forty tons of cocaine, wouldn't that be a statistic that would really make you look good, and help you and your office in promotions and things like that?"

"Yes."

"Yet you wouldn't even let Darlene and Mattivi go to the rail yard and pressure test these five tanker cars with twenty-five to forty tons of contraband For Free, would you?"

"No," Evantie replied arrogantly. This reply shocked the jury, whose gasps of surprise at his admission reverberated in the packed court room.

"I have no further questions of this witness, your honor," Gastone concluded.

The judge stared at Evantie with amazement at what he had just said. For his part, Evantie shrugged his shoulders in a "What did I do?" gesture. It was all pretty ludicrous. Afterwards, Evantie was seen rushing outside, where he puffed furiously on a cigarette while talking frantically on his cell phone with somebody.

The Honorable Yvette Pulazuelos, who had formerly been the Assistant U.S. Attorney (AUSA) on the Rite Rail case, corroborated Darlene's testimony, including the thwarting of a controlled delivery of a loaded tanker car. Yvette also confirmed the blocked checking of twenty-five to forty tons of contraband in the following five sequestered tanker cars, the lack of support Darlene got from her superiors, and the interference with the inspectors and agents on this case. Most tellingly, she informed the court of the stunning reply she got when she asked former Group Supervisor Lewis Cohen who it was who was torpedoing the Lite Rail Project. "Drake Brinkley," was the answer she said Lewis Cohen had given. This was a crucial piece of the puzzle which undergirded the whole basis of Darlene and Sandy's case. It was a Superior Court Judge telling the jury this in historic testimony against U.S. Customs.

There had been an agreement ordered by a previous Federal Court Judge to both sides in this case that the names of cooperating witnesses would not be revealed. The obvious reason for this order of inadmissability was to close the avenue for further retaliation against them by their employers. Since there is no federal whistleblower protection, it was vitally important that those who came forward to tell their stories in this case be assured that they weren't committing career suicide by their actions. Without that protection, it would have been even more difficult to get at the truth than it already was.

Yet in spite of this important order, both of the defendants' co-counsels—AUSA Thelma Ikel and Jester himself—committed a felony by doing just that. During Yvette Pulazuelos' testimony, they released Grand Jury information containing the name of a cooperating witness, literally endangering their life. Judge Pulazuelos was shocked at this action, as was the presiding Judge Quinterez. Darlene reported this unprofessional and illegal breach of confidentiality by these two attorneys to the California Bar Association.

To date, nothing has been done about it, even though the law as stated in a U.S. Supreme Court decision (Berger vs. United States) directs US Attorneys to conduct themselves in such a way that "the guilty shall not escape and the innocent shall not suffer."

Ruben Sandoval was the next witness to take the stand. He testified to the angry confrontation he had with David Gray which Darlene had witnessed. Later, when David Gray took the stand, he denied under oath that this ever took place. Ruben also testified to the hostile work environment, the retaliation, and the overt favoritism management engaged in. He also confirmed that Evantie was improperly interfering in Darlene's rail case and that he had received a letter from Customs Regional Counsel Monica Glass threatening to have him transferred or fired just two days before he was called to give a deposition on this very case.

"Customs was definitely trying to send me a message," he declared.

The next witness on the stand was Renado Giannini. He also confirmed that Evantie had impeded the rail project and hadn't allowed the pressure-testing of the five suspicious tanker cars at no cost to the government. He stated that Darlene had brought him the manifests on these cars, that he had taken them to the San Bernardino Sheriff's Department, and that before they could proceed with the investigation these tanker cars were released uninspected into the commerce of America. This was no blunder, but instead had been done by design. Why didn't Evantie and others want these cars inspected? Isn't that what Customs is supposed to do to protect the American people from what bad guys want to bring across our borders?

But Renado had more to say. He relayed to the court what he had heard while riding in a car with Lewis Cohen, specifically that Drake Brinkley was torpedoing the rail project. He also confirmed what Yvette had testified to about Lewis Cohen admitting Brinkley's role in undermining the rail project.

Bob Mattivi was the next witness and he confirmed in detail all that had been said about the case so far from the prosecution's point of view. This included everything revealed about the Lite Rail Case and also the importance of "stats" in the promotion of Customs agents. Mattivi further explained that stats can be deceiving, such as when an agent spends a long time on a case that doesn't immediately pan out and there is a resultant gap in the favorable stats management uses to promote.

When Irvin Rios took the stand after Mattivi, the jury heard more confirmation on Darlene and Sandy's side, along with making it clear that it had been Darlene who had begun Operation Lite Rail and that the so-called Think Tank Lite Rail only existed After the work had been done by Darlene, Rios, Renado,

Ruben, and then AUSA Palazuelos. Rios emphasized that Darlene had begun the Lite Rail Operation back in 1994. That date put Darlene's work years ahead of the so-called Think Tank operation which the government was claiming spearheaded Operation Lite Rail. Rios stated that this Think Tank had gotten most of its information and even its name from Darlene's operation.

It was further pointed out that SAIC/LA management's excuse for not crediting the work done by Darlene's group was that they hadn't done it. Instead, the government tried to insist that it had been a Frank Welsh who had supervised the project. Yet the government failed to produce Mr. Welsh or a single document to prove his alleged work on the operation. In addition, in a prior deposition, Drake Brinkley had asserted that Frank Welsh never worked on a rail project. Brinkley had stated that the only person he knew of in the entire L.A. region working on such a rail project was the plaintiff—Darlene Fitzgerald!

Lisa Black was called to the stand next, and just about fell apart under cross-examination. Here was Customs' and therefore Homeland Security's senior official in the L.A. Region telling the jury that Evantie did nothing wrong by blocking the free pressure testing examination of the five very suspicious tanker cars.

"Now Ms. Black," Gastone said, "there has been testimony here that one of the reasons that Darlene wasn't allowed to pressure test those tanker cars for free was that it wasn't her job—it was the inspectors job. But isn't it true that there are occasions where inspectors and agents work hand in hand as a team and tackle a project together. They work together and share the credit and everybody looks good and everybody's happy. Isn't that right, Ms. Black?"

"Yes," Lisa Black replied.

"But you didn't let that happen in this case, did you?"

"No."

During her testimony, Black also revealed that when she first took over the SAIC/LA job, out of thousands of approved ROI's (Reports of Investigations), the only ones she sent back with little negative notes on them came from the only two people in RAIC/RV who had filed EEO complaints—Ruben and Darlene. Why was she going over already approved ROI's from two agents who had filed complaints instead of doing her job and getting into the field to meet the agents under her command first hand? Was checking grammar in previously approved reports the most important work she could find to do? She was unable to provide satisfactory answers to these questions.

This kind of action from a key Homeland Security official was simply appalling. One observing attorney noted: "God, the fact that she's the head dog out there is really scary. No wonder "9-11" happened, when you have morons like this running things."

It confirmed Darlene's long held belief that the only women who advance in Customs to high levels are numbskulls who would never challenge the wrongdoings they witness by their male counterparts or superiors. Ms. Black had somehow managed to go from being a Secretary to SAIC in a flash. It's like the Mafia—you kiss the Don's ring and you'll go far. The key is control. Management won't promote women who challenge the status quo. This is how the Old Boys Club sustains itself.

Drake Brinkley took the stand next. The first thing Gastone did with this witness was demonstrate that he had lied in a previous deposition by claiming he had a four year college degree. "That is your testimony under oath in this deposition, is it not?"

"Yes."

"And you knew when you gave this testimony it was under oath under penalty of perjury, did you not?"

"Yes."

"And you knew full well," Gastone continued, "that when you answered all of these questions about having a B.A degree, you knew exactly what you were talking about, didn't you?"

"Yes." Drake Brinkley began shifting uneasily in his seat, knowing where this line of questioning was going.

"You don't have a B.S. or B.A. degree do you, Mr. Brinkley?"

"No," Brinkley answered, admitting to perjury. Brinkley then went on to state that Frank Welsh wasn't working anything with rail, and that as SAIC at the time he would certainly have known if he was. So much for the Think Tank Lite Rail baloney. In addition, Brinkley inadvertently supported Darlene's claim of retaliation when he asserted that there had in fact been a loaner car available when Darlene's was breaking down and that Evantie should have assigned it to her.

Drake Brinkley revealed himself to be a liar again when he stated that he knew nothing about the five tanker cars with an estimated 25 to 40 tons of contraband. He even claimed to have known nothing of the well-publicized demonstration by agents in front of the RAIC/Riverside Office. This from a man who also stated that his subordinate managers did a good job of keeping him informed about what was going on in all their groups. How could he not have known about potentially the largest seizure of narcotics on record sitting right in the middle of his jurisdiction? It defied logic and confirmed Brinkley as an incorrigible liar.

Darlene's former Group Supervisor Lewis Cohen was next. Of all the government's witnesses, Lewis probably came off the best. Still, he confirmed what Darlene and Sandy had learned after hiring the Documented Reference Check company to ascertain just what their former managers at Customs were telling prospective employers as they were out looking for work. This company uses certified court reporters to write down what potential employers were being told about Darlene and Sandy. The transcripts showed that Mr. Cohen had made statements which would certainly have raised "red flags" with someone considering hiring the resigned agents. In answer to the question "Would you hire Darlene back" he replied: "Only as an Intel Analyst." An Intel Analyst is a much lower position than a Special Agent. It is a job which pays and promotes at a lower level. This answer is in stark contrast to what employers want to hear, namely that an employee would be hired back in a second. So it was documented that in fact the retaliation against Darlene reached well beyond her former job at Customs.

Yet when Gastone asked him what kind of agent Darlene had been, he answered: "Darlene was a very good agent. She was very passionate about her work, and the kind of agent you'd want to have cover your back in the field." How does that square with what he had said to the Documented Reference Check Company? It didn't.

The next witness the government produced was Group Supervisor Denise Kelley. Ruben, Sandy, and Darlene had all told the jury that Denise had mentioned some bias or shenanigans with the pretext promotion board which had passed them over for promotion. Denise should have known, since she sat on that board. Denise had set up a meeting for Darlene, Ruben and Sandy with her attorney Dan Moss. As she related all of this, Denise became visibly nervous and denied ever having stated there had been irregularities at the pretext promotion board with respect to the "troublemakers." Gastone tried to pin her down. "Now Ms. Kelley," he said, "you knew that if you file a complaint against Customs that they retaliate against you, now didn't you?"

"No," she replied shakily.

"You filed your own EEO complaint, and then joined a class action lawsuit for retaliation, didn't you?"

"Well, I joined a class action, and retaliation was one of the issues raised, but that's not why I joined." Kelley was shifting nervously in her seat, having admitted joining a class action lawsuit against Customs in which retaliation was an issue yet not wanting to displease her boss SAIC Lisa Black, who was sitting directly in front of her. All evidence of wrongdoing by the pretext promotion board was, the government later claimed, either lost or refused to be provided.

Kelley wasn't finished spinning her yarn yet. "Had there been more slots for our office, then Edwin Easel (the weasel) would have been promoted into them and not Ruben or Darlene." This proved to be a complete and utter falsehood. Under the rules of the Department of Treasury Office of Personnel Management, agents have to have at least one year in grade as a GS12 in order to even be considered for a GS13 promotion. At the 1996 promotion board, where Kelley denied any irregularities, Easel was a mere GS11 and was therefore not even eligible for promotion to GS13. The jury understood the significance of such monkey business, even if Kelley denied it.

This was and continues to be the rule of cronyism which has trumped putting the best people in place from Customs Agents to the head of the Federal Emergency Management Agency—FEMA—in the debacle following hurricane Katrina's devastation of the Gulf Coast in 2005. It helps account for why the unqualified rise to such high levels in our government, and at worst it costs lives and threatens national security.

Mark Conrad, a retired Customs manager and former SAIC in Texas, came next. He revealed that in a conversation he had with the then Assistant Special Agent In Charge/L.A.—Stephen Phillsberry—that the latter admitted that suspending Sandy Nunn for three days had been "heavy handed" but that nothing could be done about it because "this decision is coming from up above."

He was followed by two brave women: Shannon Getz and Janet Somers. Their bravery was displayed by their testifying against the Department of Homeland Security even as they were employed there. They had the guts to swear to the severe retaliation they had witnessed by managers whenever an agent files a complaint. Defense attorney Jester had tried very hard in court to keep these highly damaging (to his defense) witnesses from taking the stand. He lost that fight, and the testimony they provided did a lot to bolster Darlene and Sandy's case.

In his closing statement, Jester repeatedly misrepresented what the judge and jury had heard, twisting the truth in an attempt to confuse the jury and fill them with doubt. The fact was that on the stand, witnesses for the government repeatedly claimed that they had lost or misplaced documents, although only documents which would have helped the plaintiffs' case: notes relating to the devious performance of the promotion board, Sandy Nunn's personnel file, the list went on and on. In addition, it was clear that Internal Affairs, the Customs goon squad, had never launched an investigation into what became of what was not only crucial pieces of evidence, but were "Classified Documents" as well. Somehow it all had magically disappeared and nobody tried to find out why.

This is what was presented before Judge Quinterez and the jury at this historic trial. It included what amounts to Lawrence Evantie's admission of facilitating 25 to 40 tons of contraband into this country. Whether or not such egregious conduct will ever be investigated by the government remains an open question. Still, almost all who observed this trial were absolutely convinced that Darlene and Sandy had won their case.

30

What The Jury Didn't Hear

"You want the truth? You can't handle the truth!"
Jack Nicholson from the movie "A Few Good Men"

In one of the famous Sherlock Holmes stories, a key piece of information involved a dog which was on a crime scene but didn't bark. In many ways, what was excluded in the course of the "Fitzgerald-Nunn vs. Dept. of Homeland Security" trial was more important than the evidence which was let in. First among these discarded elements was the statement made by Drake Brinkley at a Palm Springs, California, managers meeting.

In a quote supported by several different sources, what those managers heard Brinkley say was: "Anyone who files complaints against Customs is disloyal and should be treated as such. We will fight these complaints to the bitter end—them (the complainers) and their shyster lawyers." In that brief outburst, Brinkley laid his cards on the table and the assembled managers took notice. You simply cannot fight corruption without top down support, and Drake Brinkley was letting his team know that dissent in the face of wrongdoing would not be tolerated. Why would he do this?

The old Italian saying that "the fish dies from the head on down" applies neatly to U.S. Customs. If those at the top abuse the self-policing system embodied by Internal Affairs, turning that unit into a goon squad to punish those who see and report corruption, then, as they said in the movie "Ghostbusters," who you gonna call? The jury never got to hear that the top man was squaring off and using his considerable authority to punish any whistleblowers in Customs. It is fair to say that every act of retaliation and abuse against Darlene and the others was orchestrated directly or indirectly by Drake Brinkley. Being prevented from establishing the root cause of the harassment was a terrible blow against Darlene's team. That a judge would rule out the many witnesses and mountains of documentary evidence of this corruption boggles the mind, but that is what happened.

As to Drake Brinkley's motivation for attacking those who report wrongdoing in his agency, there can be only two possible explanations. The first is that such housecleaning as is required involves acknowledging that the problem is in fact there. This makes a weak manager feel threatened for what has occurred on his watch. This weakness leads such a manager to do what the ancient Greeks used to do: kill the messenger who brings bad news. It doesn't take long for the effect this approach has to spread around the agency.

The result is that those who see corruption and wrongdoing look the other way for fear of retaliation by their superiors and losing their jobs. Remember that law enforcement, particularly when it involves powerful criminal cartels, is a deadly business. An agent cannot effectively face a threat in front of him if he also has a threat coming from behind.

The second explanation for attacking whistleblowers is far more sinister. It is an indication that person or persons in management are in cahoots with the bad guys. The money involved in the narcotics trade is simply staggering. Even a tiny piece of a multi-billion dollar enterprise is huge. When you combine that money with the credible threats of harm or death that accompany it, you have a perfect formula for entrenched corruption of the kind which is present at the highest levels of parts of our government. "Follow the money," Sherlock Holmes wisely once said, and he was right.

Perhaps the saddest aspect of this situation is the reality that many of those empowered to change the way things are have absolutely no incentive to do so. They are precisely the ones who will be hurt by affording federal whistleblowers a legal defense against retaliation. Therefore such legislation is definitely not in their interest. It may be that such a change will only come about when the status quo leads to a devastating attack along the lines of—but much larger than—what we got on September 11, 2001. It's like making someone go through a head-on collision with a Mack truck before they start fastening their seat belts. Nobody loyal to America wants another "9-11" disaster. Will we really have to wait for one before our elected leaders and their appointees take action?

The jury never got to learn about the photo's and testimony concerning the surveillance pole cameras which were placed around Ruben's house the day after Darlene had received her threatening letter. Nor did the jury hear about the surveillance perpetrated on Darlene and the others by Customs Internal Affairs. It's important to remember that a lot of that surveillance was done with such clumsiness that the conclusion is that IA wanted those surveilled to be aware of it. When you keep tabs on someone discreetly, as Darlene often had against criminals and suspects, it is expressly for the purpose of learning more about their criminal activity. When, on the other hand, that surveillance is done so openly that the subject cannot help but see it going on, then the purpose becomes harassment. The message being sent is that one is not wanted, has been deemed an enemy, and can no longer be a trusted member of the team. This is crucial because modern law enforcement, unlike what movie Westerns would have you believe, is very much a team effort. A cop is only as protected as the weakest link in his team's chain. The bad guys don't like being charged and convicted of crimes. They have friends who are patient. Revenge, the Sicilians say, is a dish best eaten cold. An isolated cop is easy pickings. You get the picture.

Another piece of excluded evidence was the wrongful arrest of former Customs officer turned whistleblower John Carman. It had been Carman who had set up the meeting between seven Customs whistleblowers and the FBI agent from the public corruptions unit. That's where the suspected corruption was laid out by Darlene and the others. Also discussed was the terrorist threat that the railroad tanker cars posed. After the meeting, those present saw that they were being tailed by IA. Then John Carman was arrested by local cops at the direction of Customs IA. This arrest occurred in front of Carman's daughter, adding to the humiliation. The trumped-up charges were so flimsy they didn't even get past arraignment and were immediately dismissed. There were depositions from those same arresting officers which admitted this. That the FBI never pursued any of these phony charges was also not allowed into the case.

There also was the well-documented fact that Darlene's former Customs Group Supervisor Ivan Winkowsky had covered up for his two cronies Edwin Easel (the weasel) and Peter Blake after they had taken heroin evidence home one night instead of properly storing it in the evidence safe at Customs. The significance of this bit of cover-up was that it enabled Easel and Blake to be promoted over Ruben and Darlene. What can one say about such behavior? Why wasn't the jury allowed to hear this?

The absence of both the witness Frank Welsh and any evidence proving the government's contention that it was Welsh and not Darlene who had led Operation Lite Rail—the tanker car case—was another glaring detail the jury was kept from hearing. The same could be said of not allowing the above-mentioned Ivan Winkowsky to be placed on the stand. In addition, Darlene's team was restrained from producing evidence and witnesses with respect to over one hundred more suspicious tanker cars. Someone had gone into the TECS computer system and had overridden the holds Darlene had placed against the companies involved. These companies were connected to the outfit controlling the cars which held

8000 pounds of marijuana and 34 kilos of cocaine. Yet all of this was ruled "irrelevant" and "collateral."

An issue of profound importance in this trial was witness tampering. As an example, when Irvin Rios received his subpoena, he took it to both his supervisor and the Port Director. They gave him the green light to testify. Then he got an email from Customs Regional Counsel, the attorney Monica Glass, which gave him the opposite directive. She made it clear in that email that testifying against Customs would have a drastic effect on his career. When he got this notice, Rios immediately—and bravely—notified Darlene's legal team. The following day jury selection began. When Darlene's lawyer Gastone Bebi informed the Judge about the email, Quinterez became incensed. Judge Quinterez immediately demanded that the defense team get to the bottom of this.

"I don't like this!" the judge barked. "This smells. I want to know why the government doesn't want one of their employees to testify."

"We'll get to the bottom of this, Your Honor," defense lawyer Jester answered, even as he stumbled backwards as if the judge's anger was pushing him across the room.

"You do that," the judge replied. "I want to hear what Mr. Rios has to say." The sad fact is that nothing more came of this. During the course of the trial, Darlene's team received numerous frantic phone calls from Customs and Department of Homeland Security people telling how management had put out the word that all employees better watch what they say in front of Judge Quinterez. You could not find a clearer example of witness tampering than this. It's too bad the jury never learned of it.

One of the most important pieces of evidence withheld was an audit released by the Treasury Inspector General's Office in May of 1999. Among many other things, this report stated that Customs had created "a fear of reprisals" against employees who complained about wrongdoing and that Customs Internal Affairs so mishandled investigations that wayward agents were neither disciplined nor prosecuted. This gets right back to Easel and Blake and all the others who got away with misdeeds within Customs. Even though this report was six years old and had been given to all members of Congress and the Senate, as well as having been widely quoted in the press, it was ruled inadmissible in the trial.

That Customs has been rolled into the Department of Homeland Security created another problem. It is that the criminally malicious management style of Customs has spread through the DHS like a cancer, infecting all the other agencies in DHS as well. Darlene considers this Treasury Inspector General's report the most damning of all the evidence the jury wasn't allowed to hear. It was a report like this that seems the most likely reason the lawyer/investigator Jason Fielding was gunned down in his driveway. Whatever Fielding had uncovered—and we'll never know what that was—was deemed so dangerous by someone that Fielding paid for it with his life.

Prevented from testifying were several high-ranking managers within Customs. Chief among these was how Mark Conrad's (former Special Agent In Charge of Customs Internal Affairs) testimony was severely limited. Better than anyone, Conrad was in a position to demonstrate the "Pattern and Practice" of the IA as Customs' goon squad. He would have been able to show that this retaliation and harassment went all the way up to the Commissioner of Customs himself—Raymond Kelley. Yet all of this potentially damning testimony was ruled inadmissable.

Darlene and Sandy's prosecution team had as well a deposition wherein the former Acting Commissioner of Customs had stated something remarkable. He swore that at a managers conference in Washington, D.C., Ray Kelley had given a speech in which he made derogatory and threatening remarks against anyone who files a complaint against Customs. Drake Brinkley attended this meeting, and it doesn't take a genius to connect the dots about where Brinkley's arrogant attack against whistleblowers came from, and why Brinkley knew he could act with impunity. All of this points directly at how the climate of retaliation originated—yet it was ruled inadmissable. Where is Raymond Kelley today? As of this writing, he is the Commissioner of the New York City Police Department. There is solid evidence that Kelley was also among the top contenders being considered by President George W. Bush to head up the Department of Homeland Security.

Notwithstanding the mountain of evidence, depositions, witnesses and other material which the judge refused to let the jury hear, one would think that the jury should still have been able to see through the web of lies and intimidation undergirding the government's defense in this case. Darlene, Sandy, and the entire team sat on pins and needles while the jury went off to deliberate and arrive at a verdict. Both Gastone Bebi and Jack Stennett, along with numerous other observers and attorneys who followed the trial closely over its three week run, were confident of victory.

On March 17, 2005, the jury returned a verdict finding in favor of U.S. Customs and the Department of Homeland Security and against Darlene and Sandy.

31

The End And The Beginning

"We have met the enemy and it is us!"
Walt Kelly's Comic Strip Character POGO

When the jury had brought in their verdict, finding in favor of Customs and against the whistleblowers, everyone else in the courtroom was surprised. The government lawyers seemed as stunned by their victory as the plaintiffs were by their defeat. Even the judge sat speechless. For a moment, time simply stood still. Then the lawyers gathered up their papers and everyone filed out of the packed courtroom. What else was there to say?

It was over. "This is the way the world ends," T.S. Eliot wrote in "The Hollow Men", "not with a bang but a whimper."

Later that evening, Darlene and some of the plaintiff team were able to speak with the jury foreman. "Almost the entire jury wanted to find for you," he told them. "But we couldn't because the judge's instructions were too limiting."

"How do you mean?" Darlene asked.

"It was like trying to fit a square peg in a round hole. Most people are too naive about the government. They want to believe that their government is protecting them. Frankly, it's easier to remain ignorant than it is to face the fear that our government could behave the way you said it had."

"Did the members of the jury think there was corruption?" Darlene wondered.

"Oh yes. That's one of the reasons the jury kept going off in different directions during the deliberation process. But we kept coming back to the judge's instructions to us, and based on those we couldn't find against the government."

Then Darlene and the others told the foreman about the evidence they weren't allowed to hear. He was shocked. "I can't speak for all the others," he said sadly, "but knowing what you just revealed would have made a huge difference in my ultimate decision." By the time he had heard all of the details, he was visibly shaken. "Man, you're scaring me! How do you expect me to sleep tonight?" He then offered to write a statement that he thought might be of use in filing an appeal. After a pause, he said something Darlene and the others found absolutely amazing. It was a thought connected to the whole process Darlene and the others in Customs were engaged in when it came to stopping tanker cars and the like from entering the country with contraband. "Well," he said, "all of us want to have our cheap Sony DVD players and TV sets. You just can't stop the flow of commerce in the way that you need to in order to effect a real war on drugs. You can't have effective border security." The jury foreman looked sadly around the room as if he, too, was beginning to grasp the significance of what he had just said.

Darlene thought about his remark. Part of her wanted to throttle the guy for the ease with which he and apparently others on the jury were willing to keep the borders open and unprotected if it meant cheap prices. On the other hand, she knew she was going to go home and begin writing about this whole mess on an inexpensive computer she bought at Wal-Mart. There's the rub. The question is really about how to maintain the steady flow of goods into this country without sacrificing national security to do it. The answer is that you probably can't have both. It's more like trying to decide which is more important—your money or your life.

As disappointed as she was at losing the case, Darlene took a little satisfaction in having gotten the case in front of a judge and jury in Federal Court. Only 2% of EEO cases filed ever get that far, and this was the very first case to have any whistleblower issues tried in Federal Court. This trial had shone a spotlight on some real lowlifes who, unfortunately, are part of the team that's supposed to safeguard this nation's borders from terrorist and narco traffickers and their support systems. The court record for this case is there for all to see, should anyone care to look. And an accounting of what led up to this case, how it evolved, and what the facts reveal is at the heart of this book.

Sandy Nunn had kept her grave side promise to her father to carry the fight forward.

So what if the verdict was wrong, as long as the fight for the truth doesn't end there? What remains at stake is our national security. The people who grow the poppies in Afghanistan which makes 87% of the world's heroin and opium do so under the watchful eye of the Taliban. For their part, the Taliban operates along side Al Qaeda, the folks who brought us "9-11." The very same delivery system used to smuggle drugs into this country could and may well be used to bring in a weapon of mass destruction. Darlene's co-plaintiff Sandy Nunn did a full investigation into this possibility after receiving special training from not only experienced Customs agents but also the FBI, State Department, Commerce Department, and the CIA. If honest law enforcement is prevented from examining the cargo in pressurized rail tanker cars, tanker trucks, aviation cargo or in container cargo seagoing vessels, it will only be a matter of time before terrorists are able to bring in a nuclear, chemical, or biological device the same way drugs get in every day now.

Just because the jury in this case refused to see the truth, or was afraid of the government, or had somehow been tampered with—just because these things happened doesn't mean the truth isn't still out there. Having our borders remain wide open because the majority of politicians want it that way as they serve their own masters doesn't make it a good idea. It should be noted that in July of 2001, before this nation was attacked on "9-11," Darlene and Sandy testified to much of this before a Senate subcommittee. In February of the following year, Darlene was one of seven national whistleblowers who exposed these problems in several government agencies (see the Government Accountability Project—GAP—and the Project On Government Oversight—POGO). After this testimony was given, and while the federal government failed to take appropriate action, it is interesting to note that Washington, D.C. passed an ordinance prohibiting tanker trucks or rail cars from entering the city. At least somebody was getting the message, even if the jury in this case did not.

What the jury did in their verdict has given a boost to the corruption in government. Managers at all levels feel even more confident that they cannot be touched, no matter how they harass or humiliate their employees. Department of Homeland Security people, Customs people, all the folks in charge have been given a green light for corruption as usual. It seems there will be no consequences for mismanagement and criminal complicity, especially true the higher up you go. An example of this comes from journalist Bill Conroy, who was the first reporter to write about the harassment of whistleblowers Darlene Fitzgerald and Sandy Nunn. Immediately after the trial, and as soon as his work was published, he found himself the victim of organized government harassment. U.S. Customs Internal Affairs traumatized his family when he was not at home. "I had to explain to my son that I hadn't done anything wrong," he said after federal agents acted like he was a terrorist.

All of us who care about the future of the country we grew up in and love had better wake up to what is going on. Money talks and has bought off many of the politicians we rely on and vote for to do the right thing. Anybody filing a complaint in any of the DHS's many departments better know what they are in for.

The bosses have free rein to retaliate as much as they want against whistleblowers, and will continue to do so until we, the people, figure out a way to stop them.

America's borders are no more secure now than they were prior to September 11, 2001. In many ways, they are less secure. That is because the word has gone out to all those who could be effective in protecting this country that they had better watch their step and not get in the way of the hidden agenda of the powerful interests calling the shots.

The Old Boy System which the Drake Brinkley's have created for their own benefit operates at the expense of genuine law enforcement and national security. What we have is merely a sham of protection. How many terrorists do you think are among the eleven to fifteen million illegal aliens residing in this country right now? How many sleeper cells are waiting for the right moment, like a cancer in our body, to spread their menace and fulfill their stated objective to kill us all if they can?

Think about a meeting, as Darlene often does, in some dingy little hotel room south of the border. Seated around a table are the drug traffickers and distributors on one side and the drug producers on the other. They are discussing the movement of tremendous shipments of contraband into the United States, laughing at the ease of that operation. Imagine one other person at the table. This person doesn't speak but takes notes on what is being discussed. This person could care less about drugs, except that a good percentage of the profits from this trade finance his organization's operations. This person is Al Qaeda's man on the scene. He is smart, patient, well-funded and determined. He does not have to speak at this meeting. What his group plans, as in the case of "9-11," will do the speaking for him. Fear this person. All the wrong and dishonest moves being made by America's supposed protectors are playing directly into his hands. In answer to the question of why America hasn't been struck again by terrorists here at home, the answer is simple: Al Qaeda is biding its time while we become complacent and therefore more vulnerable.

The corruption of the governmental promotion process is ridding our nation's defense system of the very people it most needs to be effective. "Old Boys" cover for each other and root out the troublemakers who blow the whistle on their corruption. Lawmakers won't support the ones who uncover the ugly truth about what is destroying us from within. They are afraid of protecting whistleblowers who might shine the light on governmental misconduct which might come back to haunt them. Letting these agencies police themselves is a cruel joke. Internal Affairs has become the tormentor of honest cops, not the bane of corrupt officials. What lies at the beginning of an end to corruption may be the establishment of an independent Internal Affairs Division that transcends any single agency and the corrupt managers at their helm. This country cannot afford the make-believe controls currently supposed to keep an eye on the wrongdoers in all branches of government. Instead, we desperately need new ideas about how to weed out the rotten apples before their decay takes down the whole country. It really is that bad, and we'd better begin doing something about it before it's too late.

If such an elite, clean, dedicated super-department of Internal Affairs is to be established, it will require a firm and unshakeable commitment to keep it honest. Temptation is everywhere, so this new agency would have to pay its employees well enough to keep the cream of the crop aboard. It would need a much more stringent screening process than what exists now, including psychological testing and the use of polygraphs. Promotion within this agency needs to turn on a point system which measures actual achievements as opposed to who you know or what you're willing to put up with. There are many good law enforcement promotions systems, some at the state level, which could be molded to fit this federal agency. Like the hapless victims of violence in the Old West, we need law enforcers who are driven by the idea that you do what's right and not what's easy or profitable. These people exist, but instead of encouraging them to come forward and fix the broken machine we have today, we are driving them out of government with alarming speed. The low esteem with which the public holds politicians has been earned one sleazy deed at a time. But today, the stakes are simply too high for more monkey business as usual.

America was founded by people who were willing to risk their lives for an idea: that a free people living under a fair system of equal protection will protect their freedom with their lives. The further we stray from that ideal, the less likely it is that America will continue to resemble what the first Founding Fathers had in mind. Greed and selfishness are rampant in this country. Everywhere we see examples of those who put self-interest above the national interest. But the forces of moral mediocrity haven't triumphed yet. Just because turning around the rampant corruption in government is a formidable task doesn't mean it can't be done.

Darlene Fitzgerald has gone back to Kentucky. She has won a scholarship to law school. When she becomes an attorney, her focus will continue to be on protecting whistleblowers and trying to get Congress to pass laws that will allow them to shine the light on the corruption they see without fear of the kind of retaliation she has suffered. Darlene isn't alone. In fact, there is a growing cadre of Americans who are not afraid to take this fight on. All of us must make sure that we do what we can to help them.

In May 2007, Darlene would again testify before a congressional committee in Washington, D.C. Her fellow Whistleblower John Carman was also supposed to testify. Just two weeks before this testimony, John Carman was *conveniently* arrested by the San Diego, FBI office. Darlene, and many others, feel that the charges were "trumped-up" in order to silence John and send a clear message to government employees who dare speak truth to power. Darlene did not back down, and bravely testified. It is important to note that on that day it was officially read into the congressional record that over 700 federal government employees wanted to risk much (careers, retaliation) in order to come and testify as to their insider stories of government waist, fraud, abuse and corruption. This staggering number, in and of itself, is demonstrative of just how systemic this cronyism and corruption really is.

On May 6, 2008, Agents from the FBI raided and served search warrants on the Office of Special Counsel (OSC), in Washington, D.C. This followed a two year long Grand Jury investigation into criminal allegations that attorneys in this agency (who's sole function is to investigate allegations into Whistleblower retaliation and protect Whistleblowers) was itself engaging in Whistleblower retaliation as well as rejecting legitimate Whistleblower cases. Ironically, this comes five long years after Darlene and other Whistleblowers demanded an investigation into this agency in a national press conference just before Senate testimony, February 2002, in Washington, D.C. Five years ago, in a packed room of media Darlene was asked what she thought about the OSC. Darlene answered, "The Office of Special Council is a joke. It's a waste of the tax payer's money. I don't know of one single Whistleblower, including myself, that has been helped by the OSC." The second in command of the OSC at the time was sitting directly in front of Darlene as she made this bold statement.

The enemy outside this country is betting that we don't have what it takes to clean up our act. They think they can buy, scare, and kill their way to victory. If enough patriots unite to fight them, America's enemies will be defeated. It is to them—the next generation of American Founding Fathers and Founding Mothers—that this book is dedicated. The battle lines have been drawn. Which side are you on?

Epilogue

After the attacks on the World Trade Center towers in New York, the Pentagon, and the crash of a hijacked jet on a field in the Pennsylvania countryside on September 11, 2001, a special bi-partisan commission was formed to assess the threat situation and make recommendations to bolster our national security. Republican Thomas Kean and Democrat Lee Hamilton were, respectively, its chairman and vice-chairman. As of the publication of this book, practically none of the "9/11 Commission's" suggestions and reforms have been acted upon. Why is this? What possible motive can there be for disregarding the fruits of this independent commission's long and painstaking work? What else needs to happen to prod America's leaders into action?

You have now read a true and accurate first-hand account of corruption and retaliation within U.S. Customs, and by extension throughout the Department of Homeland Security of which it is a part, as seen through the eyes of a Special Agent who lived it. If what happened to Darlene was unique that would be one thing. The fact that there are literally hundreds of dedicated law enforcement people who have and continue to endure such treatment is more than an outrage. It is a national disgrace and an encouragement to those who would do this nation great harm.

Just as we witnessed the utter failure on all levels of government to respond effectively to the Hurricane Katrina debacle, so too we should brace ourselves for a repeat of this ineptitude with respect to another, and far more devastating, terrorist attack than what we saw on that fateful "day that changed everything." No one knows better than the 9/11 Commission how vulnerable we are. Yet they have been forced to issue a report card on what has been done to make America stronger and there are simply too many "F" for failures in their assessment. Those in whom we have placed our trust to carry this fight forward are simply letting the American people down.

As another example of this failure to act, the independent U.S. General Accounting Office issued in March of 2003 a report entitled: "HOMELAND SECURITY: Voluntary Initiatives Are Underway at Chemical Facilities, but the Extent of Security Preparedness Is Unknown." The report says "the federal government has identified 140 toxic and flammable chemicals that, in certain amounts, would pose the greatest risk to human health and the environment if they were accidentally released into the air...No federal laws explicitly require that chemical facilities assess vulnerabilities or take security actions to safeguard their facilities against terrorist attack." In a startling and related piece on the television newsmagazine "60 Minutes," Steve Croft was able to walk unchallenged right inside a chemical facility and stand next to a huge container of lethal chemicals which, had he simply set off an explosive charge where he was standing, would have posed a fatal risk to thousands and thousands of unsuspecting civilians in the immediate area.

Multiply these vulnerabilities by the enormous number of uninspected container cargo shipments flooding our commercial seaports, the unregulated flow of tanker cars coming by rail into this country, and the tidal wave of illegals, including terrorists, washing over our unprotected borders and you have a prescription for a disaster whose inevitability is not a matter of "if" but of "when." To put a human face on this impending disaster is why *BorderGate* was written. The alarm has been sounded again and again. Where is the response?

Appendices

"A politician thinks of the next election—a statesman thinks of the next generation" James Freeman Clark

February 17, 2006

Christopher Shays, Chairman & Dennis Kucinich, Ranking Member
Subcommittee on National Security, Emerging Threats and International Relations
B372 Rayburn House Office Building
Washington, DC 20515

SUBJECT: Witness Statement by Darlene Fitzgerald, Former Special Agent & National Security Whistleblower Regarding the Need for National Security Whistleblower Legislation

Gentlemen:

Thank you very much for the opportunity to testify for this much needed legislation. I would like to first take the liberty of briefly introducing myself, my background, training and experience. I have more than 20 years of successful experience in criminal justice: Military, federal law enforcement, and private industry. I am an honorably discharged, decorated veteran who served my country not only as a Captain in the U.S. Army Military Police Corps, but as a U.S. Customs Special Agent fighting on the front lines of the War on Drugs. I have a B.A. In Criminal Justice and a Masters Degree in Secondary Education. I am currently in Law School at William Howard Taft School of Law.

My knowledge and experience includes most facets of criminal law, complicated conspiracy investigations, federal and civil court procedures, and the rules of evidence. I have testified as an expert witness in both federal and state courts. I have worked closely with federal and state prosecutors for many years to obtain arrests and convictions on numerous high-level criminals. This involved the investigation of complex conspiracies of members of Colombian and Mexican organized crime cartels. These subjects were engaged in large-scale narcotics smuggling and distribution, as well as money laundering. As a result of my work, huge quantities of narcotics have been seized, millions of dollars in U.S. Currency have been seized, and hundreds of illegal firearms have been removed from the hands of violent criminals.

In 1998 I was running a railroad smuggling investigation. This investigation was being managed under a large scale, multi-agency operation with the Union Pacific Railroad Police, the Burlington Northern Railroad Police, The San Bernardino Police Department and Customs. This operation had received OCDTF status from the U.S. Attorney's Office, Los Angeles, CA. OCDTF—is a fancy government acronym for Organized Crime Drug Enforcement Task Force. In this operation, we had very high-level information that tons of narcotics were entering the U.S. via pressurized rail tanker cars. We learned that there was a large rail yard in Guadalajara that was controlled by the Arellano-Felix Cartel, and this yard was on of the Cartel's largest narcotics distribution points. In this yard, hundreds of these cars are loaded with narcotics each week destined for the U.S.

Our information turned out to be very accurate. In April 1998, we seized a pressurized tanker car concealing 8 thousand lbs of marijuana and 34 Kilos of cocaine. Subsequent to making this seizure, this large, successful rail operation and the two criminal investigations under its umbrella were immediately torpedoed by Customs management. An attempted controlled delivery of the seized narcotics was thwarted, my help was pulled, and my partner Ruben Sandoval and I came under immediate pressure, retaliation, and intimidation tactics on an enormous scale when we refused to shut down this operation and cease to do our job.

Several weeks after our first seizure, we identified 5 more suspected tanker cars. These cars were manifested as empty, and they were in total, 25 to 40 tons over weight. I set it up with the Union Pacific rail police to have these cars pressure tested at no cost to the government. Pressure testing is a necessary tool to further profile whether these cars should be bled out and checked. This profiling is necessary do to the fact that it cost approximately 8 to 14 thousand dollars a pop to inspect these cars. To further clarify, these are the long, metal, cylindrical shaped rail cars that many often think as carrying oil. These cars routinely carry a myriad of hazardous materials, and can only be inspected at the very few hazardous material inspection locations that exist on the southern border that also has scales that are necessary to weigh these cars. This is what makes these cars very difficult and dangerous to inspect, a fact that Narco-Traffickers know all too well.

I had these 5 suspected cars, again manifested as empty each weighing 5 to 9 tons over weight, ready to be pressure tested, and I was told not to do my job. Several days later, these cars were released into the commerce of the U.S. uninspected in any way. These cars should have never left that yard without at least being pressure tested. Subsequent to this incident, I was again pressured to shut down my operation, and Customs managers torpedoed my criminal investigations. The U.S. Attorneys office had assigned a very good, very aggressive prosecutor, Hon. Yvette Palazuelos, that was appalled as to what was going on. I found myself caught between the U.S. Attorneys Office and my agency.

I chose to continue attempting to run the rail operation. I subsequently found that someone had entered the TECS (Treasury Enforcement Computer System) and submitted over-rides to over one hundred additional suspicious tanker cars, without my permission or knowledge. These were suspect cars that I had entered into the TECS system to be secondaried and subsequently weighed, and pressure tested, both of which would be at no cost to the government. These were cars that were directly linked to my ongoing criminal investigation. These over-rides were completed in direct conflict of Customs regulations. These highly suspicious cars entered the U.S. with absolutely no type of inspection what-so-ever. We will never know what was in these tanker cars.

When other loyal Customs employees attempted to assist me on this case, they came under the same retaliation, threats, intimidation, and pressure as Ruben and I. We were submitted to endless, frivolous Internal Affairs investigations, surveillance by our agency which included surveillance pole cameras on Ruben Sandoval's home, and out right threats. Our careers, reputations, and personal lives were subsequently ruined.

What does this have to do with National Security and the Protection of National Security Whistleblowers? Consider this, the number one consumer of narcotics worldwide is the U.S. The number one way that terrorists fund their illegal activities is through the distribution of narcotics.

Ask yourself this, what happens to the price of any commodity when there's a choke hold on the supply for any reason, and the demand isn't being met? Right. The price goes up and quality usually suffers. Ask any street agent working dope today and they will tell you the current price of cocaine, marijuana, and heroin is lower than ever, and the purity is better than ever. This clearly indicates that the supply is easily meeting the demand. This stuff is coming across our imaginary borders by the ton, virtually unaffected by the efforts of U.S. Customs, or anyone else responsible for border/port security in Department of Homeland Security.

What do you have when you fill one of these tanker cars up with 10 thousand lbs. of ammonia nitrate, 100 lbs. of C-4, a shape charge, and place this container under pressure? Answer: The world's largest pipes bomb. One can place 20 times the amount of explosives into one of the rail tanker cars, than used by Timothy McVay in the Oklahoma City Bombing.

These tanker cars are the perfect instruments for a terrorist attack against the U.S. As our narcotics smuggling investigation has revealed, anyone with cash and phony identification can lease or sublease these cars using a front company as the importer/exporter of record. We were shocked as to just how easy it was for the Narco-traffickers to do this. Knowing the relationship that the terrorists have with the Narco-smuggling cartels, it is not a quantum leap to think that terrorist could easily copy the same modus operandi used by the Narco-traffickers. The terrorist would simply lease/sublease a tanker car and pay cash to set up an account with one of the major railroads. The Railroads and Customs brokers aren't trained—AT ALL—to look for any type of terrorist profile. This is a customer service industry, pure and simple. The railroad employees taking these orders for accounts make minimum wage, and they are simply "customer service reps." The Customs brokers aren't much different. They are required to check almost nothing, have no training in this arena, and have no requirements to fully identify any of their customers.

These rail customer accounts may be set up via the Internet, or over the phone. At no point does anyone in the railroad industry or Customs brokers ever require visual documentation to fully identify who the account holder actually is.

Once a person has set up an account the movement of these cars can be directed REMOTELY via the Internet or telephone. Then they can be moved anywhere in the country with extreme ease. Then the terrorist can remotely move them and if need be, abruptly change the routing of these cars via a simple phone call to their customer service rep or via the Internet, from anywhere in the world. This is truly a recipe for disaster. Terrorists can simply remotely route a hundred of these simultaneously to within a mile or two of a hundred of our national landmarks. They don't even need a suicide bomber to activate them remotely. Once this is done, the perpetrators will be extremely difficult to trace.

When my brave associates and I tried desperately to bring attention to this, our careers were destroyed. We were virtually shoved out on a limb, and Customs managers laughed in our faces as the limb was cut off. These tanker cars are a Clear and present danger to our national security, as well as what happened to the Whistleblowers who tried to stop it. The American public must demand accountability, and demand that honest cops trying to do their jobs should not be treated in this fashion.

Our story culminated in a Land Mark Case in Federal Court, and a book appropriately entitled: **"*BORDERGATE*"** (release date April 2006). It is a Land Mark Case because this was the first time in history that a Judge (the Honorable Yvette Palazuelos, Superior Court Judge) took the stand and testified in Federal Court against the government. Even the most disturbing events that you may read about in this book and/or via the court transcripts themselves, really did happen. The most significant and shocking testimony from the trial chronicled by this book, will soon be transcribed on line at www.bordergate.net (release date April 2006). The entire trial transcripts are of public record for anyone to see. They can be obtained in Federal District Court, San Diego, California (Fitzgerald—Nunn Vs. Department of Homeland Security).

In short, this story is about to become **VERY PUBLIC**. These transcripts demonstrate just how arrogant these managers really were in their testimony. Additionally, these transcripts clearly demonstrate how two very high officials, former Assistant Commissioner of Customs John Hensley, and Assistant Special Agent in Charge, (currently) Gary Pinkava were both flat out busted lying during this federal trial. Neither official has been placed under any type of investigation for any of the foregoing, even though clearly reported to the Federal Bureau of Investigations Public Corruptions Unit, and the United States Attorneys Office. These transcripts will not only be made public on the BORDERGATE web site, I plan to release them to anyone and everyone who wants to take a look at what is really happening to National Security, and the Whistleblowers trying to protect us.

Your now have a choice to do the right thing and pass this much needed Whistleblower legislation.

*"It is dangerous to be right
when government is wrong"*
Voltaire

Darlene Fitzgerald
Vice President, SIG-International
Former Special Agent
Author: "BORDERGATE,
The Story The Government Doesn't Want You To Read"

February 17, 2006

Christopher Shays, Chairman & Dennis Kucinich, Ranking Member
Subcommittee on National Security, Emerging Threats and International Relations
B372 Rayburn House Office Building
Washington, DC 20515

SUBJECT: Witness Statement by Sandra Nunn, Former Special Agent & National Security Whistleblower Regarding the Need for National Security Whistleblower Legislation

Gentlemen:

In 1988, when I became a Special Agent with the U.S. Customs Service Office of Investigations in the Los Angeles area, I truly felt that I was part of an honorable organization with the highestlevel of integrity. I was very honored and proud to become a Special Agent. And in all of the years I served as a Special Agent, I served with the utmost integrity and professionalism befitting my position as a federal agent, never once shirking or abusing my position. During the years I served, I had the honor of serving as the Case Agent on an international money laundering investigation which made national headlines and was featured in TIME and Business Week, served as the Case Agent on a case involving the illegal smuggling activity via the Southern U.S. border of tons of illicit narcotics, served as a key undercover operative on an investigation involving over 1000 fully automatic AK-47's, served as a diplomatic representative and key investigator with the Organization for Security and Cooperation in Europe (OSCE) on two European tours of duty during the UN Sanctions Against Serbia, and casework which included narcotics smuggling, money laundering, espionage, counterterrorism, arms trafficking, and national security. I took my job very seriously and I was good at what I did as evidenced by the numerous awards and commendations I received in the course of 11 years from the U.S. Customs Service, the FBI, the U.S. Attorney's Office, the Organization for Security and Cooperation in Europe, and Foreign Governments.

Nonetheless, commencing in 1997, my career as I had I known it began experiencing levels of retaliation previously unknown to me when I chose to step forward and back-up allegations made by a fellow agent of misconduct within our agency by management officials. When I stepped forward and supported my fellow agent, Darlene Fitzgerald, by telling the truth in what at the time initially was an EEO related matter, I along with Ms. Fitzgerald, also an accomplished agent, became the unwitting victims of egregious retaliatory acts perpetrated by our management as well as the Office of Internal Affairs in a concerted effort to silence and discredit us. When both Ms. Fitzgerald and I refused to back down, the heat was turned up even further as I was suddenly transferred to another office, both of us were put under investigation, our work was heavily scrutinized in an effort to intimidate and upset us, I was given adverse work assignments unbefitting an agent of my abilities and experience meant to belittle and embarrass me, and so forth. At one point, my fellow agent Ms. Fitzgerald received an anonymous threatening letter at her home advising her to "Shut up and resign or else…". And the following day, another fellow agent who had spoken out with us was also victimized when he walked outside of his home in Southern California and found two surveillance cameras pointed directly at his personal residence where he along with his wife and six children lived. For the record, I have attached photos of these cameras taken at the time of this incident in August 1998 with this statement.

During the time all of these incidents were taking place, my associate Ms. Fitzgerald was working on a major narcotics trafficking investigation which culminated in the significant seizure of over 8,000 pounds of narcotics. Information developed from this seizure in conjunction with informant-based information resulted in Ms. Fitzgerald locating 5 railway tanker cars which had entered the country. Each of these cars was manifested as empty according to the Customs Manifest. However, a subsequent weigh-in of each of these respective tanker cars at the Colton Rail Yard by Ms. Fitzgerald demonstrated that these allegedly empty pressurized railway tanker cars were between 25–40 tons overweight demonstrating to us as experienced agents and investigators that these conveyances were potentially carrying contraband of some kind. Yet, when both Ms. Fitzgerald and Senior Special Agent Robert Mattivi approached Customs Resident Agent in Charge Gary Pinkava to get permission to perform a simple pressure test at no cost to the Government and no extra manpower, Mr. Pinkava ordered both Fitzgerald and Mattivi not to do their job and not to return to the rail yard to perform their sworn duties as Customs Special Agents. This action in itself constituted "obstruction of justice" by Mr. Pinkava due to the ongoing investigation. Shortly thereafter, it was learned that the suspect tanker cars had disappeared into the commerce of the United States never to be seen again.

The concern here regarding national security is that we do not know what was in those tanker cars because none of the agents involved in the case was allowed to perform their duties thereby placing American citizens at potential risk. The question becomes: What was in those tanker cars? Was it narcotics? Or was it weapons of mass destruction, biological agents, guns, or ammonium nitrate? We don't know. We will never know. And the fact that Mr. Pinkava, a high-level management official for the U.S. Customs Service, knowingly and purposefully did this demonstrates the level of explicit misconduct inherent within the U.S. Customs Service which is now, as we all know, part of Homeland Security. What is also disturbing to me is that Mr. Pinkava, even after ADMITTING on the record in federal court during our lawsuit against the Department of Homeland Security in March 2005 that all of this happened exactly as we have always claimed it has, has never ONCE been investigated, reprimanded, or demoted for his illegal conduct. Instead, he has been allowed to continue in his fully paid full-time position of employment as if nothing had happened and was subsequently PROMOTED to a higher position of Assistant Special Agent in Charge (ASAC). However, when I attempted to look into potential links on this case involving arms trafficking connections, I was placed under internal affairs investigation for doing my job as I was sworn to do. Clearly, it is obvious that there is a problem here when someone who so blatantly admits wrongdoing in federal court in violation of the law is allowed to continue his employment as a high-ranking federal law enforcement manager in a Homeland Security agency, the very agency tasked with protecting our nation from future terrorist acts. This is a blatant example of a system that is clearly broken and dysfunctional. How many other managers like this are jeopardizing our national security and not being held accountable? One must seriously ponder this question. Because knowing what I know and seeing what I've seen, it scares me to death that even one instance of this can happen.

Additionally, when several of us reported what we felt were significant concerns of misconduct and potential issues of corruption and national security concerns to the FBI, suddenly we as the messengers and the truth tellers became the hunted and the hated. Suddenly, we became the "problem" rather than being lauded for pointing out wrongdoing, which per Customs regulations, is one of our duties.

In the midst of speaking out and becoming more public in our campaign to bring awareness to these issues, both myself and another agent were suddenly given time off without pay for frivolous reasons, again to retaliate against us for our whistleblowing and protected disclosures. It was during this time that the brunt of the suffering I was subjected to spilled over to my family. My father, himself a decorated Air Force officer and pilot, was so distraught by how egregious the retaliation was that I was suffering along with my fellow agents that he literally dropped dead of a heart attack on the 2nd day of my frivolous agency-imposed punishment of time off without pay. According to my mother, he was so upset about what my management was doing to me that he could not even discuss it. Instead, the stress and worry he had for me, his eldest daughter, was the last thing he felt when he died. Knowing that is something I will never be able to forgive or forget. My father was a good man who loved and was loved. He unfortunately became a statistic in this fight for justice as a national security whistleblower. As if that wasn't bad enough, on the day my father died, several managers (including Gary Pinkava and my immediate supervisor Rick Powell) put me under internal affairs investigation knowing full well that my father had just died. This was evidenced by a series of four memos generated by Customs management and dated on the day of my father's death which we found in the discovery phase prior to going to trial in March 2005. Obviously, Government managers bent on retaliating believe in really kicking someone at their lowest point of grief at the loss of a parent. Retaliation knows no boundaries of human decency.

But, it doesn't end there. I was forced to resign my position in protest due to the ongoing retaliation. I suffered bankruptcy and lost my retirement. Additionally, both Ms. Fitzgerald and I, both highly educated women, were time and time again denied employment opportunities. We subsequently determined after hiring a private investigation firm that U.S. Customs was blackballing us. Both of us were forced to move back home with our parents or be forced into homelessness since we could not obtain employment to support ourselves. And I might point out that this has gone on for years, which has placed an undue economic burden on those around us.

Our lives over the past 5 years have been nothing short of a nightmare not only for ourselves, but for our families and friends who have suffered along with us. We have endured a great deal and have had to work hard to rebuild what is left of our lives. Our health has been compromised due to the highly-stressful conditions we've had to undergo not to mention the emotional abuse we've suffered during this process. We have often likened the abuse we suffered at the hands of these managers as that of post-traumatic stress syndrome. I can remember nights where I would suffer nightmares and flashbacks of the incidents I was subjected to and wake up shaking in fear of what would happen next. It has taken me years to come back from that.......years of my life that I can never get back. As if that wasn't bad enough, when we finally got our case into federal court, the abusive behavior continued as the Government attempted to paint Ms. Fitzgerald and I as "loose women" and "crazy nuts." Their case never did address the real allegations at hand: Why did the Government allow 25–40 tons of contraband to enter the country illegally and then try to cover it up?

I didn't ask to become a whistleblower. I was only an agent doing my job and doing it with integrity. But, when I witnessed what I did, I was forced to make a choice: shut up and look the other way......or stand up for what's right. Being the daughter of a military officer, I did what my father had always taught me to do: be a leader. I did not shrink back from my duties but stood up and told the truth as any patriot would. And yet I was punished for that along with my fellow agents. A couple of years ago, a news reporter asked me: "If you could do everything over again, knowing what would happen to you, would you?" My response to him was: "Absolutely. Because it was the right thing to do."

Being a whistleblower is not something any of us have aspired to. Most of us were forced into this position by our strong sense of right and wrong. Therefore, I have since discovered that I am in fine company. The National Security Whistleblowers I have met are courageous and astute individuals, as well as true patriots. They are truly the epitome of the "Good Guys." Therefore, the fact that National Security Whistleblower legislation does not protect these people of integrity and true patriotism is of grave concern to me. It is also of concern to me that this legislation does not impose harsh punishments against those Government officials who engage in retaliatory activities. This illegal behavior needs to be dealt with through more stronger, effective legislation that makes it a crime punishable by fines, imprisonment, loss of employment, and loss of employment benefits for anyone who dares to engage in this activity. I have seen too many lives ruined thanks to a few who abused their positions in the U.S. Government. This has got to stop. If there is one thing I would like to see is tougher legislation that stops this abuse at the source and stringently protects those who have every right as true citizens, patriots, and federal employees to be protected for doing what they must to protect the public's interest and our national security.

Therefore, as I come to the end of my statement, I ask that you understand the sacrifices that each and every one of us has made to do the right thing on behalf of our country when we could have turned the other way and said nothing.

None of us want another 9/11. Yet, my fear as a former investigator tells me that we are a long way from being safe from terrorism coming upon our soil again. Look around you and see all of the whistleblowers who have emerged since 9/11 and subsequently destroyed. That in itself should be a signal as to the depth of the problem within. We can either choose to be part of the solution and fix it. Or, we can succumb to this sick pattern of behavior that has infested our national security agencies and risks our way of life and the security of our people because of a few people who think they are exempt from being punished after engaging in retaliatory acts against whistleblowers.

I trust that you will do the right thing and listen to each and every one of us. Please make the national security whistleblower laws as strong as possible. Protect those who speak out. They are the "Good Guys" and deserve to be heard if we are to secure our nation and its borders from future terrorist acts.

Thank you for allowing me to make my statement with regard to this matter.

Sandy G. Nunn
Sandy G. Nunn
Former Special Agent, U.S. Customs Service Office of Investigations (1988–1999)
National Security Whistleblower

"I don't make jokes, I just watch the Government and report the facts"
Will Rogers

Authors' Biographies

Peter S. Ferrara

Peter S. Ferrara was born in Charlston, West Virgina two days after World War Two's D-Day. He received his secondary school diploma from Phillips Academy, Andover, Mass and his B.F.A. from New York University's Film School. After graduation, he served as a New York State Parole Officer. During that period and for several years after, he also performed as a folksinger/humorist in clubs and colleges all over the Northeast. He writes songs that are uniquely his own, falling somewhere between his two musical heroes: Tom Lehrer and Bob Dylan.

Upon leaving the NY Executive Department, Division of Parole, he made intermission films for Home Box Office and also produced a record called "Goofy Gold" which sold well enough to pay for his move to the beach at Malibu, California. He joined the CBS Television Network in 1978 as a Writer/Producer in the Advertising and Promotion Department. There he did numerous promo's and radio spots for CBS network television shows, specials, and movies of the week. He was hired away by ABC's flagship station KABC, the most profitable television station in America, where he was responsible for On-Air Promotion. He won several awards for his work and was again hired away, this time by the NBC Television Network, where he did all of their radio promotion through his own company. He also began to write and direct television specials for HBO and Showtime, and did movie work with his comedy Guru Jonathan Winters, Martin Mull, and Tommy Chong of "Cheech and Chong," among others. He also directed Jonathan Winters, Robin Williams, Michael Richards, Milton Berle, Phyllis Diller, Mort Sahl, Louise DuArt, Jeff Altman and many others for cable comedy specials. When he got married, it was at Jonathan Winters' house, with Jonathan as his Best Man. After toiling away in Hollywood for many years, he and his wife eventually moved back East, first to New York and then to their current residence within the Daniel Boone National River and Recreation Area in the small town of Stearns, Kentucky, on the Tennessee border. He lives on a golf course where he has been known to lose his balls. Peter writes a column on anything and everything for the local paper—The McCreary County Record—called "Write On." It can be accessed on-line at "McCrearyRecord.Com". He also does a weekly two hour radio show called "Just For Fun" on radio station WHAY 98.3FM, in Whitley City, Kentucky. The "live" show can be found on the Internet at "HAY98.com". He and his wife have no kids, no pets, few household plants, and no distractions. Because of this, they both have a lot of time to contemplate what lies ahead as they watch the world going to hell in a hand basket. It is to slow down that descent that he is pleased to have co-authored "BorderGate" with Darlene Fitzgerald.

Darlene Fitzgerald

Darlene has more than 20 years of successful experience in criminal justice:
Military, federal law enforcement, and private industry. She is an honorably discharged, decorated veteran who served her country not only as a Captain in the U.S. Army Military Police Corps, but as a U.S. Customs Special Agent fighting on the front lines of the War on Drugs. She has a B.A. in Criminal Justice, and a Masters Degree in Secondary Education.

Her knowledge and experience includes most facets of criminal law, complicated conspiracy investigations, federal and civil court procedures, and the rules of evidence. Darlene has testified as an expert witness in both federal and state courts. She has worked closely with federal and state prosecutors for many years to obtain arrests and convictions on numerous high-level criminals. This involved the investigation of complex conspiracies of members of Colombian and Mexican organized crime cartels. These subjects were engaged in large-scale narcotics smuggling and distribution, as well as money laundering. As a result of Darlene's work, huge quantities of narcotics have been seized, millions of dollars in U.S. Currency have been seized, and hundreds of illegal firearms have been removed from the hands of violent criminals.

As a Customs Special Agent Darlene was also a cross-designated Secret Service Agent for the Department of Treasury. She has protect heads of state, Senators Bob Dole and Hillary Clinton, foreign dignitaries, and other political officials.

Darlene has worked extensively in the field of Counter-Terrorism as it relates to U.S. Borders and Ports of Entry. She has appeared numerous times in the national and local media including "The O'Reilly Factor" and "C-Span" as well as other television and national radio shows. Numerous news articles have been published about her story. Darlene has written for the national and international press as well.

She has had the opportunity to liaison with ambassadors, diplomatic officials, attaches, high-level military officers, business leaders, the media, and the public at large, drawing on her vast knowledge and expertise of law enforcement, Counter-Terrorism, and Whistleblower issues.

She is currently attending William Howard Taft School of Law, working to complete her Juris Doctorate Degree. She plans to put her law degree to good use in protecting the rights of National Security Whistleblowers in the future. Darlene is also the Vice President of Sig-International (Security Investigative Group International).

Recommended Reading

"Unlimited Access" by Gary Aldrich

"Borderline Security, a Chronicle of Reprisal, Cronyism & Corruption In The U.S. Customs Service," by Bill Conroy, Journalist and Editor

"Flying While Black, A Whistleblower's Story" by Cathy Harris, retired U.S. Customs Inspector

"Dark Alliance" By Gary Webb

"Poor Leadership at ICE cited as security threat" by Jerry Seper and Guy Taylor—The Washington Times, November 29, 2004—www.washingtontimes.com/functions/print.php?StoryID=20041129-010523-3159r

"Looting Homeland Security" by Eric Klinenberg and Thomas Frank—Rolling Stone Magazine, December 15, 2005—www.rollingstone.com/politics/story/_/id/8952492

"Homeland Insecurity—Leadership vacuums and ongoing turf fights are hampering government efforts to control U.S. borders" by Mark Hosenball—Newsweek, December 14, 2005—www.msnbc.msn.com/id/10469582/site/newsweek/print/1/displaymode/1098/

"Dangerous U.S. Customs" by Gary Aldrich—World Net Daily (www.wnd.com), November 1, 2001

"Whistleblowers Gone With the Wind" by Darlene Fitzgerald—World Net Daily (www.wnd.com), June 8, 2002

"The One Year Anniversary of Homeland In-Security" by Darlene Fitzgerald & Cathy Harris—Freedom Writer (www.freedomwriter.com), April 1, 2004

"Investigation Derailed" by Bill Conroy—Narco News, February 18, 2004

"Shame On Them" by Darlene Fitzgerald—The Forum (www.speakout.com), September 21, 2005

"Whistleblowers are Modern Paul Reveres Against Terrorism"—POGO (www.pogo.org) September 19, 2001

Recommended Web Sites

The "Bordergate" web site—www.bordergate.net

The Patrick Henry Center—www.patrickhenrycenter.org

The Government Accountability Project—www.whistleblower.org

Sig-International (Security Investigative Group International) www.

The Project on Government Oversight (POGO)—www.pogo.org

The Wake Up America Foundation—www.thewakeupamericafoundation.com

Customs Corruption.com—www.customscorruption.com

Customs Employees Against Discrimination—www.ceada.com

Subcommittee National Security Testimony—http://reform.house.gov/NSETIR/Hearings/EventSingle.aspx?EventID=39462

978-0-595-38984-1
0-595-38984-8

LaVergne, TN USA
16 March 2010
176039LV00003B/2/P